SO

MUCH

FOR

THE

30 YEAR

PLAN

SO MUCH FOR THE 30 YEAR PLAN
THERAPY?
THE AUTHORISED BIOGRAPHY
SIMON YOUNG

A Jawbone book
First edition 2020
Published in the UK
and the USA by
Jawbone Press
Office G1
141–157 Acre Lane
London SW2 5UA
England
www.jawbonepress.com

ISBN 978-1-911036-63-0

Printed in the Czech
Republic by PBtisk

1 2 3 4 5 24 23 22 21 20

YEAR ZERO /introduction

'We all love playing, and we love music … we're all having the time of our lives,' said Andy Cairns, over the distant throb of an outdoor show. 'If it ever stops feeling like that, then we'll stop doing it. We're just really grateful to be in the position we're in.'

Sat on the grass at Castle Donington's Monsters Of Rock festival on June 4 1994, the Therapy? frontman—joined by bassist Michael McKeegan and the band's then drummer, Fyfe Ewing—was reflecting on their rapidly growing profile during a filmed television interview with presenter Vanessa Warwick for MTV's *Headbangers Ball*. Their second full-length album, *Troublegum*, had been out for only a matter of months, and they were selling copies as fast as their label's pressing plant could manufacture them.

The Ulster trio had just played on the main stage, in a teatime slot bookended by Ozzy Osbourne guitarist Zakk Wylde's new band Pride & Glory and the sledgehammer-heavy one-two of Pantera and Sepultura. Moments before walking on stage, the band—who'd enjoyed a run of chart success with a series of irresistibly catchy alt-rock singles that year in the run up to the album: 'Nowhere', 'Trigger Inside', and 'Die Laughing'—were perhaps rightfully concerned that their blend of pop-infused punk and noise-rock may not win favour with a traditional metal crowd. But the trio's resolve and tenacity ensured that their set became a highlight of the event.

'I'd never been to Donington, and I grew up vicariously, living my Monster Of Rock dream through *Kerrang!*,' remembers Michael. 'With festivals, you're at the mercy of so many things. These were the days of bottles of piss and mudslinging. We just went on with the right attitude and did our thing. The crowd went nuts, and I was gobsmacked at the reaction. They were really on board.'

I wasn't there, unfortunately. On the morning of the festival, I was 165 miles away on a housing estate in Jarrow, in the north-east of England, preparing to trudge my way through another Saturday shift at a popular fast-food restaurant on Newcastle's Grainger Street. It paid for weekend beers and the occasional record, at least. I had been a fan of Therapy? for about eighteen months, after seeing a fellow student brandishing a Day-Glo green twelve-inch single with a razor blade on the cover, a garish punk homage to Judas Priest's 1980 album *British Steel*. It was the *Shortsharpshock* EP, which I bought that same day and subsequently played to death.

On the 533 bus to Newcastle, I remember reading *Kerrang!* and playing *Troublegum* on my portable CD player, which just fit inside my denim jacket's hidden pocket. The album's length perfectly matched the time it took to get to work. It felt like the album was written just for me. The last line, '*I'm in hell and I'm alone*', would ring in my ears as I pulled my boots on and fixed my name badge—nine months in, no stars—to my polo shirt. I'd play the album immediately as soon as my shift ended. The opening song, 'Knives', would satisfyingly drown out the voice of my bullish shift manager as I made my way home.

MTV broadcasted highlights of the festival later that summer. At a friend's house party, I nursed a bottle of warm French lager as I watched some Therapy?'s set on satellite TV. By the time they began 'Hellbelly'—the sixth song of their set—my friend Craig, a hip-hop fan, had switched off his parents' television without a moment's warning. I clearly remember a shot of Andy prowling the lip of the stage before the screen suddenly turned black.

Later that year, I moved to London to study for a thoroughly useful degree in Film and Communication Studies at Middlesex University. My first Therapy? show proper—I caught most of their set at Reading that

August—was at the Shepherds Bush Empire on November 27. I managed to watch 'Hellbelly' in its entirety this time, before I eventually exited the venue drenched in sweat, steam rising from my hoodie into the cold night.

It was the first of many, many Therapy? headline sets I'd witness over the next twenty-five years. The following year, late on June 11 1995, I jumped on the Piccadilly Line with a friend to be the among the first to pick up a copy of the band's next album, *Infernal Love*, and get my whole CD collection signed. I posed for a photo with Michael, on whom I'd clearly modelled my appearance around that time: round glasses, close-cropped hair, and a nose ring.

In 1999, I began working in the *Kerrang!* office, and I would often interview the band on the phone for news stories—one such story involved playing the song 'God Kicks' down the receiver and asking readers to guess who the drunk, mumbling singer was. I would later sit face-to-face with Andy and Michael for longer, in-depth interviews. Over the course of my career, I've seen many bands come and go, but Therapy? have been a reassuring constant in my gig diary and listening habits, as well as the architects of some debilitating hangovers.

As the twenty-fifth anniversary of *Troublegum* loomed on the horizon, I approached the band for their thoughts on pitching a book on that stratospheric era. They readily agreed, but a little later they suggested I write a book about their whole career, to mark their thirtieth anniversary.

The book you hold in your hands is the result of over seventy hours of interviews and unrestricted access to their archives. It's the story of one of rock's boldest and most idiosyncratic acts, tracing their beginnings from the politically volatile streets of Northern Ireland in the late 80s, to achieving mainstream success, overcoming line-up changes, changing record labels, and navigating countless obstacles throughout their three-decade-long career.

The secret of their longevity can be traced back to that conversation in the Castle Donington press enclosure in the summer of 1994. Therapy?

have never pandered to commercial trends: they have stuck to their guns, even during their lowest moments. They're lifers, and their passion for their music is reflected in their most dedicated of fans.

So, it's best we get started then. It's a long journey ...

On a summer's afternoon in 1989, Andy Cairns returned to his parents' home in Ballyclare, Northern Ireland, after a shift as a quality-control inspector at the local Michelin tyre factory. He was joined by Michael McKeegan and Fyfe Ewing, two students from neighbouring Larne, a fifteen-minute drive away. Their band, Therapy?, was in its infancy, its line-up having solidified only a few months previously. Later that day, they would play their first ever gig at Conor Hall in Belfast Art College, set up by the Warzone Collective, an anarcho-punk community in the capital. Decadence Within, a political-crossover thrash band from Herefordshire, were set to headline a bill that also featured local punks Pink Turds In Space and Strontium Dog.

Andy grabbed his VHS copy of Hüsker Dü's *Makes No Sense ...* and the three gathered in the lounge to watch the Minnesota trio's supercharged 1985 performance at London's Camden Palace. 'I remember being really, really nervous that day,' says Andy. 'But after watching the Hüsker Dü video we were really, really up for it. I vividly remember Fyfe noticing that Grant Hart played drums in his bare feet.'

They loaded Andy's orange Mini Metro with all their equipment and drove twenty minutes south to York Street. The band had done nothing but rehearse since May, so their plan of action was simple: play the eleven songs they had, and end with a glorious hail of feedback.

Andy, born September 22 1965, in Antrim, moved to Ballyclare as a small child. It was David Bowie's performance of 'Starman' on *Top Of The Pops* on July 6 1972 that changed his life. 'He looked like an alien,' Andy remembers. 'If it was someone with a beard and an acoustic guitar, I wouldn't have looked twice. But they were wearing makeup and outrageous trousers. I was transfixed.'

The BBC's flagship entertainment show shaped his musical education. Sparks' 'This Town Ain't Big Enough For The Both Of Us', released in 1974, was another song that lodged itself firmly in his young brain. That year, he made his first record purchase: the Sweet's 'Blockbuster'.

'I really wanted that record, and I remember my dad taking me into Belfast and saying he was going to give me the money to go up and buy the record myself,' he recalls. 'It was a big deal for me, because I was quite a shy kid, but I went home clutching this copy of "Blockbuster", which I played to death.'

When Andy was eight years old, Ballyclare Primary received a cache of musical instruments from a neighbouring school. 'Our headmaster, Mr Brown, showed us this room of dusty, beaten-up instruments,' he remembers. 'I don't know why, but I said I wanted to play the saxophone. I was kind of lost in the melee. I remember two boys called David and Marvin got a trumpet each, some girls got violins, and the only thing left was a trombone. I took it home in this battered case and got lessons from a man called Mr Cook, which got me out of class for half an hour every week. So, glam rock and the trombone ignited my interest in music.'

Andy's interest in punk piqued when the *Daily Mirror* reported on the Sex Pistols' outrageous appearance on the British TV show *Today*, hosted by Bill Grundy. 'Say something outrageous,' he prodded. 'What a fucking rotter,' replied guitarist Steve Jones. The word *fuck* had only been uttered twice on British television before, and the incident turned the Pistols into unwelcome household names.

'I remember seeing the newspaper headline "The Filth and the Fury" and being really scared of punks because we thought punks were people that had razor blades in their nose and all this kind of stuff,' says Andy. 'One lad in upper sixth had safety pins in his blazer lapel, and was sent home for having a purple streak in his hair.'

During a family holiday in Blackpool the following summer, Andy became a convert to the punk cause after hearing the Pistols' single 'Pretty Vacant'. 'The punk scene in Northern Ireland was getting really big,' he says. 'We had The Undertones, Rudi, Protex. It was all really exciting. The first record I bought with my own money was *Love Bites* by the Buzzcocks. I saved up my paper-round money and used money my grandmother gave me to get it. It was released on my thirteenth birthday, and that's when I started collecting records. I still have it now.'

Andy began to receive guitar lessons from an older teenage boy nicknamed Matilda who played guitar for a Status Quo covers band called Piledriver. He showed Andy the simplistic power of the barre chord, just like Johnny Ramone would use to devastating effect. 'I was quite slow to make chord shapes,' says Andy, 'but once he showed me how to do that, it was like a lightbulb went on in my head. I had a little guitar and amp in my room and started writing songs.'

Despite having ambitions of becoming a journalist after scraping through his A-Levels, Andy ended up on the dole in Belfast and playing in a few different bands, including Every Mother's Son with Protex drummer Gordie Walker. 'It was really just for fun,' he says. 'We'd write some crap songs and do covers. I'd left school and felt completely useless. I ended up working at a tyre factory. My dad was an engineer and had worked there, and it broke his heart. I moved back home and paid them rent and spent the rest on a Fender Twin [amp], a Fender Telecaster, an Epiphone 335, and loads of effects pedals. And lots of records. There was something really incredibly depressing about the fact that I hadn't taken my education any further and was back home living with my mum and dad.'

In 1988, Andy attended Aid For Africa, a benefit show that was held annually at Ulster University's Jordanstown campus bar, where bands were paid in beer. He watched League Of Decency, whose set consisted mainly of punk covers of Siouxsie & The Banshees, The Damned, and Dead Kennedys.

'The first thing I noticed about the band was their drummer,' says Andy. 'He was incredible. We got chatting about music, and he told me his name was Fyfe. He invited me over to his house to jam. His parents had separated, and he was pretty much allowed to make as much noise as he wanted.'

The pair would play music in Fyfe's room, with the young drummer using brushes while Andy coaxed feedback from his small practice amp. They would later rehearse twice a month at the Rathcoole Self Help Group at Merville House in the loyalist area of Newtownabbey—a practice space used by bands like Burning Kisses and Four Idle Hands.

'It was really cheap to play there, but the only thing was that you had to collect the keys from one of the most terrifying estates you've ever seen in your life,' explains Andy. 'I was working in a factory and living at home with my parents, so music, literature, and movies were the only escape I had. I really, really enjoyed being creative. We started writing songs, and we were quite prolific.'

By the spring, the pair had named themselves Therapy—it sounded good and was easy to remember—and planned to record a demo. Fyfe hit upon the idea of borrowing a bass from a school classmate.

Michael McKeegan was born on March 25 1971. Growing up, he remembers the McKeegan family home would be filled with music by the likes of Simon & Garfunkel, Cat Stevens, and The Dubliners. And, like Andy, his musical tastes were informed by *Top Of The Pops*.

'When I was eleven, I saw Motörhead on there, doing "Iron Fist", but I wasn't sure if I liked it,' he admits. 'It sort of scared me a bit but there was something about it. And with friends and older brothers, AC/DC albums started appearing on the scene. My dad and aunt took me to see AC/DC later that year at the RDS in Dublin. It was an otherworldly experience. After that, I went to see Mama's Boys.'

Michael showed musical promise and impressed his parents by bashing out the bass line to Black Sabbath's 'N.I.B.' on the piano. Gradually, he and his brothers acquired musical equipment and began to make 'an unholy racket' in a wooden summerhouse at the bottom of the garden.

'We ran an extension lead down from the house and the door had to remain shut at all times under my dad's instructions,' he remembers. 'We'd be sweltering in the summer, trying to play "Running Free" or "War Pigs", but it was good fun. My brother Ciaran already played guitar, and Charlie played drums; I took the hit and got a bass if we were to become a band, which is kind of ironic in a weird way.'

Influenced by the New Wave Of British Heavy Metal, thrash, and death metal, Evil Priest were born. 'We were originally called The Exterminators because I'd read in *Kerrang!* that KISS's Ace Frehley was in a band called that,' says Michael. 'It was a great name. Then we were called Blind Faith, until someone mentioned that had already been taken.'

The short-lived band recorded two demos—'Pretention Is No Excuse' and 'Hear No Evil …'—and played a few shows. Michael was also heavily into the tape-trading scene, and swapped cassettes with like-minded metalheads. 'Nicke Andersson was a big trader,' he says. 'He was in Nihilist, which obviously became Entombed. There was Metalion from *Slayer* magazine; Ronny Eide from *Morbid* magazine; and Fenriz, whose Darkthrone tapes came my way. Nick Holmes from Paradise Lost would trade a bit, and later I stumbled upon this band from Derby called The Beyond. You got the fanzines, read about the bands, and then you'd send off your blank tape and wait for the post. It was great, receiving all this new music in the mail.'

Fyfe and Andy borrowed Michael's bass, and, on April 8, went to Lisburn Road Studio in Belfast and recorded four songs with Colum Muinzer: 'Bloody Blue', 'Skyward', 'Body O.D.', and the jagged squall of 'Beefheart/Albini'.

'At this point in time, I was a far better bass player than guitarist,' says Andy. 'I played guitar and bass, and Fyfe said we could expand the band and I'd switch to bass. I played guitar like the bass anyway, and liked how unusual it sounded. We met with Colum—he used to be in a band on EMI called Cruella De Ville—and charged us £50 to make the demo.'

Fyfe took the four-track demo cassette into school and played it to Michael on his Walkman. 'He was like, "This is what I did at the weekend,"' says Michael. 'I don't think it was even mixed, but I thought it was unbelievable. It was such a huge step up from anything I'd heard locally; it was catchy, had loads of energy, and was well-recorded.'

Therapy?—the question mark was added to fill a gap on their demo, which they'd named *Thirty Seconds Of Silence*—needed a bassist, and they asked Michael to try out for the band later the following month. 'They had a gig booked in the summer,' he says. 'I think they thought Evil Priest was more of a serious concern than it was, but we didn't really do much. We maybe played three or four gigs in total.'

The band would return to Merville House to practise regularly. Andy—who had a Protestant upbringing—insisted on getting the key to the rehearsal space. Michael, who was raised in a Catholic family, would wait in the car. 'Andy did that because if I went in there and someone said, "Oh, where are you from?" or asked what my surname was, there might have been some trouble,' he says. 'There were murals and all sorts of graffiti. It was a real loyalist stronghold.'

At the time, Northern Ireland was in the grip of violent unrest over the splitting of Ireland into two countries. Nationalists—who were usually Catholic—believed that Ireland should be a united, independent country. Loyalists—who were largely Protestant—wanted Northern Ireland to remain part of the United Kingdom. The Troubles had begun in the 1960s, after British soldiers began to patrol the streets in Northern Ireland and clashed with paramilitary organisations. But inside that Mini Metro were just three lads who wanted to let off some steam and play music.

'When it came to music and gigs, people had the good sense to leave that kind of nonsense at the door,' Michael continues. 'People weren't interested in religion but more about what good records you'd heard recently. The worst thing about gigs at the art college was there'd be a load of aggressive skinheads who'd hang around. God forbid whoever was picking you up after the gig was late and you ended up around there on your own. I mean, we're talking people with swastika tattoos on their foreheads. I suppose every town in the late 80s had them, but Belfast had a unique breed.'

The band's first gig at Conor Hall lasted half an hour. Opening with 'Bloody Blue', their eleven-song set was received well.

'I broke a string,' Michael remembers. 'I don't think I've ever broke a string apart from then! It was E string, during "Body O.D.". I didn't panic. I just thought, *Oh, great.*'

'People came up to us and said we were either amazing or just said it was bizarre,' adds Andy. 'We didn't look like anyone else in the building. Decadence Within were this smart punk band, and the others had undercuts and crusty garb. We didn't have any fashion sense and just looked like three young farmers had wandered on stage.'

Gerry Harford, a concert promoter, first saw the band shortly after the show at the art college. When The Senseless Things got their dates wrong and failed to show up at Belfast's Errigle Inn, Gerry's colleague Elaine McDonald suggested a local band who could fill in at short notice.

'She went around Belfast looking for them and found Andy and Michael,' says Gerry. 'Their gear was in Ballyclare, so Michael and I drove out there to collect some of it. Michael, being a heavy-metal fan, was impressed with some of the metal acts that I worked with—like Kreator and Death—and shyly offered me a copy of their first demo. We got the gig going and I stayed to listen, although I had planned to leave, as my car had been giving me trouble all that day. I still had to drive from Belfast to Dublin late at night; this was not something lightly undertaken in the Troubles!

'I still remember getting home at about 2am and telling my wife, Susan, that I had just heard the most interesting and original band to come out of Ireland since God knows when,' he adds.

In September, Michael underwent an operation on his stomach. In his absence, Andy and Fyfe worked on some new ideas and, in one rehearsal, came up with a clutch of new songs.

'They came to visit me in hospital, and they showed me this tape they'd been working on,' remembers Michael. 'It was just the drums, guitar, and vocals.' Among the songs they'd written were 'Meat Abstract' and 'Window Wall', which would later become 'Brainsaw'. 'It's nuts to think that, in a three-hour practice, they managed to write two big signature songs for the band. That's the rate of how quickly things were moving.'

On September 22, in a single rehearsal, they added 'Fantasy Bag' and 'Potato Junkie', and they also had 'S.W.T.', which featured what would become the 'Screamager' riff. 'Things were on a roll,' Michael adds.

By November, the band were ready to record their second demo— their first as a three-piece. Towards the end of the month, they booked in a day at Active Studio in Banbridge and thrashed through four songs— 'Multifuck', 'Here Is …', 'S.W.T.', and 'Punishment Kiss'—for a limited-run cassette demo they named *Meat Abstract*.

'I got the impression it was definitely a step up from the studio that the *Thirty Seconds Of Silence* demo had been recorded in,' says Michael. 'It was a commercial studio, but I don't think it sounded as good. It was a bit thin-sounding.'

'We did the first demo in Colum's attic with a 16-track, but this was in a proper 24-track studio,' adds Andy. 'We'd rehearsed the songs within an inch of their life. A lot of country acts and folk musicians recorded there. It was quite a busy studio, and there was definitely a feeling, when we turned up, of *who the fuck's this?*'

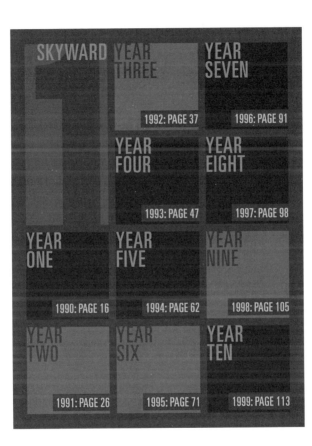

SKYWARD

YEAR ONE/wake up!
time to die!

In early January, Therapy? recorded their debut single at Randalstown's Homestead Studio, with production duties being handled by Shaun Wallace, a local legend otherwise known as Mudd. The studio was a popular residential recording facility in County Antrim that had once hosted Northern Ireland's 1986 World Cup squad for their single 'Come On Northern Ireland', produced by Mudd himself. The band immediately warmed to him.

'Mudd was really well known, and a shit-hot guitar player, too,' says Andy. 'When we started thinking about the first demo, I called the studio up, and he answered. I asked how much a day in the studio would cost, and he asked how much we had. I said about £100, and he replied, "I'll make you a cup of coffee for that." I was working in Michelin, and Fyfe was working in the Kiln [pub] in Larne, and I think Michael had a part-time job as well. For two days, it came to about a grand. We just thought, *Let's do this*, and scraped the money together.'

Before they recorded 'Meat Abstract' and 'Punishment Kiss', it was noted that Michael's load-in was unusually quick. 'I didn't have a bass amp with me,' he explains. 'Mudd started laughing and told me I couldn't just plug straight into the desk and sound like Rob Wright from Nomeansno. A display of brilliant naivety there.'

The single begins with a rapid-fire drum pattern, punctuated by a sample of *Blade Runner* character Leon Kowalski barking 'Wake up … time to die!' into the face of a near-unconscious Rick Deckard. 'I went to Amsterdam for a weekend and heard Belgian new beat in a club,' says Andy. 'The next day I bought a compilation that had Erotic Dissidents on it. I played it to Fyfe, and he liked it. For the song, I had this drone-y Eastern thing on the guitar.

'Steve Albini's songs would tell stories, and I was influenced by that,' he adds. 'Fyfe had read in the paper that a kid had killed a family member and when the cops came, he was wearing a T-shirt that said *No one knows the trouble I've seen.* It's about the dark side of human nature. We didn't have a title for ages, and then I saw some art by Helen Chadwick, who'd taken a series of photographs of meat and called it *Meat Abstract.*'

The grinding, insistent riffs that informed the single's B-side, 'Punishment Kiss', were inspired by the Big Black albums *Atomizer* and *Hammer Party*. In the song, Andy tells the story of three people who take a life-changing trip abroad: '*Little Leslie, fond of the sun, came back with more than a tan, tried to change the shape of their lives carved from concrete with a welfare knife ...*'

'One of them was recently divorced, so they'd saved up for ages and went on holiday to somewhere like Spain,' explains Andy. 'When they came back, it turned out all three of them were diagnosed with HIV. What started out as a hedonistic fling had turned into the worst case of bad luck.'

To release the seven-inch, the band set up their own label and named it Multifuckingnational. Andy called a pressing plant in north London and ordered one thousand vinyl records. 'It was something like £580,' he remembers. 'I found their number in the back of the *NME*. We were going to get five hundred made, but it was cheaper to get more done, so they told me to wrap the tapes in tinfoil, in case the package came into contact with magnets. I put the cheque inside and posted them. It was a bit of a leap of faith because we could have lost our music or just got ripped off. We just needed to decide on what to have as a cover.'

Local artist George Smyth met Fyfe through his cousin, Harry McKay, who attended the same university as the drummer. 'He'd been studying over in Scotland but returned here to go to [Ulster University in] Coleraine,' says George. 'In 1989, my cousin landed at my door and was a whirlwind full of chat, and he mentioned a band called Therapy?. He reckoned they were going to be massive. He played me the *Thirty Seconds Of Silence* cassette, and it was excellent. Later on, I met Fyfe, and we talked about all things art-related: film, music, and painting. I showed Fyfe some of the work I'd recently completed, and he asked if I could do the artwork.

'I painted the cover straight after meeting Fyfe,' he continues. 'His energy and enthusiasm were infectious, but I realised that the imagery had to be as visceral as the music. It grabbed you by the throat, stared you down until you got it, so both had to go hand in hand.'

The sleeves were printed, while several boxes of vinyl were delivered to Andy's parents; the band spent hours sitting at the kitchen table putting their single together. 'We folded and glued a thousand of the sleeves with Pritt Stick and put each record into its sleeve, while my mum made us cheese on toast and cups of coffee,' says Andy.

The following month, the band secured a gig at the Monster Club, a night of music and comedy held the Errigle Inn in Belfast on February 28. In the days leading up to the booking, the band arranged a rehearsal in Newtownabbey. With Michael living in Larne and Fyfe residing in Portrush, Andy faced a round trip of 130 miles. He and Michael arrived at the drummer's home to discover Fyfe wasn't there.

'We didn't have mobile phones in those days, so I found a callbox and rang his house, but there was no answer,' Andy remembers. 'We knocked on every window and started visiting bars we thought he might be in. Someone at his student union told us that he'd been asked by a band called The Impossibles to fly to London to mime the drums for a performance of their single on a kids' TV show. He'd not left a note, and he was aware that our gig was scheduled to take place during his trip to London.'

Furious, the pair arranged a rehearsal with Michael's brother Charlie in an attempt to salvage the show. 'The gig went ahead and was short and energetic, and Charlie was well up to the task,' Andy recalls. 'We managed to get a hold of Fyfe several days later, and he refused to discuss what he did.

What he *did* talk about, though, was how furious he was with us that we'd played the gig without him. This was a big blow to me, as I'd naively thought we were a team—that this band was something special we'd built together.'

Around this time, Andy was in another band called Catweazel with Paul Chapman of Strontium Dog. 'It was a good way to keep playing music with a musician I admired, and it was all very relaxed and easy,' he explains. 'The music itself was a mix of Misfits, Screaming Trees, Dinosaur Jr., and melodic garage-punk. It was never serious, though, and we only ever played one concert, supporting a fledgling Quicksand at Belfast Art College. I was focused on Therapy?, but it helped diffuse my frustration.'

As the year rolled on, Therapy? were building a cult following in Northern Ireland—much to the chagrin of the headline bands they were supporting. On June 20, they supported Oxford shoegazers Ride at the Limelight in Belfast. 'You had to feel sorry for Ride, as most of their set was drowned out by the crowd chanting "James Joyce is fucking my sister" [from "Potato Junkie"],' remembers George. 'I don't know what Ride thought, but their singer didn't look too pleased. People were meeting new people all the time, friendships being formed; it was like a tribe was emerging.'

Meat Abstract was released in July. The band earmarked one hundred of the vinyl copies for promotional use and mailed them to the likes of SST Records, Dischord, Steve Albini, and Thurston Moore, and magazines like *NME*, *Maximum Rock And Roll*, *Forced Exposure*, *Film Fret Magazine*, *Hot Press*, and *Kerrang!*. They also contacted radio stations and local DJs like Mike Edgar, Mary Carson, and people at RTÉ in Dublin. The rest they would sell at gigs and through local record shops.

'We had no master plan but wanted to release a single,' says Michael. 'We just wanted to have a record on the shelf alongside the Sub Pop, Touch And Go, and Dischord stuff in Caroline Music in Belfast—that was the dream. Everything was moving quite quickly.'

That month, the band were invited to play a handful of dates with

Derby progressive metal four-piece The Beyond, including dates in Edinburgh, Hull, and Derby. On drums was Michael's tape-trading contact, Neil Cooper.

'We'd released the *Manic Sound Panic* EP,' says Neil, 'and our manager, Mike Stack, was in Belfast and went into a record shop and asked for some local recommendations. He was given the *Meat Abstract* single. I've still got the promo tape. We listened to the songs and thought it sat well with what we were trying to do. We didn't sound the same—we were more metal. Therapy? were more punky, but we had a similar mindset.

'Around that time, I didn't think much of rock and metal; it was all Poison, Warrant, and Aerosmith, and it meant nothing to me,' he adds. 'So when we found out Therapy? were coming over, we were over the moon.'

'The first time I saw Neil drum, I went, *Holy fuck!* And the second thing I thought was, *How old is that guy?*' laughs Andy. 'It was a bit like with Fyfe; you didn't know if he was seventeen or twenty-five. But with Neil, he looked like [pint-sized *Home Alone* hero] Macaulay Culkin. He was really baby-faced. The thing about Fyfe was he hated most drummers—he only liked Rey Washam [Scratch Acid], John Stanier from Helmet, and Stewart Copeland from The Police. I remember Fyfe watching Neil and going, *Oh my god, that guy's amazing.*'

'Fyfe and I got on pretty well,' says Neil. 'When we got chatting, we discovered we were listening to similar stuff. He'd talked about bands like Skinny Puppy, and I mentioned these white-label dance records I'd been listening to. After the tour, we traded cassettes. He'd send me industrial stuff and I'd send him stuff by [Leeds acid-house duo] LFO and [Sheffield techno two-piece] Sweet Exorcist. I'd drum along to this stuff and nick the grooves, if I'm honest. So, when I watched Fyfe play, I completely got what he was doing.'

Towards the end of the tour, the band drove their big orange transit van, dubbed Big Bertha, to BBC Radio's Broadcasting House in London. Their mission was to press a copy of *Meat Abstract* into the hand of John

Peel. 'We had a day off before a London gig, so I drove the van to the BBC and double-parked it,' explains Andy. 'This is how naive we were: I walked into the reception and said, "I'd like to give this record to John Peel." The receptionist explained how this wasn't the way things worked, and, besides, he recorded his show in another building.'

A kindly concierge overheard Andy, took the single along with some details, and promised that the music would find its way onto the legendary DJ's desk. 'I got back into the van and told Michael and Fyfe what happened,' he recalls. 'They both were like, *Fuck, that's the end of that!*'

The following night, the band supported Massachusetts hardcore band Moving Targets in New Cross, then drove over the river to catch up with The Beyond, who were headlining the Stick Of Rock pub on Bethnal Green Road. 'I'm not sure what happened, but we had a food fight after the gig,' explains Neil. 'We covered them and their van in food as an end-of-tour prank. I don't know why, because they were lovely. I remember phoning Michael after those dates because I felt really bad, but with Michael being Michael, he was completely fine about it.'

'There were a lot of practical jokes between the bands,' adds Michael. 'They got eggs and flour and covered Big Bertha, which was an eyesore to see anyway. It was old-school, proper revenge. Whatever happened to their drummer?'

Shortly after the tour with The Beyond, Therapy? were back in Northern Ireland. Andy was visiting Michael's flat when they heard a shout from the next room. It was Michael's brother, Charlie. 'He came running in and said, "John Peel's playing your single!"' he remembers. 'We all ran into the kitchen and caught the end of "Meat Abstract". John Peel said something like "That was Therapy?, and if you want to hear more …", and then he read out Michael's address—which we were standing in at that very moment. That was a really big night for us.'

On September 15, the band ticked off a dream support slot from their bucket list—if bucket lists existed in 1990—when they shared a bill with Fugazi at McGonagles in Dublin. 'When the band started, we all discovered Fugazi at the same time,' remembers Andy. 'It wasn't metal, it wasn't straightforward punk, and it wasn't noise rock, but there were elements that we all loved. Ian McKaye has such an aura about him, about what you do and you don't do. I drove down to the gig and I began to overthink it—*Oh, god, what are you meant to say to Ian McKaye?*—and was self-conscious about buying a beer, because Fugazi didn't drink. They turned up and they were really nice guys, no airs and graces.'

'I just sauntered in and went to Joe Lally, "Um, can I borrow your bass amp?"' adds Michael. 'He was lovely about it, but imagine doing that. Again, that was incredibly naive of me—who turns up expecting to play with no equipment?

'The gig was phenomenal, and it was absolutely rammed,' he adds. 'I suppose, for us, Fugazi were like—I dunno, they were our Rolling Stones, do you know what I mean? The Fugazi stuff was musically so much more our vibe, we were so excited to play that night.'

'I had goosebumps watching them from the side of the stage,' says Andy. 'It was a life-affirming experience.'

The following month, the band were invited to record a session for Dave Fanning's show at RTÉ 2FM Studios, engineered by Paddy McBreen. They performed 'Reality Fuck', 'Innocent X', 'Body O.D.', and 'Dancin' With Manson'. 'We'd done some interviews and had our single played on the radio, but to record a session was a big validation of what we were doing,' says Michael. 'We did an old version of "Die Laughing" called "Reality Fuck", and it really felt like things were starting to happen.'

Towards the end of the year, the trio closed their 1990 account with a handful of shows in Northern Ireland and Ireland. On November 27, they supported Teenage Fanclub at Coleraine. The headliners' frontman, Norman Blake, ponied up some hard cash for a copy of *Meat Abstract*, and had an unusual request. 'He asked me where he could buy a kite,' remembers Andy, 'as he wanted to go to the beach and fly one. The whole band were really lovely.'

Gigs followed in December at the Attic in Dublin (supporting Shred and Pig Ignorance), Sir Henry's in Cork, and McGonagles in Dublin (supporting Loop). Then the band's attentions turned to committing much of their current setlist to tape. Over the Christmas period, they spent two days with producer Mudd at Homestead Studios in Randalstown, where they'd recorded their *Meat Abstract* single eleven months previously. Now, they recorded 'Animal Bones', 'Skyward', 'Loser Cop', 'Innocent X', and 'Dancin' With Manson'.

'We recorded over Christmas because it was dirt cheap,' explains Michael. 'We just played the songs like we were doing our live set.'

'The first night we were there, Mudd said we needed to be a bit livelier,' remembers Andy. 'He suggested we go to the off license to get some beers, and that relaxed us.'

Under Andy's sludgy guitar tone, 'Skyward' is a pop song, based partly on Robert De Niro's antihero in the 1976 film *Taxi Driver*. 'For some reason, I wanted to try to write a piece of music like Jimi Hendrix,' he says. 'I know I can't play like him. I'd just bought my first wah-wah pedal, and I used to hate the fucking things. Being from a punk background, they were considered a self-indulgent toy for boring old hippies. Then I heard *Living All Over Me* by Dinosaur Jr. and played the opening track, "Little Fury Things", over and over again. I couldn't believe the onslaught of wah. It was amazing—a wall of noise.

'I started looking desperately for other records in my collection that might have wah on them, and the nearest was a collection of Hendrix singles. I had these three chords—B Minor, G, and D—which sounded good together. I started playing them trying to use the wah. I was rubbish, and it sounded like a terrible 70s cheese-rock band. The chords themselves sounded good enough on their own. The song is about listlessness, zoning out, and Generation X.'

'Animal Bones' was written after watching a documentary about the Vietnam War and the use of 'nonhuman mammal remains' to give decimated soldiers' coffins added weight without telling their grieving families. The line '*Honey, I'm home*' is a nod to Hüsker Dü's iconic *Land Speed Record* album cover, which features a row of American troops' coffins draped with the stars and stripes.

The song itself is a frantic thrash, opening with a 'wonky cassette speeding up' vocal by Andy, who yells, '*You're a piece of shit!*' It was almost lost when it came to collating the five tracks. 'Mudd couldn't find the master tape version of "Animal Bones",' says Michael. 'I think it had been recorded over with a country-and-western session. So the version we used for the album was a cassette of the rough mix, because it was the only version we had. It sounds considerably thinner in comparison to the rest of the tracks, but what can you do? That was the chaos element coming into play.'

The band's love affair with free-jazz saxophonist John Zorn loudly makes its presence felt on the largely instrumental blast of 'Loser Cop', which is bolstered by sampled dialogue from the films *Electra Glide In Blue* and *Easy Rider*. The chaotic jazz squall was provided by their friend Keith Thompson, a Caroline Music employee, who performs saxophone on the song. 'He drank a load of tequila when we were in the studio and got completely shit-faced and fell asleep in this empty Jacuzzi,' says Michael. 'In between blowing chunks, he had to blow some sax.'

The song itself recounts a student house party in Portrush that went awry. 'There was loads of hash floating around,' remembers Andy, 'and there was this stuff called Sputnik, which was hash laced with coke. I didn't have any, so God knows what it was like. There was something like fifty people there, but what we didn't know was that the landlord had taken ill—he'd maybe had a heart attack or something—and his daughter drove past while the party was happening. I remember being sat in the corner and these two people ran in. We thought they were gate-crashers, then the daughter kept shouting about her dad. The guy who was with her started lifting people up by the scruff of the neck and kicking them out of the house. Upstairs, Harry—who did our lights—was there, and he drew a pentagram on a mirror with shaving foam and wrote "Satan" above it. Bear in mind this was Northern Ireland, and very religious.

'All these cops steamed in,' he adds. 'They threw us in the back of their police trucks and got us in, one by one, and asked what we were doing there. I remember them asking about all the drugs in the house and who drew the pentagram. One police officer kept muttering "Fucking assholes … absolute fucking assholes …" under his breath. That's who the song is about.'

'Innocent X', written by Andy, is cautionary tale about drugs and family visits. 'The lyrics are about me trying to talk myself down off an acid trip in my old bedroom in Ballyclare,' he says. 'I'd inadvertently taken acid the night before, and it was about four in the morning when I started freaking out about having to go to my parents' house. The roads would have been empty, so I drove home and got to their house. They were both out, luckily.'

Andy's distorted vocal was inspired by the Bad Brains song 'Sacred Love', which frontman Paul 'H.R.' Hudson sang down the phone from Lorton Reformatory in Laurel Hill, Virginia, while serving time for marijuana possession. 'Mudd rigged up all the telephones with an intercom and Andy recorded his vocals that way,' explains Michael. 'Things like that were no problem for Mudd. Some people would have preferred to just record it clean. He was a good ally in that respect.'

The final track, 'Dancin' With Manson', was based on old riff meant for a song idea called 'Winona Ryder' that, according to Andy, eventually became 'a noise-pop fest that would be a pointer for *Troublegum*'.

'That song was influenced by Sonic Youth's "Death Valley '69",' says Andy. 'Me and Fyfe watched a documentary about Charles Manson and wanted to write a narrative about him. I don't know why it ended up being six minutes long. It's a very convoluted way to get to the heart of a pop song, but it's one of my favourites from that time.'

With the recordings done, Andy had to go back to work his night shift at the Michelin factory while Mudd worked on the mix with Michael and Fyfe. Bleary-eyed, he returned to Homestead to find an exhausted producer at the studio desk.

'I told Mudd that I couldn't hear any guitar or bass in the mix,' says Andy. 'He said his ears were fried, so we all mixed it together. Fyfe was going, "Turn the drums up!" I'm shouting, "I'm going to turn my guitar up!" And Michael wanted his bass turned up. I kid you not—it was like something out of a cartoon. Mudd got all the faders and pushed them up to the top and said, "Are yous fucking happy?" And that was it.'

As 1990 melted into 1991, the trio had five new tracks. The untitled, one-sided demo would be later nicknamed the Michelin Tape, on account of the tyre-company mascot that adorned the photocopied sleeve. 'We were delighted with it,' says Michael. 'It was essentially our set at the time—everything was played live and a couple of things were overdubbed. I think it really caught the energy of the band. We then started talking about how we were going to release it properly.'

YEAR 1991
TWO / acid, knives, and an angry phone call

With five new recordings completed the previous month, Therapy? continued to plough their own furrow in the UK and Ireland throughout the winter and spring.

On January 26, Andy and Michael boarded a ferry and crossed the Irish Sea to see Ministry's Al Jourgensen's industrial side-project Revolting Cocks and Silverfish at Glasgow's College Of Building And Printing. (The gig was originally set to take place at the city's university, but after complaints about the headline act's name it was moved to a smaller, more intimate venue.)

'We took a *Meat Abstract* seven-inch, and a cassette, too,' remembers Andy. 'The cassette was for Al Jourgensen. When we got to the venue, we went straight to the bar and asked if someone could pass it along to Al. The guy behind the bar said we could give it to him ourselves, and we ended up in their dressing room. We saw Al doing an enormous line of speed off an ironing board. It looked like there was a bit of carnage going on and we felt a bit out of depth, so we had a quick chat and left.'

The band knocked on Silverfish's dressing room door, too, and handed vocalist Lesley Rankine a copy of their record. 'We got chatting to Lesley,' adds Michael. 'They were signed to Wiiija Records. It was a fantastic gig, and we also saw Silverfish in Edinburgh the following night. A few days later, Gary Walker from Wiiija called and said, "Look, Leslie passed on your single, and we'd love to hear more stuff."'

On February 14, the trio supported Stourbridge fraggle-rockers Ned's Atomic Dustbin at Ulster University's Coleraine campus. 'Gerry Harford, who was tentatively beginning to manage us at this point, had a main gig as a promoter, and Ned's were one of the bands he looked after,' explains Andy. 'Fyfe was already at Coleraine, studying Combined Humanities, so it made sense to have us as a support band for the gig in the student union. The gig was uncomfortably rammed, and, with a bunch of Fyfe's student mates in the crowd, we had a fantastic reception.

'The band themselves were really sweet and all bought T-shirts and seven-inch singles, which we were selling ourselves from a box beside the bar,' he adds. 'It was very nice to see one of the band sporting a Therapy? T-shirt in an article in either *NME* or *Melody Maker* the following week.'

On February 22, the band played Belfast's Conor Hall (formerly part of the Belfast campus of Ulster University) and met with Southern Records' John Loder, whose company was in a label partnership with the aforementioned Notting Hill-based Wiiija Records (whose postcode was W11 1JA) and also handled their distribution.

'He recorded Fugazi, Big Black, Crass, and that kind of thing, so we were just like, *Wow, it's THE John Loder!*' says Michael. 'The Art College show was sold out—four hundred people—and people were going nuts. The next day we signed a contract. I say contract—it was a sheet of A4 paper with a couple of paragraphs. We were incredibly naive, but John sold the idea to us. He said if we need to get into a big contract, then he said we can't really work together, because this was how he did it. Just a formality. We started writing more songs around that time: "Accelerator", "Skinning Pit", "Summer Of Hate". We planned to release *Babyteeth* in the summer: the two songs from the *Meat Abstract* single and the five tracks we'd recorded around Christmas.'

By April, the band found themselves crisscrossing the Irish Sea, playing more and more shows in England and Wales in the run up to the release of *Babyteeth*. 'We opened for Dr Phibes and The House Of Wax Equations on April 25, in Newport,' says Andy. 'We stayed on the floor of [late, legendary TJ's owner] John Sicolo and his wife and got to meet a lot of the Cheap Sweaty Fun crew, including Simon Phillips, who had put on many gigs by bands like Fugazi, Swans, and Big Black. Not much sleep was ever had at Newport shows, as we'd sit up all night with the Cheap Sweaty Fun lot, asking them to tell us more war stories about all the fabulous noise and punk bands they'd booked.'

A week later, they played the 1-in-12 club in Bradford, a not-for-profit initiative that the organisers say was 'founded on the anarchistic values of self-management, co-operation and mutual aid'. 'We were so excited—it was such a legendary punk venue,' says Andy. 'Most of our shows at this point were beginning to pick up a word-of-mouth following, but the 1-in-12 was different. I think eleven people had turned up for the show. The staff in the venue felt so sorry for us that all of them stepped out from behind the bar and stood at the front of the stage. That meant a lot to us, and, afterwards, we hung out with them all and had a good laugh about it.'

'After playing in Bradford, we actually drove to a motorway services and spent the night in the car with all the gear,' says Michael. 'That was grim.'

Following a show at Dublin's McGonagles in early June, the band ran into trouble while parking their van. 'We heard a commotion outside, and some lads took a bass from the van,' explains Andy. 'Michael's brother, C.J. [Ciaran], chased them and tried to thump one. The person we were staying with said they'd call the police. While we were waiting, there was a knock at the door, and we were faced by eight people with hurling sticks, the same age as us: "Where is he? He took a swing at one of our lads! You had no fucking right to hit him." We said he'd stolen one of our guitars and he replied, "I'll get my fucking gun and I'll shoot you, you northern cunt!" The police arrived and we said we were just talking, so they drove away.

'The next day, one of the lads came and said he knew where the bass was—it was in a park, dumped in a hedge,' he adds. 'A few days later, a group of people surrounded the person whose house it was and told him to get the fuck out. He had to move. That was a Republican area.'

During the summer, the band played the Underworld in Camden, London. Music agent Paul Bolton was in attendance. 'For some reason, in the early 90s, I seemed to be putting a lot of my other clients through this Irish promoter called Gerry Harford,' says Paul, who still works with the band to this day. 'We had had a good run of shows and had not fallen out, despite an issue with a PA catching fire during a show we had in Drogheda. When Gerry suggested I checked out a band he was managing when they played at the Underworld, I trusted his comment about them being special. I wasn't disappointed. Their songs were clever, aggressive, and catchy all at the same time, and it was obvious they had potential.'

On July 15, seven months after the band finished recording it at Homestead Studio in Randalstown, their debut album, *Babyteeth*, was released by Wiiija. It reached the top of the British and Irish indie album charts, and would later be reissued by Wiiija's distributor, Southern. 'The reviews were really good,' Andy remembers. '*Select*, *NME*, *Melody Maker*, *Sounds* all gave it a good review … I remember Fyfe was really unhappy with the reviews because none of them had mentioned the drums. One review mentioned that it sounded like it had been recorded on a Walkman on a passing bus!'

For artwork, the trio called once again on the services of George Smyth, who had painted the surrealist cover for their *Meat Abstract* seven-inch. 'I was given free rein to paint what I wanted,' says George. 'I just let my imagination run riot, inspired by the sound and energy they were creating. I did a couple of preliminary paintings for *Babyteeth*, but I knew I'd nailed it with the final version. Fyfe was delighted when he saw it. He said, "What the hell is going on in your head, George?" My mother's face on seeing the cover is a different story.'

Shortly after *Babyteeth*'s release, John Loder and Gary Walker from Wiiija met with the band to discuss recording another mini-album in the coming months. 'We wanted to do an EP,' says Michael. 'We had "Skinning Pit", "Fantasy Bag", "Prison Breaker", and "Potato Junkie". John Loder took us to one side and said it cost the same to make a mini-album. We had the tracks: "D.L.C." was an instrumental, and "Shitkicker" did what it said on the tin.'

In late July and August, the band supported Minneapolis trio Babes In Toyland in Cork, Dublin, Belfast, London, and Newport. 'I think the tour came at the suggestion of John Loder,' Andy recalls. 'There was a lot of really good vibes at the shows, and we got on really well with the band. Babes In Toyland didn't suffer fools, and they were very inspiring in the way they dealt with touring. They were really good fun, and I look back on that time with much fondness. Kat [Bjelland, guitarist] was friendly, Michelle [Leon, bassist] had a fantastic sense of humour, and Lori [Barbero, drummer] was brilliant and would offer to drive us if we wanted to have drinks. She took the Polaroid of the band on Brighton beach, which was used on the back of [US compilation album] *Caucasian Psychosis*.'

Pleasure Death was recorded on August 14 and 15, and mixed over the following two days. The night before the band went to Southern

Studios, they secured a gig at the now-closed Square in Harlow, supporting Spiritualized, featuring former Spacemen 3 guitarist Jason Pierce. 'I remember we were really excited about that,' says Andy. 'Fyfe and I were fans of Spacemen 3, but we didn't know them at all as people. Their album, *Lazer Guided Melodies*, wasn't out at that point, but they were already *NME* darlings.'

The band arrived at the venue and waited for a soundcheck that never came. They were delighted to discover they were going to receive a meal before the show: 'We couldn't believe it, because we weren't eating very well at that time,' says Andy. The trio took their meal to the backstage area, where they discovered the headline act had commandeered both dressing rooms: one for the band, the other for their equipment. A question of where to eat their dinner was met with a shrug. The doors opened and the audience started to drift in.

'We were sat on the stage eating our jacket potatoes and beans and chatting to the people who came down early to check us out,' remembers Andy. 'When we went to leave our plates backstage, a crew remember told us we couldn't go back. Fyfe tried to push past a tech, and, when we saw him getting grief, Michael and I piled in with full Ulster wrath. We saw Jason Pierce looking terrified. We were so fucking furious because we were so humiliated, and had bitten our tongues. They were arrogant, spoiled indie wankers in our eyes, but things calmed down, and we went on stage and played a blinder.'

Afterwards, Andy apologised, and the band were given a room, but it made for an awkward atmosphere. Spiritualized left after the show; Therapy? stayed behind for a club night. Andy, still bristling from earlier, was hooked up with some speed by a punter. 'The dealer arrived in a navy blue Ford Granada and looked like Barry Grant from [British soap opera] *Brookside*,' says Andy. 'Getting whizz wasn't a good look, because we were in the studio the next day. On the way back to London, I was that guy in the back of the van that wouldn't stop talking.'

By the next morning, when it was time to go to the studio, Andy hadn't slept at all. 'We did the guitars and drums for "Potato Junkie", and I was absolutely wired,' he says. 'I thought my Fender Telecaster was the best it had ever sounded. The session went really quickly, and we went to the pub that night.'

Pleasure Death was produced by the band's sound engineer, Harvey Birrell, who'd worked with Crass and alongside Steve Albini and Ian MacKaye. 'He was just a lot more professional and would be like, *It's late, let's go home*, rather than suggest we open a second bottle of whiskey, like Mudd would,' says Michael. 'We certainly didn't need any encouragement at that stage to be lairy. Harvey was like a cheerleader and got everyone on the same page really quickly.'

Opening track 'Skinning Pit' starts with yelling and a rolling drum pattern and a sample of Ray Liotta's character Henry Hill in Martin Scorsese's 1990 crime classic *Goodfellas*: 'Every once in a while I'd have to take a beating. But, by then, I didn't care. The way I saw it, everybody takes a beating sometime.'

'Me and Fyfe were talking about child abuse and how people deal with it,' explains Andy. He describes the lyric '*I was born your punch bag and you, you know I'll never punch you back*' as being about 'the helplessness of feeling alone in a place where you're meant to be guarded and safe. I think we'd taken the inspiration from a still from the movie *La Rupture* by Claude Chabrol, which ended up on the back of the album artwork.

'There's a bit in the middle-eight where it breaks down into almost a techno beat and trance guitar, which was inspired by The Beyond,' he adds. 'We called it the "Beyond Bit" in rehearsals. I've no idea why we put the *Goodfellas* sample in, but Fyfe was obsessed with Scorsese at the time.'

'Fantasy Bag' was originally conceived as a fast-paced riff with an Eastern melody. During rehearsals, it evolved into a sinister, lurching tune befitting of Andy's lyrics about a serial killer: '*I wanted you but what could I do? Now my hands are all covered in you.*'

'I've got Michael and Fyfe to thank for that,' says Andy. 'I was listening to a lot of Loop at the time; they were loud and did hypnotic riffs, and smothered the vocals in delay. I had a James Hetfield moment, where I was really proud of the riff and played it and the other two said I should slow it down. Ten minutes later, it sounded amazing. I could play that riff all night.'

'Shitkicker', a frantic song with a noisy riff inspired by the playing style of Silverfish guitarist Andrew 'Fuzz' Duprey, tells the tale of a musician friend who lived in a Republican area of Belfast. 'It was basically run by a paramilitary organisation,' explains Andy. 'The thing about paramilitaries in Northern Ireland that we found strange growing up—on both sides— was the little foot soldiers who got involved. They thought they had carte blanche to do what they wanted under the umbrella of this political organisation. If you pissed off a kid, they'd go, "I'll tell my da, and my da will get you done." They were empty threats half the time, but if you knew they were connected, you'd keep your mouth shut. It was just part of growing up.

'Our friend told us this story about him and his friend were into psychobilly and had bleached-blonde quiffs,' he adds. 'He was approached by some people representing a paramilitary organisation and they said some old ladies had been complaining about his haircut. "It upsets them, so get rid of it," they told him. "We brand it antisocial behaviour." It could get you beaten up—or worse. They didn't get their hair cut. Later, someone had got into his house and written a message on his mirror in lipstick: *This is warning number one, next time we're back, we'll bring the gun.* That's when he started growing his hair out.'

The title of 'Prison Breaker' was coined by Tad frontman Thomas 'Tad' Doyle, who told the band it was slang for smoking hash out of a can. The song itself is about absence. 'We'd been away from home a lot and relationships were being tested,' explains Andy. 'We took the term, prison break, for being away from a confined environment.'

Like 'Shitkicker', the instrumental 'D.L.C.' was not originally intended to appear on the band's second Wiiija release. 'We had this riff that had an absurdist, NoMeansNo, Eric Dolphy jazz swing, and it sounded like someone was sneaking into your house,' says Andy. 'It stands for *Dark Lord Cometh*, which was named after someone we knew who was a sponger and would help himself to your food and lager, or borrow something from your video collection that you'd never see again.'

The final track was 'Potato Junkie', a song that has remained an integral part of the band's live shows throughout their career, despite nearly being scrapped for being 'too grunge' and 'too rawk' in rehearsals. It's most notable for its blunt refrain: *'James Joyce is fucking my sister.'*

'I don't have a sister, and I like James Joyce,' says Andy. 'There was a thing in Ireland called *raggle-taggle*. It was a post-war gypsy ruffian look, like Dexys Midnight Runners in the 'Come On Eileen' video. It was like a Hollywood version of the Irish, with fiddles involved for a good old Celtic knees-up. "Potato Junkie" was our diatribe against that. *James Joyce is fucking my sister* didn't really mean anything; it was just a way of saying that it was ripping my own culture apart.

'When I brought the song into rehearsal in Rathcoole, Fyfe said, "Are we a Sub Pop band now?"' he adds. 'Fugazi are masters of using stops, so we got Fyfe to play through them, and we said it sounded like "Fire" by Jimi Hendrix. We kept the song. If Michael and Fyfe hadn't liked the song, it would have been dropped and never played again. A year later, someone at Trinity College in Dublin did a thesis on the song, which is incredible.'

The band took one and a half days to record the mini-album, and, on the second day, they recorded a John Peel session in Maida Vale Studio 5. Fuelled by Tennent's Super—one of the stronger beers, favoured by hardened drinkers—they recorded 'Innocent X', 'Meat Abstract', 'Prison Breaker', and a new track called 'Perversonality'.

Following the studio session, Therapy? headed across town to see Silverfish perform at London's ULU—with a smashed Andy hanging out the back of the van while being admonished by label boss John Loder—and, from there, went to a party at RAK Studios near Regent's Park.

'Fyfe was friends with this two-piece called The Impossibles, and they were recording a single there,' says Andy. 'It was one of those mad nights. The Impossibles put make up on us all and we were running about in drag. I had a microdot of acid, and then things took a turn for the worse.'

Michael went downstairs and discovered Andy carrying some kitchen knives; with a little gentle cajoling, they were removed from his grasp, and he was ordered to lie down in a darkened room. 'I found sanctuary in the bathroom, which had this silky wallpaper,' Andy remembers. 'I took a marker and decided to write *Mickie Most, shit host* in big letters on the wall and tried to sleep,' he adds—Mickie Most being the studio's owner and a legendary producer responsible for hits by The Animals, Donovan, and Suzi Quatro. The next morning, a RAK employee told the 'saucer-eyed Wurzel Gummidge with the Ulster accent' that his bandmates had returned to Southern Studios to mix the album with Harvey. And, also, to get the fuck out—in the politest way possible.

At Southern Studios, Andy took refuge under the mixing desk, yelling, 'Turn up the feedback!' and 'Sounds amazing!' to anyone in earshot. By the close of the night, the exhausted, fearful frontman decided to sleep in the studio. 'The next morning, I found out that Cathi Unsworth and Steve Gullick had come down to the studio for a *Melody Maker* piece,' says Andy. 'It was a really big deal, because we liked what they did. That was quite a week.'

Shortly after returning to Belfast, Andy's phone rang. On the other end of the line was a well-spoken woman from RAK Studios. She didn't sound happy. 'Is this Andy Cairns?' she asked. 'I'm phoning up about the wallpaper in our toilet. We know you wrote *Mickie Most is a shit host* on the wall. Would you do that in your own house?'

The terse phone call ended with the shamed frontman promising to pay for the damages. He duly emptied his bank account to cover the cost.

On September 15, Therapy? set out on a headline tour, the final date of which, at the Camden Palace on October 1, marking the night when their now legendary merch seller and raconteur, 'Diamond' Dave Thompson, first starting selling shirts for the band.

'I met them the year before, at the Limelight in Belfast,' he says. 'I was over visiting my relatives, and my cousin Nicola and her husband-to-be Willie took me to see a band called LMS, which actually featured Michael's brother Charlie on drums. After the gig, I heard 'Meat Abstract', and it was an absolute stomper. The band were there, and we were introduced; it changed my life forever.

'I'd started my studies and the Central School Of Speech And Drama in September—a decision I regretted very quickly, as my acting skills were rather limited,' he adds. 'I was spending most of my time following these rogues around on tour.'

In December, the band played a run of shows supporting Hole. 'They were a bit hit and miss live, and we were not hit or miss at all, so it was fucking great,' says Andy. 'They were really good shows, all sold out and there was a lot of madness.'

Of the four shows, it's the one at TJ's in Newport that will live long in the memory, largely thanks to Hole's Courtney Love and her guest of honour. 'Daisy Chainsaw were on the bill that night, too,' says Michael. 'We'd just played, and we had to get all of our stuff off the stage. My brother C.J. was on tour with us, and he saw someone was sitting on our flight cases. He said, "Sorry mate, I really need to get those cases," and was blanked. He said, "Right, mate, you need to get the fuck off my cases right now." The guy got down and shuffled off. He only found out later that it was Kurt Cobain. C.J.'s dined out on that story ever since.'

Legend has it that Kurt proposed to Courtney that night. Around the same time, Nirvana—who were touring the UK in support of their new album, *Nevermind*—made their debut appearance on British TV by way of Channel 4's late-night show *The Word*. He told the audience, 'I'd like all of you people in this room to know that Courtney Love, the lead singer of the sensational pop group Hole, is the best fuck in the world.' In its day, *The Word* was many things, but no one expected such romantic declarations.

'I remember that we got an advance copy of *Nevermind* and *Mush* by Leatherface and played them in the van all the time,' says Michael. 'I actually preferred the Leatherface album, to be honest. But you could tell there was a big change coming for the underground music that we liked. We'd watched it build and build.'

YEAR THREE/'in my sleep, i grind my teeth ...'

Pleasure Death was released on January 27 1992. Following favourable reviews in the *NME* and *Melody Maker*, it reached no. 1 in the UK indie chart. But behind the scenes, the band—now playing the biggest shows of their career—were struggling financially. Andy was still working night shifts in the tyre factory, while Michael and Fyfe were juggling the demands of their college courses with the band's growing itinerary.

With two successful mini-albums to the band's name, Southern Records planned for them to record a full-length album the following year with Steve Albini. But something had to give. 'We were playing bigger and bigger gigs and we were either losing money or just about breaking even,' says Andy. 'I was working in the factory, trying to make ends meet, pay rent and my car insurance, just so I could drive to work. We were all finding it hard.'

'It wasn't like we wanted a tour bus,' adds Michael. 'We'd eat cornflakes out of the box and buy a loaf of bread and coleslaw and see how far that would go. Our equipment was on its last legs. Everything was fucked.'

Chicago-based label Touch And Go teamed up with its UK distributor, Southern, for the North American release of *Caucasian Psychosis*, a thirteen-track compilation of *Babyteeth* and *Pleasure Death*, in April. However, it was decided at the last minute that because the album featured previously released material, it would appear on Touch And Go's Quarterstick subsidiary instead. Southern urged the band to tour North America to support the release, but with barely enough money to eat or pay rent, paying for transatlantic flights without any tour support posed its own set of problems.

'They suggested we get jobs to pay for it,' says Michael. 'It was Northern Ireland—there weren't any jobs. Southern said we would have to sort it out. There were a lot of opportunities we couldn't take because we didn't have any money.'

A few months earlier, Nirvana's *Nevermind* had changed the landscape of the music industry forever; gigs would be soon populated by eager A&R men brandishing chequebooks clamouring to sign any alt-rock band and their grandmother, whether they were in a band or not. Southern boss John Loder got wind of the fact that big labels were courting Therapy?, and called the band's manager.

'He phoned up Gerry and said that I was the one who wanted to be a rock star and sign with a major,' says Andy. 'Where the fuck did that come from? The three of us had sat down and decided that we needed to sign to another label. I felt I was being singled out for it. It wasn't me being a rock star. It wasn't me and Michael scheming away. We needed to do it if we wanted to be a working band.'

'We experienced every A&R cliché,' says Michael. 'We did a European run and one label came out and it was nuts. He was like, "We've got to get the beers in, lads! Who's up for banging hookers?" That kind of thing. It was weird.' One label, A&M—founded in 1962 by Herb Alpert and Jerry Moss, and home to Soundgarden and The Police—pursued the band relentlessly. 'They were the only label we liked,' says Andy.

According to Michael, Southern's two-record deal with the band was for two full albums, which meant that *Babyteeth*, *Pleasure Death*, and *Caucasian Psychosis* didn't count towards fulfilling their contract. 'It was really unpleasant,' adds Andy. 'The label weren't happy. Touch And Go—who put out our records in America, and were heroes to us—weren't happy. Wiiija weren't happy. Everyone thought we were dickheads, but we needed to do this.'

'The whole punk-rock trust thing suddenly turned to talk of lawyers,' remembers Michael. 'Harvey Birrell and Gary Walker were caught in the middle. It was one of those situations where we could move on but we couldn't go back. To their credit, A&M bought us out of the deal for £65,000, which Southern were more than happy to accept.'

It wasn't a grand gesture. The band would have to pay it back incrementally: £20,000 would be taken from their publishing, £10,000 from their advance for *Nurse*, £10,000 from *Troublegum*, with a further £15,000 to be recouped from royalties and sales. But it meant they could move forward.

The band signed with A&M on June 5 1992. The following day, they played the In The Park festival at Finsbury Park, North London, sharing a bill with Pearl Jam, L7, PJ Harvey, Shudder To Think, and The Cult. 'We were given £100 each in cash,' says Michael. 'That was probably the most money we'd ever seen from the band, and we had one hell of a weekend.'

The band started writing songs for their new album, *Nurse*. At their initial rehearsals in Rathcoole, they wrote the opening track, 'Nausea', its title taken from French philosopher Jean-Paul Sartre's first novel, *La Nausée*. 'It was about trying to escape from the shit-storm that was going on around us,' says Andy. 'Signing to a major label was a turning point for us, and people took it personally. It was seen as a mass betrayal; people would call us sell-outs, and we lost a lot of friends. I remember one person in Scotland—a fashion designer who looked like she was in the show *Nathan Barley*—told me, "I don't like the new stuff you played. It's too mainstream." But we hadn't played any fucking new songs. She'd got it into her head that we were playing Boston or some REO Speedwagon nonsense.'

On August 1, the band shared a bill with Simply Red and The Saw Doctors at the third-ever Féile, an annual festival at Semple Stadium in County Tipperary, Ireland. During an interview, they were asked, 'Do you ever reckon you'll be like The Rolling Stones and still be around in twenty years?' Once their laughter died down, they answered, 'Don't be ridiculous.'

Soon after, the band travelled south to a house on a farm in County Carlow, to spend two weeks writing, free of any distractions. Andy recalls bringing enough alcohol and speed to last the duration of his stay. The environment, it turns out, would not help his chemically fuelled state. At all. 'There was a very odd atmosphere in the house,' he remembers. 'There was one room which was like a child's room, but the drawings on the wall looked like they would be on a Swans album cover. A few days after we moved in, we found a dead crow hanging in the barn.'

After solidly plugging away at new material for two weeks, the trio needed to let off some steam, so they headed into the nearest town to drink. 'It got a bit *Lord Of The Flies* towards the end,' Michael admits. 'I think after all the stress of changing labels and the amount of investment in the band, the house didn't really help our mental state. We all fell out with each other over something trivial and went back to the house separately. We carried on drinking and started to trash everything we had.'

Their gear was wrecked. Guitars were thrown through windows. Drums were burned on the lawn. A massive antique mirror was smashed. In the corner of the room, Michael's voice-activated tape recorder switched itself on and documented the entire melee. The recording can be found hidden among the rare gems in the band's 2013 retrospective set, *The Gemil Box*.

'There's just a lot of noise and people shouting, "This is it! Burn it all down, destroy it!"' laughs Michael. 'In a way it was good, because it cleared the air before we started recording the album. But we had to get a glazier in to repair all the broken windows.'

With Harvey Birrell at the production desk, the band recorded 'Gone' at the Barn in Annamoe, a village twenty miles from Dublin. 'It was one of the first songs we wrote in Carlow,' explains Andy. 'It's about a friend of ours. She got pregnant at a young age and was disowned by her parents. She had an abortion and then tried to take her own life.'

Andy explains that he had intended 'Gone', a funereal-paced song befitting of the lyrics, to have a Slint-like feel. 'At the time, we thought the song was verging on being a ballad,' he says. 'Signing to a major label coloured everything for us. The second we wrote anything catchy, it was like, *Oh, no, we're corporate rock dickheads*. It seeped into the water table of creativity. "Gone" was put on the back burner for a while.'

Long before strings added new textures to their albums *Troublegum* and *Infernal Love*, the band employed the services of local cellist David James to give the six-minute song extra depth and gravitas. 'Bob Mould used the cellist Jane Scarpantoni on a couple of tracks,' says Andy, 'so we thought we would see how it would sound.'

The rest of the album was recorded in August at Loco Studio in Caerleon, a town on the outskirts of Newport, Wales. This time, Andy swapped amphetamines for acid to pass the time while waiting to record his vocals. 'I was quite impatient,' he reasons.

It was a documentary about bruxism—a condition that causes an individual to involuntarily grind their teeth or clench their jaw—that sparked the inspiration for the album's lead single, 'Teethgrinder'. 'I wrote the riff when I got raging drunk,' says Andy. 'It was an earworm that wouldn't go away. It sounded like NoMeansNo and Fugazi. I came up with the vocal melody. We saw a documentary on Channel 4 and wrote the lyrics with Fyfe. My only regret is that I sang "teethgrinder" twice in the chorus, which is pretty lame.'

Like several of the band's previous releases, 'Teethgrinder' features samples. The voiceover 'He's losing his mind and he feels it going' was taken from a public-information film about LSD and had been included in the 1986 documentary *The Beyond Within*. The second, of a woman describing her bruxism ('I'm a teethgrinder; in my sleep, I grind my teeth') featured in a programme called *American Conversations*.

'Nausea' begins with a clip of Nick Cave screaming 'Here I am, motherfuckers!', taken from John Hillcoat's 1988 prison drama film *Ghosts … Of The Civil Dead*. The Bad Seeds frontman gave his consent and was handsomely compensated for doing so. But that would be that, said the label.

'The moment the album was done, they said, "There's samples?"' says Michael. 'They said it could take up to six months to clear them all. The verses on "Hypermania" were meant to be all made up of samples, but there were so many of them it would have taken us months to find out who did what. They couldn't be cleared in time, so Andy and Fyfe did some vocals, but it didn't really come out how we wanted it to.'

'Disgracelands' was inspired by a button badge found in a tourist shop. Using its pithy phrase, 'Fuck Columbus, he was lost', Andy and Fyfe took turns writing lines for the track, later described by the frontman as a 'fucked-up nursery rhyme'. 'Accelerator', on the other hand, was informed by dialogue from Walter Hill's 1978 crime thriller *The Driver*.

'I wanted to write a fast riff like a mix of Dead Kennedys and early Black Flag,' says Andy. 'The lyrics are about joyriding in Northern Ireland, true antisocial behaviour. It was happening everywhere, but if you were caught, you got kneecapped.' Several lines were 'taken verbatim' from the film.

In hindsight, some of the tracks weren't fully realised. 'Zipless', which took its title from Erica Jong's phrase 'zipless fuck', from her book *Fear Of Flying*, is, according to Andy, 'the very definition of an album track. I don't know what we were trying to do with the song. It's quite forgettable.' Similarly, 'Deep Sleep'—a dub-heavy song about smoking the devil's cabbage—was written and recorded but never revisited following the album's release.

'Summer Of Hate', which appeared on the B-side of 'Teethgrinder' and the Japanese version of *Nurse*, remains one of Andy's favourite Therapy? songs. 'It was written on the hoof in the studio,' he says, 'and we didn't overthink it. It took five minutes. Fyfe said my riff sounded like The Cult, but once I mentioned I was trying to do a Helmet riff, he relaxed. I think it should have gone on the album instead of "Zipless".'

Fun fact: the band made festival T-shirts featuring the American flag, a peace sign, and a phrase from the song's lyric, 'Fuck Woodstock', across the chest. Thanks to the band's one-time US agent Marsha Vlasic, the garment made its way into the hands of Neil Young, who performed at the original festival. 'He apparently burst out laughing and took it,' says Andy.

During the sessions, the band found time to record a forty-five-minute avant-garde song named 'Penis Temple', which they considered sending it to their new label's A&R department for a laugh. They chickened out, but the atonal jam is buried deep inside the band's extensive archives.

Shortly after completing the album, the band opened the main stage at Reading on August 29 at midday, sharing a bill with Rollins Band, Smashing Pumpkins, Manic Street Preachers, and Public Enemy. Their seven-song set featured three songs from their forthcoming album: 'Teethgrinder', 'Perversonality', and 'Summer Of Hate', which was then simply named 'Woodstock'. 'It felt like we'd made a step up into a different league,' remembers Michael.

Nurse was released in Europe in October, while the band toured North America, where they played their own headline tour and opened for Screaming Trees in New York. 'That tour was brilliant,' Michael continues. 'We played with the Melvins at the Kennel Club in San Francisco. Loads of people came out to the shows, and you'd have people from Hole popping in.'

'I remember that San Francisco show,' Andy adds. 'Jello Biafra [formerly of Dead Kennedys] came backstage to say hello and talked about Irish punk. I was elated, until Michelle [Leon] dryly piped up, "I don't mean to burst your bubble, but he's always backstage."'

Andy felt a backlash following the band's decision to sign with a major label, which tainted the transatlantic trip for him. 'Obviously, playing venues like CBGB was great, but people kept asking why we were leaving Touch And Go, and I think it did a lot of harm,' he says. 'People had liked *Caucasian Psychosis*, and now they thought we were trying to do a Nirvana. I was heartbroken.'

The album would be released the following month in the UK, but, in the meantime, lead single 'Teethgrinder' peaked at no. 30 on the UK singles chart.

The *NME*'s Edwin Pouncey awarded the band's major-label debut eight out of ten: 'Therapy? kick off sounding like Nirvana and end with a final guitar stroke that imitates The Beatles. In between, *Nurse* is solid Therapy?. Pure and simply staggering.'

'Local band Therapy? make a thunderous major label debut that should establish them in rock's premier division,' declared Northern Ireland newspaper *Sunday Life*. 'It's brutal, uncompromising stuff, and about as subtle as a breeze block across the knees.'

'The critical reception was brilliant,' remembers Andy. 'James Sherry reviewed it for *Metal Hammer*. He liked it but made a good point when he said the guitars were a bit thin-sounding. *Rolling Stone* called us Punk Floyd. There'd be people in Lard t-shirts going "I fucking hate you guys" who never saw us again, but *Nurse* brought a lot of new people to the band.'

Even independent retailers were singing the band's praises—notably Alan's Records in Wigan, whose small advert in the *NME* caught Andy's eye. 'I remember we used to buy a lot of records by mail order from there,' he explains. 'If you wanted records by The Hard Ons or Fugazi, that's where you went. When we put the record out, in the advert it had something like, "Therapy?—*Nurse* (it's actually good)".'

The band ended the year with an extensive tour, beginning with a slot supporting Daisy Chainsaw at London's Metro Club on November 6, followed by their own headline shows across the UK and Ireland, which ran until December 21. They recorded sessions for the Mark Goodier *Evening Session* and John Peel in November, both of which would be included on the 2007 album *Music Through A Cheap Transistor: The BBC Sessions*.

'As one of the highlights of The Cult's In The Park festival earlier this year, Therapy? blew the cobwebs off a large field full of sunbathers in the middle of the afternoon,' wrote *Kerrang!*'s Paul Travers, following their November 9 show at Manchester University. 'In a very much smaller, darker and more enclosed environment, they are virtually unstoppable. The power and energy which pours from the stage is inspirational, yet despite the sledgehammer heaviness, there exists in their music a myriad of subtleties and deviations. All too often, it's the heaviest bands who are the most repetitive and boring, but Therapy? are blessed with a canny knack for songwriting and a whole host of different approaches.'

For their show at the London Astoria on November 27, the band decided to add 'Gone' to their setlist. To replicate David James's haunting cello on the *Nurse* track, they enlisted the services of Martin McCarrick, a Luton-born cellist who had worked with Siouxsie & The Banshees, This Mortal Coil, and Dead Can Dance. 'I think it was Gerry who tracked Martin down,' remembers Michael. 'We rehearsed briefly with him on the day before the gig and then hung out a bit after the show, and we clicked with regard to humour, outlook, and influences. I remember he was wearing a Pigface t-shirt when we first met, which was a good sign, as I was expecting a more "traditional" type of cellist from a more classical background. Martin was definitely punk rock. We were also big fans of the This Mortal Coil records he had played on, so it made sense to have him play strings on any future records or at shows.'

Towards the end of the run of shows, the band were resting in their hotel before playing Nottingham Polytechnic on December 5. Andy and Michael were watching the *Smash Hits Poll Winners Party* on BBC 1. Hosted by Simon Mayo and New Kids On The Block's Jordan Knight, the cheesy pop awards ceremony took place at London's Docklands Arena. It was watching Take That's performance of 'A Million Love Songs' and their cover of Barry Manilow's 'Could It Be Magic' that prompted Michael to pass comment on the highly excitable crowd.

'I said, "Look at all those screamagers,"' he remembers. 'There was a big surge of boy bands that we hadn't maybe seen since Bros, and the crowd were going nuts.'

The UK tour wrapped in Colchester in December, and the band had a week off before two final shows at the SFX Centre in Dublin and a hometown show at the Ulster Hall in Belfast, where one thousand copies of a free seven-inch promo single titled 'Have A Merry Fucking Christmas'—featuring covers of The Undertones' 'Teenage Kicks' and U2's 'With Or Without You'—were handed out to fans.

However, while the band had had their most successful year to date, tensions were beginning to mount. 'Around this time, Fyfe announced that he wanted to take a year off,' remembers Andy. 'We had a meeting with our manager, Gerry, and it emerged that he was led to believe that Fyfe wrote all the songs.'

'It was a myth that was … I wouldn't say perpetuated, but not necessarily denied by Fyfe, that he was the musical brains behind the band,' adds Michael. 'But me and Andy weren't two bevvy-loving bozos that were instructed to do this stuff.'

'We were really shocked,' Andy continues, 'because me and Michael were like, *Wahey, three lads from Northern Ireland taking on the world*, and the whole time this was going on in the background. A few weeks later, Fyfe approached Gerry and said he'd noticed a power shift. I was like, *Who uses a term like power shift in this band? What's going on here? We're not Guns N' Roses!* We were good friends, and I fucking loved the guy's drumming, but this just made for a surreal atmosphere for a few months.'

With studio time booked in January to record a new EP, there was the small matter of finding a new producer to work with. They contacted

Steve Albini, but he politely declined because of his friendship with Touch And Go's Corey Rusk. 'We met a few producers, but the person that we really, really liked was Chris Sheldon,' says Andy. 'He was just like us.' They decided to give it a go: 'If we liked the results, then we'd keep him on board and see what happened.'

Chris met up with the band when they played at Wulfrun Hall in Wolverhampton on December 4. 'Their A&R guy, David Rose, took me to see them,' he recalls. 'I immediately felt at ease with them. They had zero pretensions and wonderful humour that I latched onto straight away. Everything clicked, so we decided to go ahead with the recording.'

YEAR FOUR /the making of troublegum

With their differences seemingly resolved, Andy, Michael, and Fyfe headed to Ritz Studios in London for two days in early January to begin pre-production on four new songs: 'Screamager', 'Auto Surgery', 'Totally Random Man', and a re-recording of 'Accelerator'.

'We worked on the song structures,' explains Chris. 'That way, when we hit the studio, there were no cross words or misunderstandings, just a desire to really deliver. In the studio they took direction extremely well, and were as eager as I was to really make something special.'

On January 7, they decamped to Black Barn Studios in Surrey to record their new EP over the course of a week. 'Considering what had happened with Fyfe just before, it was really good fun,' says Andy. 'Chris was refreshing, because he's a no-bullshit guy, which we liked. He just said, "Do what you're doing, but make it direct and make it aggressive."'

The EP's opening salvo, 'Screamager', had been kicking around since the band formed and its irresistible hook had been tagged on to the end of 'S.W.T', a song from their 1989 demo, *Meat Abstract*.

'I'd always thought it was a bit of a waste,' says Andy. 'I didn't know what to do with it, because I didn't have songwriting chops then. I had a song called "I've Got Nothing To Do", which was written on the acoustic, and it was very Ramones-y. It sounds like a modern version of "Rudy", or a little bit like Stiff Little Fingers, or it could be an Undertones track— it's like an Ulster-tribute pop song. Obviously, it had more of a metal influence than those bands, but that was very much what it was.

'I grew up very working class, and I got into a high school where I was very much made to feel like I didn't belong there,' he adds. 'It talks about the ennui facing us, I suppose, that as kids who've got nothing to do but try and find something to hang on to.'

The song quickly took shape in the studio. A meandering drum fill was quickly replaced by a simple, thundering intro on the toms and snare, and bolstered by a stabbing riff inspired by Helmet's album *Meantime*. 'I have to give Chris credit for the drum intro, because it was quite ridiculous, initially,' says Michael. 'We're talking [late Rush drummer] Neil Peart territory. Chris was like, "No, it needs to be immediate." With the new intro, you're straight in and there's no messing about. Everything in that song has a hook. There's no fat.'

'The prolonged drum intro was totally unnecessary in my opinion, and didn't serve the song well,' adds Chris. 'To me, it needed something short and memorable, like the intro to "Teenage Kicks" by The Undertones. I put this to Fyfe and the band and had them try alternatives, which worked better for the song. Fyfe took it in good grace and nailed that shortened intro and made it his own. In hindsight, I'm glad I stuck to my guns about it.'

Chris had reservations about including 'Screamager' on the EP. 'The funny thing is, when I took the initial recording of the song, I took it home on a cassette to listen to it, pre-mixing, and was really unsure about it,' he reveals. 'I had been so into the group's earlier music, like "Teethgrinder", and this was such a departure that I worried what people are going to make of it. These worries didn't last long, however, and I realised that we had created an absolute banger of an EP and set about mixing it with a vengeance. I mixed the songs at Livingston Studios in north London from January 16th to the 19th, and "Screamager" just sounded fantastic.'

Before the *Shortsharpshock* sessions were completed, the band filmed a video for 'Nausea' with Jon Klein, which would be used to raise their profile in the USA. 'Because we all still lived in Northern Ireland, the label set up so many things for us to do when we were in England,' says Andy. 'We'd finish in the studio at 5pm, then go to do the video. They wanted to fit in as much as possible while we were in England. I don't think we ever had any time to take it all in.'

Following a session for BBC Radio 1's *Friday Rock Show*, the band toured Europe with Derby alt-rock quartet Bivouac and German indie four-piece The Notwist. 'When we went over with *Nurse*, we were playing three-hundred-capacity venues, and, this time, the sizes had doubled,' says Andy. 'I absolutely loved that tour.'

March 8 saw the release of the *Shortsharpshock* EP, which paid distinctive homage to punk with its Day-Glo green cover and the various formats depicting a zip, a safety pin, and razor blade. Three days later, the band began a short tour of the UK with Silverfish and Gallon Drunk. The EP reached no. 2 in Ireland and no. 9 in the UK, earning the trio a slot on *Top Of The Pops*.

'The first time I saw the show was when I was about six,' says Andy. 'It was where I saw the Buzzcocks and Motörhead for the first time. You'd often see something that was almost magical.' In Mr and Mrs Cairns's eyes, however, not even an appearance on BBC 1's flagship music show could lend an air of legitimacy to their son's chosen profession. 'I think my dad was expecting a mansion because we were on *Top Of The Pops*,' laughs Andy. 'I think he just made some comment about my hair and our black shirts.'

By the end of March, the band had recorded a further five songs with Chris at Livingston Studios. Four of them—'Turn', 'Speedball', 'Bloody Blue', and 'Neck Freak'—would make up the *Face The Strange* EP. 'Opal Mantra' was kept for a follow-up release—its title a pun on assistant engineer John Mallison's Opel Manta car—to be bolstered by live material recorded in New York the previous year.

'I was writing like crazy,' says Andy. 'It's the confidence that comes with success, I think, and, as a band, we were a lot more open-minded and felt like we had nothing to lose.'

'The band were on a roll, for sure,' adds Chris. 'We recorded the *Face The Strange* EP at Livingston Studios in four days. One thing I remember is working on Michael's bass line on "Turn" to make it much more driving, to push the song along and add some menace to the track. Generally, the vibes in the studio were good, as far as I was concerned. I remember taking a bit of time out with Andy and going for a walk and maybe a visit to the pub to put him at ease, as the pressures of shows and recordings were pretty intense; Andy delivered as only Andy can, and the vocals and guitar playing on those sessions were fantastic.'

'Turn', the EP's lead track, was inspired by Jay Stevens's book *Storming Heaven: LSD & The American Dream*. 'It talks about the crossover between Aldous Huxley, LSD, the CIA, and revolutionaries in America,' explains Andy. 'One of the chapters was called "Turn And Face The Strange", which is from "Changes" by David Bowie. I never thought about it at the time. I wrote the riff when we were in Malmö. It had three droning, psychedelic chords, with delay and chorus on it, and I played it over and over until I had the bare bones of the song.'

In April, the band travelled to North America for a six-week tour, opening up a dream bill that featured Chicago sluggers The Jesus Lizard and New York alt-metallers Helmet. 'That was quite a run,' remembers Michael. 'At the time, they were two of our favourite bands, and everyone really clicked with each other. On stage, The Jesus Lizard were feral. There was a real danger to their performances, which was probably helped by David Yow drinking twenty-four tins of Budweiser before going on. Watching Helmet felt like someone was sitting on your chest and getting heavier and heavier. They both made us massively up our game.'

While the trio were in New York, they entered producer Gary Katz's studio to work on a collaborative track with the rapper Fatal. The song, a ferocious collision of discordant, looped riffs and aggressive vocals, was titled 'Come And Die'. It was written and recorded in twelve hours, especially for the soundtrack to the film *Judgment Night*. The idea for the album was relatively simple; eleven rock bands were paired off with a range of established and rising hip-hop stars for this groundbreaking release: Helmet and House Of Pain, Teenage Fanclub and De La Soul, Living Colour and Run DMC, Biohazard and Onyx, Slayer and Ice-T, Faith No More and Boo-Yaa T.R.I.B.E., Sonic Youth and Cypress Hill, Mudhoney and Sir Mix-A-Lot, Dinosaur Jr. and Del The Funky Homosapien, Pearl Jam and Cypress Hill.

'In the early days, we'd listen to Public Enemy, NWA, and all that, so we were really up for it,' says Andy. 'We didn't have long to do the track, but Fatal turned up late with his mates. There was loads of strong weed and the studio was filled with this green fog, like a scene in *Scooby Doo*. The track came out well, I thought.'

'Diamond Dave was with us, and we found him relaxing in the lounge with Fatal's mates,' laughs Michael. 'We caught him attempting to do a freestyle rap, and he kept calling Fatal "Fat Al" for some reason. They thought he was hilarious.'

Unbelievably, Diamond Dave's involvement on this tour was part of his drama course. 'This may be best piece of blagging or bullshit ever seen in the whole of higher education,' he explains. 'I had to enter the world of "work" for three weeks, which was followed by an Easter holiday, so I went on tour with the band, and got to see The Jesus Lizard and Helmet every night, too. That day, I was recovering from a rather demented bus trip that had ended with me listening to Christy Moore's "Ride On" constantly and stage diving in the bus while doing an impression of David Yow. I got up late and honestly thought the band were working with someone called Fat Al. He was a thoroughly decent chap.'

When the tour reached Los Angeles, all three bands on the bill were invited to a party at the home of psychologist and psychedelics advocate Timothy Leary. 'He lived in the hills,' says Andy, 'and his home was right at the end of one of those long, winding roads you'd see in a David Lynch movie. I remember Billy Idol was there, and House Of Pain, who'd worked with Helmet on the *Judgment Night* soundtrack, were there, too. Timothy was giving a lecture to some students in one room and the rest of us were drinking beer in the garden. There were loads of drugs flying around, and it was carnage. All of a sudden, his assistant walked in and said, "OK, party's over," so we got cabs into downtown LA and carried on drinking. It was a surreal evening, just drinking and talking about punk with Billy Idol.'

Following the tour, the band returned home and entered Homestead Studios with Chris Sheldon. Over the course of ten days, they wrote and demoed songs for their next album.

'The songs came together pretty quickly, if my memory serves me well,' says Chris. 'For the band, it was a nice vibe, to come back to where it had all started for them. I joined the band there for six days in June of that year to finish the writing and arranging. "Nowhere" was fantastic straight off the bat. I remember using Andy's delay pedal to sample the iconic guitar figure that starts the song, so the band could play along with it while Andy could also play rhythm guitar. In the end, when we did the album, we recorded it as two separate parts rather than rely on the sampler pedal, but while we were routining the song it worked well. We certainly worked on "Die Laughing", and for whatever personal reasons Fyfe didn't show up at the studios for a day or two, so we pressed on with routining the song and working on the arrangement with me playing kit, which was slightly awkward, as Fyfe was left-handed and I'm not, but it came out well. When Fyfe did show up, he learned it pretty quickly, and we got going again.'

Some of the songs already existed in other permutations. 'Reality Fuck'—which was first recorded during a Dave Fanning session for RTÉ 2FM—formed the basis of 'Die Laughing'.

'I'm going to call a spade a spade here: it's basically "Waiting Room" by Fugazi,' says Andy. 'It's about not exactly knowing your identity or what you really want. One beautiful day, I'd taken acid and listened to Sonic Youth's album *Goo*. I was with some friends and someone asked if I was staying the evening and I was like, "I don't know, I can't remember." Then someone jokingly asked me what my name was, and I didn't know that either! I really started to panic.'

The music for 'Stop It You're Killing Me' was largely a reworking of 'Body O.D.', a song from the band's *Thirty Seconds Of Silence* demo. 'There was a bit of consternation about the main riff, because at some point we wondered if it sounded a bit like "Owner Of A Lonely Heart",' says Andy. 'We speeded it up, and it had a Black Flag and Hüsker Dü feel to it. I'd been listening to The Byrds when I came up with the middle eight. When I said I wanted to add a 12-string to that part, Chris said, "Over my dead body!" and reined me in.'

'Hellbelly' was written in Carlow, during the pre-production for *Nurse*, when the band stayed in a creepy farmhouse and discovered a crow hanging in a barn. 'Whenever I was stuck for riffs, I'd think of Big Black, Black Sabbath, and Black Flag,' explains Andy. 'I was inspired by the Pixies' [1991 album] *Trompe Le Monde*, too. At the time, I was reading a lot of Flannery O'Connor, who wrote in a Southern gothic style, and I wanted to write about people who grew up working on farms. Most of these people in Northern Ireland, and especially in County Antrim where I lived, flew under the banner of Protestantism and religion to get away with anything, from underpaying labourers to getting certain benefits from the local council, belonging to the Freemasons—that kind of stuff.'

A rough version of 'Nowhere' had been kicking around for a while, along with riffs for 'Femtex' and 'Lunacy Booth'. 'So many people have used that chord progression in "Nowhere",' says Andy, citing 'Another Girl, Another Planet' by The Only Ones, and 'Just What I Needed' by The Cars. 'Initially, the song was very fast but it sounded ordinary, and, to Fyfe's credit, he added some swing to the song. For the lyrics, it goes back to when I was working in a factory. I'd been really lazy; I had a good education but I didn't do anything with it. In order to buy myself records and pay my rent, I got a job in a factory. At one point, I just thought, *What am I doing with my life?* I thought of [Irish novelist] Flann O'Brien—how would he introduce the song? So I came up with the line "*Heaven kicked you out, you wouldn't wear a tie*", and that brought the spiritual and the quotidian into one sentence.'

The dark humour of Flann O'Brien also informed 'Femtex', a song that bravely opens with the lyric '*Masturbation saved my life*'. 'I'd watched *Whore*,' says Andy, referring to the 1991 film by Ken Russell. 'The main character, played by Theresa Russell, stands up to all this horrendous abuse. And I thought about how women are treated in the music business, which can be a horrible environment. We would always call out and pull men up on their behaviour. We were very vocal about it, and we tried to write a song like Fugazi's "Suggestion"; it had the right intention, but it didn't come out as strongly.

'I wanted to keep that loser mentality that ran through *Troublegum*: impotent rage,' he adds. 'I mentioned the masturbation line to Chris, and he said it was brilliant. I remember saying, "Is it not a bit much?"'

Face The Strange was released on June 1, with cover art befitting its title. The band's concept involved a stark black-and-white image of a man smartly dressed in a suit jacket and fishnet stockings, with flippers on his feet and a gas mask on his face. Think of a politician caught in a compromising situation.

'I loved the band as people, and I had been working with them for a while and watched as their career had gone from strength to strength,' says Andy Prevezer, A&M's head of press at the time. 'There was a casual—or possibly drunken—conversation about who they could get to do it. I knew the photographer, a lovey chap called Simon Fowler. I think I randomly suggested that I could be that person, to which the band readily assented!

'I remember driving past a huge billboard on Barlby Road in West London when the EP had just came out,' he adds. 'It had my image emblazoned all over it, and some fucker had graffitied the word "CUNT" over my body. It had me in total hysterics at the time.'

The single earned the band another appearance on *Top Of The Pops*, peaking at no. 18 in the UK singles chart and no. 5 in Ireland. 'To be on the show twice in six months was crazy,' says Michael. 'We never thought to swap instruments or piss about like some bands. It was such a big thing for us. Sisters Of Mercy were on, and we were in awe of them. *Floodland* was such a big album for me when I was young, and it was so fucking cool to meet Andrew Eldritch. That year was full of things like that.'

That month, Therapy? decamped to Chipping Norton Recording Studios in Oxfordshire. While tracking, the band played a cover of Joy Division's 'Isolation', a song from their 1980 album *Closer*. 'Chris loved the riff, and I had to fess up and say it was a Joy Division bass line,' says Andy. 'I'd been playing that riff for years, but the cover came together really quickly. Joy Division fans will hear I've added the keyboard line from "Atrocity Exhibition" as a guitar solo, too.'

With Fyfe preparing to move to Brighton and Michael about to go on holiday, the producer paired them off and, astonishingly, they tracked their parts for the fourteen-song album over the course of two days. 'I set the guys up to play together, but with the idea of only keeping the drum performances,' explains Chris. 'Fyfe nailed his parts in a couple of days, with only "Die Laughing" proving tricky to get right, but eventually we had that in the can. Michael recorded all his bass parts in an evening, pretty much—anything left over we finished the next day. The man is a machine!'

'I was there for the full two weeks,' adds Michael. 'After I recorded my parts, I was mostly watching *The Simpsons* while Andy was recording his guitar parts, because Sheldon had this extensive video collection.'

'Michael and Fyfe both nailed it,' remembers Andy. 'All I had to do was put rhythm guitars over it and sing. It was fucking amazing because the bass and drums alone sounded incredible. There was a uniformity to the whole album.'

'One of my fondest memories is recording the guitars,' says Chris. 'We'd often record the guitars with Andy being in the studio control room with me while the guitar speakers would be in the recording room, mainly so we could talk about the parts and performances. My back would be to Andy while I was listening to the studio monitors and he was playing behind me. On one occasion, the most ferocious din was being produced with unearthly noises; when I turned around to see what Andy was doing, I found him holding the guitar by the whammy bar, bouncing the guitar up and down with it to create a total sonic explosion. Needless to say, Mr A. Cairns remains one of my favourite guitar players!'

Their next stop was RAK near London's Regent's Park. 'It was bizarre, because I had been there before,' explains Andy, recalling his drug-fuelled night while making *Pleasure Death*. 'When I found out we were heading there to continue work on the album, I was hugely embarrassed. I was in the studio for literally five minutes and this attractive woman in her fifties with a posh voice appeared and said, "Oh, there he is, there's the graffiti artist …" I apologised again, and she was an absolute sweetheart. But every time I saw her, she'd tease me about it.'

It was that chaotic night that inspired the lyrics to album's opening track, 'Knives'. 'It started off that theme of impotent rage,' says Andy. 'It's almost like the story of somebody that's so angry at the world, but all he can do is talk to himself in the mirror: *I'm gonna get drunk / Come round and fuck you up.* The music itself was very inspired by Big Black's "Cables"; it's almost merciless and unfeeling.'

At RAK, Silverfish vocalist Lesley Rankine recorded vocals on 'Lunacy Booth', an Ulster-noir song rooted in religion, with a riff inspired by another Big Black song, 'Fists Of Love', from the Illinois band's 1986 debut album, *Atomizer.*

'When Lesley starts singing, the harmony could be from a 50s country song,' explains Andy. 'The term hillbilly comes from Northern Irish people [followers of King William Of Orange, or Billy] emigrating to America in the seventeenth century and moving up into the mountains. They brought their folk music with them, which evolved into country music. In Protestant Northern Ireland, country music and religion are very, very heavily entwined: the old rugged cross, and songs about waiting on God coming … there's a very stoic aesthetic to that as well.'

During the RAK sessions, Andy contacted Helmet's Page Hamilton to add a suitably discordant solo to 'Unbeliever', a song about entering into platonic and romantic relationships with the unreasonable belief they would be short-lived, often helped by self-sabotage. 'The "Unbeliever" riff is a total Helmet rip-off,' laughs Andy. 'I called him and he agreed to do it straight away in New York. He did exactly what we wanted, and it fits the song perfectly.'

The album was finally mixed and sequenced at the Church Studios in Crouch End, a facility owned by Eurythmics' Dave Stewart. 'There were Harley-Davidsons there and a white grand piano—real rock-star stuff,' remembers Michael. 'There was a big leather sofa behind the mixing desk, and, when we sat down to listen to the mixes, there'd be this unholy stench.'

The aroma was thanks to a previous studio guest—an 80s singer who'd taken a handful of magic mushrooms and vomited down the back of the sofa, which rained through the gaps in the wooden floorboards. Whenever the heating was switched on, the smell would wrestle the nostrils of everyone inside the control room. 'That singer went right up in my estimation,' laughs Michael. 'Good lad.'

'Brainsaw' reworked a riff from one of the first songs the band ever wrote, 'Window Wall', which was a regular sight in Belfast—when buildings were bombed, the broken windows would be bricked up as a cost-effective way to replace the glass—while on 'Trigger Inside', Andy dredged up a childhood memory that had parallels to the formative years of Jeffrey Dahmer, the serial killer dubbed 'The Milwaukee Cannibal'.

'In Brian Masters's book *The Shrine Of Jeffrey Dahmer*, there's a part where Dahmer remembers being a very young child and giving something to the teacher, who threw it away—that memory really affected him,' he explains. 'I had a similar experience at school when I gave my teacher a little cake, who put it in the bin. I was destroyed by that and remember the feeling vividly. That's where the line *"I know how Jeffrey Dahmer feels"* came from.'

The lyric would draw some criticism from the press. The late Andy Gill of the *Independent* called Andy a 'twerp' for even suggesting such a thing. 'I don't think I thought that through, properly to be honest,' he admits. 'I read an interview with Nicky Wire from the Manics, who said he hated that line. Maybe it could have been phrased a better way, but at that point in time, I just thought it really suited the brutish nature of the album.'

After the album's sheer onslaught of impotent rage, betrayal, and loneliness—*Troublegum* is not an album for lovers, it must be said—the band added a crackling cover of 'You Are My Sunshine', the 1939 song first recorded by the Pine Ridge Boys, hidden away at the end of 'Brainsaw'.

'We wanted to use an old recording of "You Are My Sunshine" or have a sample of Winona Ryder in *Heathers*, where she says, "My teenage-angst bullshit has a body count!" The label said the sample would cost a small fortune. So I sang that song instead. I think it adds a sense of levity to it all. *Troublegum* might have been mentioned in the same breath as [Manic Street Preachers'] *The Holy Bible* or [Nine Inch Nails'] *The Downward*

Spiral, but with "You Are My Sunshine", or lines like "*masturbation saved my life*", it was unlikely to happen.'

'We'd spent a lot of time getting the running order right, and I'm glad we did,' he adds. 'I wasn't happy with the production on *Nurse*, and our first two mini-albums were very much the work of three lunatics let loose in a studio. But this actually sounded like a proper album, and I was really over the moon with it.'

'I wasn't surprised at how quickly the band worked, having already recorded a few times with them,' concedes Chris. 'We were all enthusiastic about the project and very much had a punk-rock work ethic to not get bogged down and keep the songs and recordings as punchy and ferocious as possible. I certainly liked to record that way, and I wasn't one for labouring over parts. It was a great time, and I have only fond memories of the experience.'

From July, the band spent much of the year on the road, taking in an appearance at Denmark's Roskilde festival and a French tour with Living Colour. 'I was a big fan of their albums *Vivid*, *Time's Up*, and *Stain*, so I was interested to see them live,' says Michael. 'It was insane. On stage, it looked like a music shop; there were so many pedals and amps. They were absolute gents and we were well looked after. Diamond Dave was in the thick of it and made sure everyone was chilled out as they should be. Every band needs someone like him around.'

'I was a sort of a merchandiser and court jester, a man to lift everyone's spirit while trying to sell t-shirts and provide quality nonsense at the drop of a hat,' adds Diamond. 'We were playing near a beach—I remember that Andy had gone paragliding for photos in a music magazine—and we were discussing my role in the Therapy? crew, and Doug [Wimbish, Living Colour bassist] felt in many ways I was a moral technician, and made me the official Ambience Director, which is a term that should be used at all times.'

While the band were on tour, they would regularly receive the producer's *Troublegum* mixes to sign off. 'I mixed the album on my own, at the Church Studios in north London,' explains Chris. 'I used to send them cassettes to hear, but was pretty much left alone to get on with it. Even the album sequencing—joining the songs together and choosing the short gaps—was pretty much my decision; we had discussed some of this before the band went on tour, so we had an idea of what we wanted. I remember being a bit worried about the mixing, as I couldn't seem to get it to sound right when I started the mix. After a couple of false starts, I thought I had got the sound and balance we had been trying to achieve, so I asked David Rose to come to the studio and see what he thought. David had been the perfect A&R man for the band at that time. After putting the band and me together, he left us alone to make the record with minimum interference. Anyway, he came down, heard "Knives", gave me the thumbs up, and I was off. I remain indebted to him for his support with both Therapy? and Gun, another of his bands I worked with.'

'Opal Mantra' was released as a single on August 16. It placed at no. 16 in the UK singles chart and no. 6 in Ireland, and with it the trio notched up their third *Top Of The Pops* appearance. Two weeks later, they played the main stage at Reading Festival, placed just two spots under Saturday headliners The The and Siouxsie & The Banshees.

Born In A Crash, an EU-only compilation of the *Face The Strange* and *Opal Mantra* EPs, was released ahead of the band's European tour with Paw. A fortnight later, the *Hats Off To The Insane* compilation—featuring the songs from the *Shortsharpshock*, *Face The Strange*, and *Opal Mantra* releases—was released in North America and Japan, where the band were due to tour for the first time.

'We arrived in Tokyo,' says Andy, 'and there must have been fifty fans waiting for us at the airport. They had gifts for us and were really sweet.'

'It was the first time I'd felt completely alien,' remembers Michael. 'We were at sixes and sevens following a really long flight, and we couldn't read the signs or understand the language, but it was a fantastic experience.

We'd been warned that there wouldn't be mosh pits or anything like that, but the shows were great.'

Manic Street Preachers were also touring Japan at the same time, in support of their album *Gold Against The Soul*, which had been released in June. Calls were made, and Manics frontman James Dean Bradfield hit the streets of Tokyo with the band. After some 'amazing' late-night sushi and beers, they returned to the hotel.

'James was interested to hear what the new album sounded like,' remembered Andy. 'I had it on cassette and played it through these little speakers. He sat and listened to the whole thing. At the end, he said, "That's fucking amazing." He liked "Die Laughing" in particular. I was really flattered because I loved the Manics. He could have easily turned around and gone, "This doesn't sound like 'Teethgrinder', what the fuck's this?" I remember waking up the next day and heading out being really over the moon about that.'

The band closed the year with a tour of the UK and Ireland with New York City post-punks Cop Shoot Cop and British hip-hop collective Gunshot.

'That was a great, noisy bill,' remembers Michael. 'We've always tried to take out different types of bands like that. Cop Shoot Cop did the Dublin and Belfast dates as well, but luckily we were never pulled over by the police. Fair play to them, playing Northern Ireland with a name like that. Imagine if they'd been being stopped by the RUC [Royal Ulster Constabulary]! It was great way to end the tour, but we were really ready for a break.'

YEAR
FIVE/'and i will kill
for a good night's sleep . . .'

In early January, the band travelled to Suite 16 on Rochdale's Kenion Street, the studio (formerly named Cargo) where Joy Division recorded their 1980 single 'Atmosphere'. There, John Robb, frontman of Blackpool post-punks The Membranes, produced three songs that would appear as B-sides on 'Trigger Inside' the following month. (A companion twelve-inch was also released, featuring remixes by London techno collective The Sabres Of Paradise and New York DJ Joey Beltram.)

'When the band formed, we were all fans of his,' says Andy of Robb. 'He'd just started doing work with other bands, and we decided to record some covers: "Nice 'n' Sleazy" by the Stranglers, "Reuters" by Wire, and "Tatty Seaside Town" by The Membranes.'

The studio wasn't a residential facility, so the band stayed above a 'really rough pub' nearby. Sensing some long hours in the studio, Andy sourced a local entrepreneur and waited for a special delivery at the pub. 'At this point, I'd developed quite a taste for coke,' he says. 'A local dealer turned up and went, "Oh fucking hell, it's the guy from Therapy?" I wanted to start small, because I didn't want to come across like some rock star, so I asked if he had any speed.'

'You dirty bastard,' the dealer sneered, before brightening when he was asked for some coke instead. 'He asked for my autograph,' laughs Andy. 'But when we were in the studio, John was like, "We're here to work, boys—we're not here to do drugs and drink," which is fair enough. We had a good old laugh. I remember Fyfe loving the drum sound from that session.'

'The original Stranglers song has this very ornate bass line, which I didn't know how to play,' remembers Michael. 'John insisted I used his Precision bass, and the action made it excruciatingly painful to use. But we were excited to be there, given the studio's history.'

The band headed south to London to record a session for the BBC's *Radio 1 Rock Show*, which was broadcast on January 7: 'Brainsaw', 'Trigger Inside', 'Isolation', and 'Knives' gave fans a tantalising taste of *Troublegum*, which was set for release the following month.

Two weeks later, the trio appeared on Channel 4's flagship culture show, *The Word*, with each member wearing a 'Pogo On A Nazi' t-shirt— originally intended for a future *Alternative Press* cover shoot. Their performance of 'Nowhere' could be best described as enthusiastic.

'They gave us a load of beer,' explains Michael, 'and bear in mind that we hadn't really played the song since we'd recorded it. Everyone was complicit in the carnage. I remember the label were pissed off—*Fuck, nice one guys!*—but everyone was talking about it afterwards.'

'By the time we went in to do soundcheck, we were all plastered, and I'd taken loads of coke to stay awake,' remembers Andy. 'I remember [actress] Anna Friel was interviewed by *Melody Maker* about two weeks later, and was being asked what music she liked. She replied, "I like bands with a singer who can sing, not like the guy from the band Therapy?" I remember being absolutely heartbroken, because at that time everyone fancied her. When you look back at that performance, it was absolutely shambolic.'

'Nowhere', which was released on January 17, entered the UK singles chart at no. 18. In Ireland, it charted twelve places higher. Another appearance on *Top Of The Pops* beckoned, and this time saw the band nestled in the half-hour show alongside ZZ Top and Richard Marx.

'Maybe I'm just being paranoid, but every time we did *Top Of The Pops*, they'd make the kids go right to the front of the stage, and they'd look at me as if to go, *Is that the singer?*' says Andy. 'That was always weird for me, but I enjoyed the whole experience of getting to meet celebrities like the Pet Shop Boys for a fleeting moment in the canteen.'

The following month saw the first of two North American tours that took the band from Atlanta to San Francisco via Seattle, with Stabbing Westward and Swervedriver. 'I remember one of the first conversations I had with the label while we were out there was about image,' remembers Andy. 'You think that people in the music business aren't like that, but they fucking are. The conversations went along the lines of, "Green Day and Offspring are massive, so it might help if you shaved off your beard and spiked your hair. We could do a new video and take 'Screamager' to radio again." We couldn't live with ourselves if we suddenly started looking like Green Day. We'd look like their dads. Our manager had our back and told them it was fucking ridiculous. You could sense they were disappointed.'

'I think the success of "Screamager" caught them out a wee bit,' says Michael. 'I'm glad we didn't back down on that, because that would have been a whole fucking can of worms if the American label had started getting involved.'

Advance reviews for *Troublegum* were hugely positive. '*Troublegum* sees Therapy? relying solely on basic instinct, inflammable material and adrenaline,' wrote *Kerrang!*. 'The result is loud, without being trite. Obnoxious without being dumb.' Elsewhere, *RAW* magazine asked, 'Were Therapy? always this good? *Troublegum* is the sort of album that gets you out of bed early in the morning, then sends you to the nearest stereo just so you can listen to it again and again … and it gets better and better with each and every play.'

While they were on tour, the band received a fax—this was 1994, after all—to say the album had entered the UK charts at no. 5. 'We went out for a meal to celebrate, except Fyfe,' says Andy. 'We just had a sense of vindication, you know: we took this chance and it's paid off.' (When Andy phoned his father to tell him, however, his dad simply replied, 'Who's no. 1?')

'I think it was the best thing we had done at that point, by a long stretch,' adds Michael. 'The singles had charted, so I thought it would do well, but not that well.'

'I was certainly excited by the album as a body of work, and I was really looking forward to people hearing it, but its success was a shock to me,' adds producer Chris Sheldon. 'I knew it would do quite well, but nothing like what it actually did.'

Later that month, the band returned to the UK for an eleven-date tour of significantly larger venues, aided and abetted by rising Kilkenny four-piece Kerbdog and British hip-hop collective Credit To The Nation. 'It was a great tour,' Andy remembers. 'We'd played with Kerbdog before and had great fun; they were almost nerdy or geeky in their tastes, like we were, and there were no airs and graces about them at all. When people talk about seeing us in the 90s, that's the tour they talk about.'

March saw an extensive tour with Canadian alt-rock band Doughboys. Two days into the tour, Therapy? were preparing for a show at Pumpehuset in Copenhagen on March 11 when the phone rang. It was Sharon Osbourne, inviting them to record a cover of Black Sabbath's 'Iron Man' with Ozzy for the *Nativity In Black* tribute album. Four days later, they were in Metropolis Studio in London with producer Chris Tsangarides to record the music before heading back to Stockholm to resume the tour. They would later join Ozzy while he recorded his vocals. 'Michael and I had learned the parts, but it was obvious Fyfe hadn't listened to it,' says Andy. 'We finally got a version we could use. Michael nailed it in two takes, and I was there to the fucking death doing the guitars.'

Following the European dates, the band returned to the USA as support to Texas trio King's X. 'This is absolutely no slur on the band, but that tour was the first time we'd encountered what we imagined an old-school road crew to be like,' remembers Michael. 'I think they'd been out with the Scorpions and were complaining about how they hadn't got any sound checks, then literally did the same to us. Then the band would turn up, and they were lovely. I was a big fan of theirs, especially their *Out Of The Silent Planet* album. That experience reinforced a lot of the things about how lucky we had been on previous tours.'

On April 25, during a day off, the band flew to Los Angeles to finish work on their 'Iron Man' cover. 'Terry Date, who was producing Ozzy's part, told us not to turn up while he was singing his parts,' remembers Andy. 'We arrived when we were told, but Ozzy hadn't shown up yet. Ozzy asked us to stay anyway, so we watched him work. I remember that when he was in the booth, Terry asked him to take his jewellery off, because the mic was picking it up. He sang it again, and I was like, "That was amazing! Nailed it in two takes!" Ozzy said, "I've only been singing it for over twenty years!" We got a Polaroid with Ozzy, sang our part, and flew back to Minneapolis to re-join the tour.'

Following the King's X dates, Therapy? went out on the road with Rollins Band, whose video for 'Liar'—directed by Dutch photographer Anton Corbijn—was a near-permanent fixture on MTV. 'I remember being really nervous before that tour, because Henry Rollins was a hardcore legend,' says Andy. 'He was really driven but really approachable and accommodating. He loved "Nowhere" and said it had a "righteous melody". They couldn't do enough for us.'

'I loved that tour, and I had a lot of good times hanging out with their bassist, Melvin Gibbs,' remembers Michael. 'There were a lot of surreal moments. I remember seeing Henry at the side of the stage in his shorts, doing press-ups, during "Screamager". I also saw him lift an Ampeg 8x10 from the floor onto a two-metre-high stage by himself. It was nuts.

'The punk police didn't like the success of "Liar", and there was one show where some people had put up flyers outside of the venue, calling him a sell-out,' he adds. 'So both bands went and collected them and put them across their backline. I have a lot of respect for the way the whole band and crew handled themselves.'

Henry Rollins, who famously doesn't drink alcohol, was convinced by Andy to join the band and Helmet's Page Hamilton at a bar in New York City. What could possibly go wrong?

'I remember asking him about drinking, and he explained that he just didn't like it,' says Andy. 'I invited him out, and there was a girl there who we'd been drinking with. She'd been drinking margaritas and shots and sat in the booth across from us. Henry turned up and the girl was violently sick. She had vomit all over her hair, and, as I helped her up to get a cab, it got all over my shirt. He just gave me this bewildered look!'

'Die Laughing' was released on May 30 and peaked at no. 29 in the UK singles charts and no. 14 in Ireland. Its promo, filmed earlier in the year, was directed by Matt Mahurin, known for his work with Metallica, U2, Alice In Chains, and Soundgarden. Soon after, the band were subject to tabloid claims that they'd used patients from a psychiatric hospital as extras. Their manager, Gerry, denied it, telling an Irish newspaper, 'It would be exploitation, and Therapy? would never agree to that. They've been stung about these allegations, which are downright lies.'

'I have no idea where that story came from,' Michael recalls, 'although I have a sneaking suspicion that someone from the A&M press office was trying to get some sort of ill-advised hype going about the single. Of course, we were oblivious to it all until a couple of newspapers had run a story, and people started asking us if we used real inmates in our video. We were horrified and had to explain that not only was it untrue, it would be literally—and legally—impossible for a touring rock band to turn up at a hospital in North America and whisk some patients off to a random location to shoot a video. Ridiculous.'

The remainder of the summer was packed with festival appearances across Europe that did little to provoke any further tabloid scandal: Rock Am Ring, Pinkpop, Eurorockeenes, Phoenix, Provinssirock. But it was their Monsters Of Rock appearance at Donington on June 4 that will live long in the memory. 'I was really, really nervous before we played,' Andy admits. 'Phil Alexander [at the time the editor of *Kerrang!*] had painted a picture of all these bottles of piss raining down on us. I thought this would be the end of my career—this chubby guy with a beard walking off stage like Sissy Spacek in *Carrie*, but covered in urine, with eighty thousand boos of the unwashed metal masses ringing in my ears. But it turned out to be one of my favourite festivals that I've ever played.'

The trio closed their summer run with an appearance at Reading on August 28. Soundgarden had pulled out of the festival at the last moment, allowing Therapy? to move up one place, directly below the headliners, Red Hot Chili Peppers. 'At that point, we'd had a gold-selling album, had singles go into the Top 20, and had been on the cover of *Kerrang!*, *NME*, and *Melody Maker*,' remembers Andy. 'It did feel like we'd deserved to be in that place. It was a shame that we didn't get to see Soundgarden, but to play to something like fifty thousand people in the darkness was brilliant.'

'That summer had been mad—they seemed to perform breakthrough shows in every country that year,' remembers agent Paul Bolton. 'Reading was just another amazing show for them.

'What I remember most about that day was drinking with James from the Manics, who'd played the day before,' he adds. 'He was with a guy called Jeff, who I thought said he was from their label. We had a few drinks and went back to the hotel. I remember telling James I thought Jeff, the A&R guy, was a nice guy. It turned out that it was Jeff Buckley.'

The following month, the band attended the Mercury Music Prize awards ceremony. *Troublegum* had been shortlisted for the prestigious award alongside albums by Paul Weller, Primal Scream, The Prodigy, Pulp, and Take That. Manchester dance-pop act M People were the surprise winners with their album *Elegant Slumming*.

'We went into the awards with the right spirit,' says Andy, 'because we knew we weren't going to win. We know how these things work, but I felt bad for Blur, because everyone thought their album, *Parklife*, was going to win. There were a few of the Britpop greats who were really cocky about their chances of winning, so I was pleased it went to a wild card like M People. They're not my cup of tea, but they're really nice. We hung out with the Prodigy that night, in the bad lad's corner. They took it all with a pinch of salt.'

The ceremony was the band's first taste of the red-carpet treatment, and they appeared in the tabloids' reports the following morning. Andy received a call from his father—not to offer his condolences, but to enquire about something else entirely. 'One of the newspapers had said I'd got a tattoo on my arse while we were on tour,' says Andy. 'But it was my arm.'

Soon after that, the band undertook a tour of France with support from the Manic Street Preachers. Guitarist Richey Edwards, who had missed their Reading set to undergo treatment at the Priory Clinic in Roehampton for 'nervous exhaustion', was back in the line-up for the three-week trek.

'They were very, very bright, working-class lads who didn't have any sense of arrogance or entitlement, unlike so many other rock stars I'd met,' says Andy. 'It was because of their background. To be honest, it could be quite intimidating, but they weren't like that at all, once you met them.'

On that tour, Andy gave Richey a copy of Thomas Moore's book *Dark Eros: Imagination Of Sadism*. In return, he was given *Elegy Written In A Country Church* by Thomas Gray, which he signed 'Love, Richey'.

'There was no inkling, certainly among us, that Richey wasn't in a good place,' remembers Andy. 'It was just a great tour to do. We'd have Subbuteo [table football] tournaments with Sean [Moore, Manics drummer], and I remember that we wanted to buy them presents before we went home. They'd been wearing camouflage gear on tour, so we bought four Action Man dolls and left them in their dressing room.'

'Richey was understandably a bit shaky, so we gave them their own space, but, fuck, they were inspirational,' adds Michael. 'I'd say that tour is probably a career highlight. We were only getting into a groove and then it was over.'

A week after their tour of France, Therapy? were invited to appear on the TV show *Taratata*, presented by Nagui Fam, an Egyptian-born TV and radio personality. As part of the show, they performed a cover of The Police's 'Next To You', from their 1978 debut, *Outlandos d'Amour*.

'I think Sting had mentioned in a magazine that he thought Fyfe's drumming was similar to Stewart Copeland's, which was spot on, because he was a huge fan,' says Andy. 'Sting came up to me and said that he hadn't played the song in years, so we grabbed a couple of acoustic guitars and went through it together in his dressing room. It was surreal, being sat a foot away from Sting, singing it with that voice he has. He had a drink with us afterwards and asked what we were up to next. We mentioned we had a UK tour coming up. He had a charity thing with Eric Clapton and Elton John coming up. He lives in a completely different world.'

In November, just ten months after the release of *Troublegum*, the band began writing material for their next album. 'We were on a roll, and it got to the point where we were just saying yes to everything, says Andy. 'I was drinking a lot and doing a lot of drugs, and people would ask me questions whenever I was in that state. I remember someone from the label saying they wanted to book some time for us to work on the next record, and I said yes. I really should have said that we needed some time off. It's easy to say that now, but that's what we should have done.'

'We should have taken some time off and given America another crack,' agrees Michael. '*Troublegum* hadn't been out that long, and it was just about to sell a million copies. But we'd written a few new songs and had some ideas,' he adds—among them 'Bad Mother', 'Stories', 'Diane', 'Me Vs You', and 'A Moment Of Clarity'. 'It was quite a stressful time. Once we finished there, we went off to Berlin for the MTV Europe Awards, which was frankly proper showbiz territory.'

Manager Gerry credits the album's success to a number of factors. 'Firstly, it was, and still is, a brilliantly strong album, full of hooks,' he says. 'The timing was right, too. We came out with that album when people were looking for powerful songs with attitude, melody, and interesting lyrics; the album connected with people.

'Secondly, they had a very committed team at the record company in London and in Europe,' he adds. 'They all loved Therapy?—not just as musicians and as a band but as people, too. They go out of their way to make people welcome and comfortable; when you have that type of personality, people respond to it and make the extra effort. The band worked, and continue to work, very hard, and people around them respond to that and respect that.'

The trio saw out the year with a seven-date UK tour, starting off with a two-night stand at Shepherds Bush Empire in London, with thirteen more dates in Germany. Andy and Michael both admit that by the time the tour ended, at Musik-Zirkus in Dortmund on December 20, they were running on fumes, having spent much of the year on the road.

'By the end, I was worn out,' says Michael. 'Sore neck, sore hands, sore back. I just felt broken.'

'I was drinking all the time and found it hard to stop when I came home,' adds Andy. 'If I was home for a couple of days, I didn't rest and do my laundry. I just kept on going. The only difference was there wasn't a gig at the end of the night.'

YEAR SIX/fear and loathing in wiltshire

This is not a year that Andy Cairns has ever looked back upon with any degree of fondness.

By the previous year's close, he and Fyfe were barely on speaking on terms, their near-silent relationship exacerbated by a packed schedule in support of *Troublegum*. Over the course of the previous eleven months or so, their rift had deepened. The band had embarked on two separate trips to North America, plus two UK headline tours, festival appearances, multiple dates in Europe, and two shows in Tel Aviv during the summer. It was relentless.

Flying back to Dublin after their performance at Dortmund's Muzik-Zirkus on December 20, Andy was met by an old friend who remarked that his mid-length, dyed-black hair made him look like an 'old goth'. As the band's profile grew in the past year, the frontman had been subjected to barbed comments about his appearance in the press, and he'd had enough. Before heading to his favourite pub, the White Horse on George's Quay—don't look for it now, it's a Starbucks—Andy and his friend made a pit stop at the friend's home. Dumping his case in the hall, he borrowed some clippers and proceeded to give himself a close crop. After that, he gave himself a clean shave—something that he'd not done for several years. The *Troublegum* goatee was off, swirling down the plughole.

Perhaps hoping for a symbolic fresh start before the holidays and rid himself of the emotional baggage of the past twelve months, Andy stared into the mirror and immediately regretted his decision. *Fuck.* 'I didn't like what I saw,' he says. 'I was constantly seeing us in the press that past year, and I think I got sick of looking at myself. Shaving my head didn't turn me into Ian MacKaye, as I thought it might do. It just made me hate myself even more.'

Exhausted, Andy returned to Northern Ireland for Christmas. A few days later, he headed back to his home in Dalkey, just half an hour's drive south from Dublin, and spent the rest of the holidays drinking excessively. He did so in part out of routine, but also in an attempt to combat the nagging thoughts of writing new music for their next album, which the band were due to begin pre-production of in a matter of weeks.

'I didn't know if I was coming or going,' he admits. 'I developed quite a healthy drug habit and was drinking a bottle of Absolut vodka every day. I thought that if I gave up drinking, I'd spend the next two weeks lying in bed and feeling sick. I decided to keep going and see if inspiration would hit.'

It didn't.

Instead, he was paralysed by a dilemma. Britpop was in full swing, and the indie music press had pitted Oasis and Blur against each other in a North vs. South soap opera. After the success of *Troublegum*, Therapy?'s label was seemingly keen to strike while the iron was hot and get the trio back into the studio before they'd even had a chance to finish their current tour. Their set at London's Shepherds Bush Empire on November 26 featured three new songs in a somewhat embryonic state: 'Me Vs You', 'Bad Mother', and 'Jude The Obscene', the latter of which was based on 'This Isn't (Where It's At)', a song Andy had originally penned for his short-lived side-project, Catweazel. The following night saw the band drop the latter in favour of '30 Seconds' and 'Loose'. Each of these songs, even in their early incarnations, was different, and offered no firm pointers as to where the hell album number five was heading.

The idea of recording *Troublegum II* didn't sit well with Andy. It would be too easy to make another album of metallic pop-punk, and he kept coming back to the same idea: to write music that reflected his listening habits, which meant bands like The Afghan Whigs, This Mortal Coil, and The God Machine. 'I found it very difficult to deal with the pressure, if I'm totally honest,' he admits. 'It was horrible. I had all this going on in my head, on top of a bottle of vodka a day, as well as speed and coke. I'd got myself into a right old state.'

On January 21, Andy, Michael, and Fyfe returned to Chapel Studios in Lincolnshire, to follow up on the pre-production they'd begun in November with producer Al Clay. The time off had been far from prolific in terms of songwriting, and Andy was beginning to panic. He'd barely touched his guitar during the break, but did bring along the urgent, jagged riff to 'Epilepsy', which he'd conjured up in a 'fucked-up state' just a couple of days before flying to England. Inspired by San Diego's Drive Like Jehu—the now-legendary band featuring Rocket From The Crypt frontman John 'Speedo' Reis and his Pitchfork bandmate Rick Froberg—the riff was intended to thaw the chilly atmosphere between himself and the drummer.

THERAPY?

'We both saw them at the Garage in London after *Yank Crime* came out, and it was incredible,' says Andy. 'Going into the album, I was looking for a connection, so I came up with a slightly off-kilter riff, and he liked it. The track itself is passive-aggressive, and it's like two cats fighting in a bag: it stops, yelps, and there's some relief in the chorus. I think Fyfe liked it from a drummer's point of view because it was more complex.'

That day, the trio set up their equipment, and their producer urged them to run through any ideas they had, no matter how small, in order to get a grasp of the task at hand. 'I'd say the album was about 15 percent there,' remembers Andy.

Michael was facing his own struggles, too. At just twenty-two years of age, the prospect of going into the studio to record a follow-up to a hit album unsettled him, as he feared the process may highlight any perceived shortcomings he had as a bass player. 'There was a lot of talk, like, "Let's make the bass like John Entwistle here" and stuff like that,' he says. 'I could see what Al was doing, pushing the band a wee bit further. When you're stood there and people are picking through your bass lines ... I didn't feel like I was up to the job. I'm not the sort of person to pull things out of the bag; I prefer to go away and do it in my own time.'

Later that week, with pre-production over, Michael and Fyfe headed down to London to attend the *NME* Brat Awards on January 24. In a surprise to absolutely no one, Blur and Oasis dominated the ceremony, with Blur winning five awards and Oasis bagging three.

'There was a very heavy, druggy vibe there,' remembers Michael. 'I saw people smoking heroin in the toilets, and I was offered every drug under the sun. I didn't like it at all. I've never told anybody this, but I had a bit of a meltdown the next day. I was massively hungover and had a panic attack. I thought, *Fuck this*, and got a flight home. After a couple of days, I came back. It was a bit awkward, but the lads were great about it. I just thought I couldn't do the album.'

Next stop: Milton Keynes. The drums were tracked for one week at the beginning of February at Great Linford Manor, a studio chosen for its spacious live room. Both Andy and Michael played live while Fyfe thrashed away at his kit. This labour-intensive week presented its own problems, however. According to Michael, even though they had 'seven solid songs', new ideas presented themselves, and the band found themselves reworking those as well.

By February 12, the band had relocated to Real World Studios, a state-of-the-art recording facility owned by Peter Gabriel in the Wiltshire village of Box. 'I was like a canary down a mine when it came to choosing the studio,' remembers Andy. 'I'd volunteered to have a look at some places while we had some time off. I visited Real World, Parkgate in Battle, and Wool Hall in Bath, which was owned by Van Morrison. The thing I liked about Real World was that there was no clutter; I thought that since my head was full of enough rubbish, it would be good to record there.'

'It was incredible,' adds Michael. 'There was a massive live room with a grand piano, instruments from Peter Gabriel's travels, and lots of vintage guitars. I also experienced the internet for the first time while we were there and spent a lot of time playing the game Myst.'

The studio, which was originally an old mill, was purchased by the former Genesis frontman in 1987. Far away from any distractions, the facility was patrolled by a flock of aggressive geese that kept the band on their toes, especially in the early hours of the morning. 'They would attack anyone they thought might have some bread, in a pincer movement,' laughs Michael. 'You can imagine having a load of beer in you and trying to ward them off.'

With drum tracks ready to work from, Michael and Andy entered the studio with a gung-ho attitude. The sessions began enthusiastically enough, with the bassist overcoming his crisis of confidence and recording his parts early on. Andy burned the candle at both ends; focussing on tracking his guitars during the day, he kept himself up at night with alcohol and a dab of speed or two, and pored over his notebooks. One book in particular helped inform the romantically damaged tone of the new material: *Dark Eros: Imagination Of Sadism* by Thomas Moore, a Detroit-born psychotherapist who once spent thirteen years as a Catholic monk—the same book Andy had given to Manic Street Preachers guitarist Richey Edwards during a tour of France the previous year.

'The book looked at the darker nature of humanity and he challenged people who were reading it to look squarely at their own unfathomable, revolting truths,' says Andy. 'When I look back at the lyrics I was writing at Real World, they were so verbose. *Troublegum* had pithy, angsty haikus. Little punch lines to dark jokes. With all the cocaine and alcohol, it got to the point when I couldn't write anything pithy; it was all loquacious. I had loads of notebooks full of words.'

Every night, he repeated the same pattern: he'd track guitars during the day and then go off to his bedroom at night, wired on uppers, and attempt to slot words into the music they'd recorded just hours previously. He was sleeping perhaps three hours a night and was rudely awakened by a phone call each morning at the ungodly hour of 11am. It was Al, saying it was time to start work.

Over the weeks, the sessions began to drag on, and the band would keep unusual hours in order to meet the record label's deadline. 'We'd be sat there and the cleaner would come in at seven in the morning,' says Michael. 'There was a fridge full of beer that magically restocked itself, which didn't help.'

A trip to the magic fridge—other fridges are available—was fraught with danger. It was located in the kitchen, which was situated in a small building adjacent to the recording studio. The residents would draw straws to see who had to make the short trip from the studio, over a small bridge and into to the kitchen. More often than not, those bastard geese would make their presence known and try to nip those foolish, or brave enough, to run the errand. Sometimes they'd bump into Peter Gabriel, too.

'One night, it was my turn to go to the kitchen and grab some drinks,' says Andy. 'The kitchen was in total darkness, and when I opened the fridge door, this face, which was about a foot away, lit up. It was Peter. When he saw I was holding a bottle of wine, he said, "Whatever it takes, eh?" and walked off.'

The frosty atmosphere between frontman and drummer showed no signs of thawing. When the band sat down to work out any kinks in a song's arrangement, there were no rows between the two—just a deadly, awkward silence. 'It got very passive-aggressive,' says Andy. 'If Fyfe didn't like a certain section of a song, he wouldn't say anything, but, eventually, word would get back. It wasn't a nice place to be. I don't know how it got to that point and I'm not blameless in any of it.

'I'm sure my constant partying didn't help,' he adds. 'When I got very drunk or high on coke or speed, I'd be very in-your-face. I'd go from someone that's quite thoughtful to being that guy in the studio who won't shut the fuck up. It must have been difficult for all the other people to deal with.'

Al credits Michael's diplomatic skills as an important factor in the album getting made, a 'peacekeeper' between the silently warring factions, about which Michael laughs, 'Isn't being a peacekeeper the default setting for any bass player?'

Growing up in a family of seven children, the bassist quickly learned how to deal with different personalities: 'You know when someone's having a bad day or know when not to tell them their hair looks ridiculous. You learn the hard way and get a slap from an angry sister.

'With some of the tension in the studio, everyone was saying the same thing, but in a different manner,' he adds. 'Because of the exhaustion and the stress, people would read things the wrong way. I like meeting people in the middle and making sure they're happy. Letting everyone know they've contributed is like solving a little puzzle. Life's too short for grievances.'

'Michael doesn't see the sense in creating problems when there are none,' says Andy. 'Fyfe and I were the masters of that. We could take a sunny day and turn it into a horrendous torrent of rage and angst. You need someone who's proactive, and that was Michael. He rescued the album.'

That's not to say their stay at Real World was all *sturm und drang*. There was a Subbuteo table and an ever-growing Scalextric set, whose track would grow any time someone went into Bath or Bristol to run an errand. 'During the time of *Troublegum* and *Infernal Love*, I used to get quite lonely,' explains Andy. 'One place where I found succour and comfort was in toyshops. If I ever felt flat or alone, I'd go to a toyshop. I bought a Scalextric set in when we were in Milton Keynes, and it got out of hand.'

'We wanted to make the track go around the whole studio, but there were so many adapters it was making the amps buzz,' adds Michael. 'The two engineers were stationed at particularly tricky corners to put the cars back on. Those poor fuckers, babysitting these Northern Irish idiots: you've played bass for a couple of hours and want to have some fun.'

The band also worked on 'Duck Symphony', a hare-brained scheme dreamt up by Andy and Michael in a bid to ease the studio tension that became a sort-of successor to 'Penis Temple', the avant-garde jam recorded during the *Nurse* sessions. The pair would climb into the rowing boat on the small lake surrounding the studio and record the pleasant, ambient sounds of the local wildfowl. The geese made an appearance too, of course. 'We had to do something like that or we were going to go absolutely mad,' laughs Andy. 'But it seemed to work.'

Slowly but surely, the album began to come together. The band made contact with Belfast DJ David Holmes, who'd done two different remixes for a twelve-inch release of 'Die Laughing' the previous year. He was briefed to create ambient interludes that would ebb and flow in between each track. 'Early on, we discussed having a DJ do these segues,' remembers Michael. 'David could conceptualise things we couldn't. We had reference points like [*Twin Peaks* soundtrack composer] Angelo Badalamenti and classic soundtrack stuff he was into already, so he grasped what we wanted quickly.'

The lyrics, though, were a little less forthcoming. The ideas and words were there, but combing through Andy's notebooks and condensing his amphetamine streams of consciousness into songs was proving to be something of a Herculean task. Melodies came easy to the frontman, but picking a line to match was something else entirely.

'Every single song had a different approach,' Al later told *Team Rock*. 'Lyrics seemed to be a challenge for Andy, to really nail certain things, and I definitely let him run, because I absolutely felt that he knew what he was doing. We'd be talking long into the night about lyrics. It really did feel like we were on a mission to do something new and fresh that hadn't really been done before.'

Michael took the frontman aside and urged him to put his notes to one side and just focus on what he wanted to say. After several days, 'Stories'—the album's infectious lead single in the vein of Rocket From The Crypt, helped along by Simon Clarke's squalling sax break—was the first song to benefit from this simple suggestion. With its insistent refrain of '*Happy people have no stories*', the song details the frontman's teenage years in Northern Ireland, spent hanging around with his friends and a group of wealthy girls from 'very big, posh houses' in County Antrim. 'They were slumming it with us because we were the kids from the estate,' says Andy. 'They hung about with us because we were a bit rough and liked music.'

The music for 'A Moment Of Clarity' was inspired by San Diego trio The God Machine's second and final album, *One Last Laugh In A Place Of Dying*. Recording in Real World's huge live room, producer Al was tasked with achieving what the band described as a 'haunted ballroom' feel. The idea was informed by the classic scene in Stanley Kubrick's 1980 horror masterpiece *The Shining*, in which Jack Torrance (played by Jack Nicholson) wanders through the middle of the Overlook Hotel's bustling dance hall and orders a drink from the Lloyd the bartender. The words, meanwhile, were about a giving up on a failing relationship. The opening line, '*I thought of you tonight*', was taken from Paul Muldoon's poem 'Incantata', written in memory of the American visual artist Mary Farl Powers.

The music and melody for 'Jude The Obscene' were written several years earlier, around the time the band recorded *Babyteeth* at Homestead Studio. The lyrics came to Andy during one of his chemically fuelled late nights as a repressed memory from his childhood in Ballyclare bubbled up from out of nowhere. The opening lines—'*He was born the same time as me / To a small-souled woman who died twenty-three / Now you're here, they can't shove you back*'—are about a school bully who would make Andy's long walks to and from school a living hell. One day, the bully caught the young Cairns, tied him to a lamppost, and threw bottles above his head, showering him in shards of broken glass. A neighbour caught him and the police were called, and Andy was escorted to the safety of his mother's workplace. The bully ended up in a youth centre and eventually took his own life.

'The boy was excluded from school for a while,' Andy remembers, 'but I was absolutely terrified about going to school for the next couple of years. I'd completely buried that memory until we started doing the album. I have no idea why it came back to me.'

'Bowels Of Love' was the first track on the album to feature touring cellist Martin McCarrick. Andy says that the track—a fucked-up troubadour song in the vein of Nick Cave and Tom Waits—came to life after Martin's contribution. 'We were going for a David Lynch and *Blue Velvet* thing, like a drunk torch singer with these Marquis de Sade-type lyrics, singing it to an empty room as they're brushing up bottles at the end. It nearly didn't make the record, but after Martin added his strings, it took on a life of its own.'

Martin's frantic, cascading riff at the beginning of 'Bad Mother' earned him a co-writing credit. The verses, which have a bouncy reggae rhythm, were based on XTC's 1979 single 'Making Plans For Nigel'. 'The song had been in the set towards the end of the last tour and it was me palm-muting two chords, which is really bog standard,' admits Andy. 'Martin saw what chords we were playing and changed the nature of the song.'

The lyrics were inspired by a chapter in Moore's *Dark Eros*, examining how 'writers always put themselves in desperate situations—drugs, poverty—to help the creative process. I think that Jesus-martyr complex can go too far.'

'Me Vs You'—a brooding song about regret—was informed by one of Andy's favourite songs of all time: 'Miles Is Dead', from The Afghan Whigs' 1992 album *Congregation*. 'One of the things I like about their lyrics are the way they write about masculinity. They were unflinching, like a John Cassavetes movie.' The opening verse—'*I just came to get my things / I'm not drunk or anything / I saw a light on in your house / Undo the chain and let me in / I want to talk*'—imagines the narrator as a stalker standing outside a former partner's home, wondering what went wrong and what could have been. 'When we did the song live the year before, it sounded like something off *Troublegum*,' he adds. 'It had big, blocky power chords and was a bit pedestrian. When we got into the studio, we got the tremolo pedal out and made it more atmospheric and not an AOR ballad.'

Therapy? had long worshipped Minneapolis punks Hüsker Dü and often played a cover of 'Diane', a chilling story of the rape and murder of a Minnesota waitress Diane Edwards by Joseph Ture in 1980. The original, composed by drummer Grant Hart, appeared on Hüsker Dü's 1983 EP *Metal Circus*. At Real World, Therapy? recorded a version as a full band and it was only until Martin added strings that the song was reworked into something altogether more haunting.

'Martin got a cassette of the track—this is how long ago it was—and sent Al a demo, which was like chamber music,' Andy remembers. 'We got him back to Real World to record it properly, and I sang over it. It was something a bit different, and Al was jumping up and down in the studio, saying it was amazing.'

By now, the band were running two weeks over schedule, and, due to a prior booking, had to relocate from Real World's main studio and complete the remaining tracks in Peter Gabriel's private studio upstairs. The overrunning schedule also meant they had to regrettably cancel a trip to Russia. By March 31, the frontman and producer were working around the clock to complete '30 Seconds', *Infernal Love*'s final song, as a courier had been dispatched by A&M to pick up the master tapes and return them to their offices in London.

'The song had been around for a long time and had a Minor Threat or Motörhead feel, but it didn't have lyrics or vocals,' explains Michael. 'Al suggested we write a verse each and sing it ourselves. I'm neither a lyricist nor a strong singer by any means. So Al was sat there recording a bassist who had never sung before in a professional studio. We were in *Some Kind Of Monster* territory,' he adds, referring to Metallica's toe-curling documentary.

'To his credit, Michael recorded his verse, and it was really good, but Fyfe didn't bother trying,' says Andy. 'In the end, I finished the song while the courier was on their way. I was singing the second verse with Al, who by this point was a broken man. I was looking for excuses to avoid doing it, but it had to be done.'

After six weeks of stress, broken sleep, and aggressive wildfowl, *Infernal Love* was complete. In London, David Holmes was adding his ambient interludes, which ebb and flow throughout the eleven tracks. With the master tapes packed off to London, the band packed their belongings and climbed into a people carrier and headed down the M4 to catch a flight from Heathrow to Japan, where they'd see out the remainder of their current tour. 'It seems like a peculiar dream now,' says Michael. 'You can imagine the state our heads were in.'

Therapy? landed at Tokyo Narita airport on April 2 to begin the final leg of their *Troublegum* shows. After the stress of recording their new album, the nine-hour time difference did little to dampen their spirits.

Well, for a moment, at least. 'I remember thinking, *This is going to be great*,' says Andy. 'We'd played in Japan in 1993, and it was incredible. We'd got to the airport and there were loads of kids with gifts there and wanting autographs. I had a shaved head and no beard, wearing a green hoodie and these two girls looked at me and burst into tears. They asked what had I done to myself. I was so exhausted by that point, I couldn't enjoy it.'

Following their show in Osaka and two nights co-headlining with New York hardcore four-piece Sick Of It All in Tokyo, the band flew south to join the ill-fated Alternative Nation festival in Australia, a three-day event launched to rival the Big Day Out. Both headlining acts—Red Hot Chili Peppers and Stone Temple Pilots—had dropped out, but the rest of the bill was strong, with Therapy? joining the likes of Faith No More, Lou Reed, Nine Inch Nails, Body Count, The Prodigy, L7, Live, and Pennywise, as well as local acts. The three shows, in Brisbane, Melbourne, and Sydney, were hampered by bad weather, with the latter event turning the Eastern Creek Raceway into a mud bath.

With the album's June release looming large on the horizon, the band were dealing constantly with faxes about choices for the lead single, video shoots, and a blunt representative from their label. 'People wanted to know what the new songs sounded like, and there was a guy who worked for A&M who had a Hüsker Dü tattoo, so we let them hear a promo CD,' says Andy. It was evident that this particular listener was taken aback by the new material. He really didn't have to say a word, really. In fact, it might have been better all round had he swerved the topic entirely. Instead, after hearing one song, he said, 'What the fuck was that? I don't get it.'

'That put me on a firm, downward trajectory,' admits Andy.

The man with the Hüsker Dü tattoo wasn't the only one who didn't immediately embrace the band's latest full-length. As they kept busy approving mixes on the road, they were getting it from all angles over the days and weeks that followed: Why didn't they record another *Troublegum*?

Why the fuck are there cellos on the album? Why did Andy cut all his hair off? On and on it went. Andy started to self-medicate with a renewed enthusiasm until Roger Pattinson, the band's tour manager, took him to one side and had a word.

'He wanted to take me to see a doctor,' Andy says, 'because he thought I wasn't well. He said something like, "If you don't behave yourself now, something really bad is going to happen."'

An appointment was made, and a prescription for tranquillisers was written out on the spot, with a repeated warning to not even think about drinking alcohol. 'The pressure became too much, and it got worse and worse,' Andy admits. 'People were beginning to receive promo copies of the album and the label were feeding back; a lot of people hated the record when they first heard it, especially in the rock press. I thought I was going to go mad.'

While the band were in Sydney, Andy and Fyfe briefly reconnected over 'Epilepsy', the new album's chaotic opener. 'We ended up chatting on a night off and playing this song which, briefly, broke down any barriers,' Andy told *Team Rock* in 2015. 'Both of us loved the track: the twisted riff, manic, bop drumming, and guttural bass work. The "free jazz" freak-out section was inspired by Ornette Coleman.'

The *NME* caught up with the band on April 29, before a show at the Espace Médoquine in a suburb of Bordeaux, France. Mark Sutherland's cover story caught the trio in a defiant mood as they played the final date of their *Troublegum* tour, with their set including new tracks 'Stories', 'Misery', and 'Loose'.

'We're desperately kicking against the doom right now,' Andy told the *NME*. 'Which makes us ahead of our time or completely fucking stupid. I'm so cynical of these little Nirvana rip-off bands who use depression as some kind of creative yardstick. Happiness is not an invalid experience.' He went on to describe 'Loose' as 'the happiest thing I've ever written. Kurt Cobain made some beautiful music that means a lot to me, but I don't want to end up like him … and I won't. The survivor in me has really come out recently. I have this special mechanism that keeps me alive through it all. It's just a pity that happy songs don't have the impact of depressing ones.'

'Stories' was released as a single on May 22. The cover photograph, which was taken by Anton Corbijn in a sleepy Portuguese fishing village, became something of a talking point in the rock press. Andy, Michael, and Fyfe dressed in red frilly shirts and stick-on moustaches—a decision that stemmed from an afternoon at Real World with the Dutch photographer, who had directed the videos for Depeche Mode's 'Enjoy The Silence' and Nirvana's 'Heart-Shaped Box', and worked extensively with U2. We may as well address the suave elephant in the room, then.

'I've always like him because of the stuff he'd done with Joy Division,' says Andy. 'When the record company asked who we wanted to do the shots, it was almost like a joke when I said, "Why don't we get someone like Anton Corbijn?" We thought he wouldn't do it, because he'd done U2 at this point.'

Anton brought what was essentially a 'dress-up box' to Real World and produced a set of flamboyant garments, suggesting that it would play with the band's men-in-black image. 'We thought it was like a piss-take of entertainers and the business of show,' laughs Andy. 'We were quite shocked to begin with, but eventually we thought, *OK.*'

'The frilly shirts and moustaches were only a small element of the shoot,' remembers Michael. 'A lot of fans got quite annoyed about it, actually. Those photos were just poking fun at stereotype we'd been saddled with, but what can you do?'

On May 22, 'Stories' was released as a single. It debuted at no. 14 in the UK and no. 15 in Ireland, which meant the band earned another appointment at Elstree Studios for a *Top Of The Pops* appearance.

In the run up to their headline tour with Schtum and Skunk Anansie, the reviews started to roll in. *Kerrang!* awarded *Infernal Love* full marks, with Paul Rees describing the album as a 'songwriting tour-de-force that runs the gamut from adrenalin-gobbling anthems to twisted torch songs … quite simply, a classic.'

Q's Sam Taylor was similarly impressed, awarding the release a five-star review: 'Though still a trio, Therapy? seem to have extended their sound in all directions. This album ranges from the pop accessibility of "Loose" (which could have been lifted from Sugar's *Copper Blue*) through heaving epics like "A Moment Of Clarity" to an actual Bob Mould [sic] cover, "Diane", which is a work of pure dark genius. Transformation complete, Therapy? are ready for anything.'

Select said it was 'an album that'll thrill the fanbase [and] welcome lovers of the fetchingly turned-out chorus'. *RAW*'s Howard Johnson gave it four and a half out of five, remarking, 'If there's the occasional fleeting thought that maybe the lyrical likes of "Jude The Obscene" and "Bowels Of Love" are tying a touch too hard, then it would be churlish to linger on them. Therapy?'s growth is assured in their music. They've made a damn smart move.'

'*Infernal Love* will undoubtedly both consolidate Therapy?'s mainstream status and alienate the purists,' wrote *Vox*'s Lisa Verrico in a seven-out-of-ten critique. Other periodicals weren't so kind. *NME* gave the album five out of ten, while *Metal Hammer*'s Pippa Lang gave it a proper kicking. 'Even after repeated plays, you struggle to grab a hold of anything concrete within the sludge of rock balladry that consumes this record,' she wrote. '*Infernal Love* is a very poor album indeed.'

The album was released on June 12. On June 11, Virgin Megastore on London's Oxford Street was opened just before midnight to allow fans to buy the album and meet the band. 'It was nuts,' remembers Michael. 'To me, that's what Guns N' Roses did. I was like, *Who in their right mind goes to central London at midnight to go to a record shop?* There was always the risk of having an Artie Fufkin moment, where no one comes to a Spinal Tap signing—but it was actually pretty cool.'

Andy's memories of the midnight signing are vastly different. 'I remember the shop played the album crushingly loud while we were signing stuff,' he remembers, 'and people were saying stuff like "I'll need to listen to this two or three times", or "What the fuck's this?" A lot of it was paranoia, because of the uppers I was taking. I'd be signing stuff and having my photo taken, but a voice in my head was saying *this person doesn't like this record.*'

The next morning, the band took a train to Manchester for two more signing sessions, at Virgin and HMV. 'It was a bad time,' recalls Andy. 'I remember shouting at Fyfe over something stupid like a cup of coffee. At the Virgin Megastore, one of the staff mentioned that the album looked like it was going to go to no. 9 in the charts. We were kind of hoping it would go to no. 1. I was like, *Don't tell me shit like that.* I was in such a negative frame of mind.'

On June 28, the night before the band performed at Libre Antenne in Paris, the band were invited to meet Metallica drummer Lars Ulrich backstage at the Élysée Montmartre, where Slash's Snakepit were performing. 'We got a call saying Metallica would like us to play Donington as their special guests, but Lars would like to meet us,' says Andy. 'Lars was there with either his agent or his accountant, and said it would be great to have us on the bill. Two things I remember were that Lars wanted a cold beer, and the person he was with had building plans for a helicopter pad.'

'I think he was just wanted to know if we were on the same page,' adds Michael. 'I talked his ear off about the *New Wave Of British Heavy Metal '79 Revisited* compilation he put out in 1993.'

July and August was spent largely on the European festival circuit, by which point Andy was beginning to see things in a more positive light. 'I took myself off for a while to clean myself up,' he says. 'The pressure got so much and I thought I was going mad at that point in time, from the pressure of the *Infernal Love* sessions to going straight out on the road.'

And so to Donington, for Therapy?'s second appearance in as many years. The show, billed as 'Escape From The Studio'—as Metallica were recording their *Load* album—boasted a roster featuring Corrosion Of Conformity, Warrior Soul, Machine Head, White Zombie, Slash's Snakepit, Slayer, and Skid Row. Therapy? were placed second from the top—a billing that caused some consternation backstage.

'Behind the scenes, there were so many bands saying, "Who the fuck are these guys? Why are they second from top?"' says Andy. 'They were furious, and there was a really bad vibe back stage.'

'I hated playing Donington that year,' he adds. 'There was a small section of the crowd chanting "Therapy? are shit" before we went on stage. We wanted to go on to [Thin Lizzy's] "The Boys Are Back In Town" because it was the second year we'd played. Word got back to Metallica, who said that's what they were going to use for their intro tape. I think people were disinterested, and I really didn't enjoy it. Metallica were great, but it was quite deflating after the experience we had the year before.

The following month, the band joined the Monsters Of Rock tour of South America, taking in shows in Brazil, Chile, and Argentina. During their show at Santiago's Teatro Monumental, they endured 'a hail of spit' during their nine-song set.

'That was the most feral crowd I've ever seen,' remembers Michael. 'The gig was like playing in *Mad Max Beyond Thunderdome*. I wasn't on the mic, but poor Andy was, and he got spit in his mouth early on.'

'People were leaping from the third balcony into the mosh pit,' adds Andy. 'It looked like a Hieronymus Bosch painting. It was incredible, a seething pit of denim and skulls. Three songs from the end, I dropped my trousers and started waving my genitals about.'

When they returned to the hotel, the band's tour manager suggested they catch an earlier flight to the next show, in Buenos Aires, which they did. Half an hour after they'd left the hotel, the police arrived, demanding to know where the genital-waving rock star was. But in Spanish.

'The whole event was broadcast on live TV,' explains Andy. 'It's a very

Catholic country, and very strict on the issues of nudity. I'd have been arrested.'

'We're banned from playing Chile again, apparently,' adds Michael. 'The crowd was great but the spitting was too much. The police and the army were there, and they were all carrying guns. I'm not good with any kind of firearm, and there was a real, horrible edginess to it all.'

Due to the nature of the tour and enthusiasm of the fans, the bands bonded as they took refuge in their hotels on the three-date festival tour—notably Michael and the frontman from Megadeth. 'Dave Mustaine rang my room while we were there and wanted to go for a drink,' he says. 'We had a cocktail and told me he was a big fan of *Troublegum*. He was like, "I know what it's like, and you're probably very close to burning out." He said if I ever wanted to chat about it, call him, and gave me his number. I think he was possibly concerned about Andy, who was burning the candle at both ends.'

Paradise Lost were on the bill, too, which gave frontman Nick Holmes a chance to catch-up with his old metal tape-trading friend from Larne. 'I knew Michael from his Evil Priest days,' says Nick. 'He sent me an Evil Priest sticker, which I put on the wall in my mum's kitchen. I think it's still there. The band were great—good fun and down to earth.

'There were some real heavyweights on that bill, and sharing a bill with the likes of Ozzy was a scary few steps up,' Nick adds. 'I seem to remember Andy was encouraging the spitting [at the Santiago show]. It was weird because it's never happened since. My Chilean mates actually seem pretty ashamed about it, even though it was generally accepted as a term of endearment at the time.'

Much of the remainder of the year was spent on the road. A few days after the Monsters Of Rock tour, Therapy? were back in Europe, playing shows in Scandinavia, Germany, Italy, and France. On November 6, they released their cover of Hüsker Dü's 'Diane', which peaked at no. 26 in the UK and at no. 20 in Ireland. It achieved Top 10 status in many countries across Europe, and its expensive, high-concept video, directed by W.I.Z. (known for his work with Oasis and Marilyn Manson, among others) was a fixture on MTV's alternative-rock playlists.

'The video was absolute lunacy,' Andy told *Team Rock* editor Paul Brannigan in 2014. 'It was a huge production, and I distinctly remember that it cost the price of a house to make—the most money we'd ever spent on a video. At one point I had to lie naked under a shower of ice cold water while a model stroked my hair, which just made me wonder what the hell I was doing there.'

The trio embarked on a nine-date tour of the UK, then journeyed into Europe, before returning for a show at London's Brixton Academy on December 13. Former Hüsker Dü drummer/vocalist Grant Hart, Honeycrack and Joyrider were also on the bill.

'Getting Grant on the bill stemmed from our cover of "Diane",' explains Andy. 'When we were in the studio, we wrote the lyrics down from memory and recorded the song. When it was released as a single, there was a *Kerrang!* headline which read, "Grant Hart slams Therapy?." He talked about why we'd changed the song so much, which I thought referred to the cellos. I got his number and apologised, promising we wouldn't play the song again. He explained it was the fact we'd changed the lyrics—but that was due to remembering it wrongly. I invited him to play with us at Brixton, and he was fantastic.'

While Therapy? took to the stage, several hundred people gathered outside nearby Brixton Police Station to peacefully protest the death of a black twenty-six-year-old man called Wayne Douglas, who had died while in police custody. A five-hour riot broke out, and much of the area was sealed off, leading to twenty-two arrests.

'There were people in masks holding bats, running up the streets,' remembers Michael. 'We were advised by the police to stay inside. It was a brilliant show and everything was super tight, but the riot was a massive dampener and a total nightmare for people getting home.'

'We thought we'd be kept inside until maybe 1am and get taxis back to the hotel,' adds Andy. 'But it's bizarre that in rock'n'roll, the after-show must go on, so our band and crew and Grant's band and crew had five or six police officers flank us for a five-minute walk to the boozer.'

The band ended their year with two final shows, at the Point in Dublin on December 28, and at Belfast's Ulster Hall two nights later. After the Belfast show, Michael and Andy went to the band's after-show at the Limelight, and Fyfe didn't show up. They thought nothing more about it and drank into the early hours.

YEAR SEVEN/exit fyfe, enter light

A few days after their Belfast show, Fyfe rang Gerry to say he was quitting the band.

'The atmosphere between Fyfe and me had become so toxic towards the end,' says Andy. 'After the last show, he'd held a party for his friends but didn't tell us. It was shit because of the amount of time we'd spent together. It hurt a little bit when he told us he hated touring, then told the *NME* a week later he thought we were turning into a traditional rock band. Anyone who'd heard *Infernal Love* knows that wasn't the case.

'I wish we'd discussed it face-to-face, and that it had been on better terms,' he adds. 'That's the only regret I have about it. I haven't seen him since. It's quite strange, but I think when people in bands run their natural course, it tends to be the end of that relationship, because they're so deeply entrenched with each other. I don't hold any ill feeling towards him.'

'It's horrible to say this, but there was a sense of relief when he left,' says Michael. 'It had been building long before *Infernal Love*. It was his call, but

Andy and I had discussed it, when he wasn't pulling his weight. He just didn't seem to be into it, and he constantly complained. It was getting to the stage where the relentless cheerleading to get him on stage was really hard work. Any radio session was a drama, because he'd turn up late.

'We should have sat down and had a word but because we hate confrontation, it was a bit weird,' he continues. 'Deep down, I knew he was probably going to go. But, to his credit, he was fantastic at the Dublin and Belfast shows.'

A press release was drafted and sent out to the media. 'Therapy? have parted company with drummer Fyfe Ewing,' it read. 'The split is totally amicable, Ewing being unable to cope with the rigours of touring. With Therapy? about to embark on a five-month US tour to coincide with the release of *Infernal Love* in America, a parting of ways was mutually agreed.' Plans were made to hold auditions for a new drummer as soon as possible.

On January 4, Andy and Michael were back at the Point for the second time in a week, making an appearance at Vibe For Philo, a concert to mark the tenth anniversary of the death of Thin Lizzy frontman Phil Lynott. The show featured members of Thin Lizzy, Def Leppard's Joe Elliott, Henry Rollins, Whipping Boy, and Midge Ure performing songs before an eight-thousand-strong crowd. Andy and Michael played 'Bad Reputation', the title track from Thin Lizzy's 1977 classic album, with Brian Downey, Scott Gorham, Darren Wharton, and John Sykes.

'That song really suited Andy's voice, as it's one of their heavier songs,' remembers Michael. 'That night was a bit of no-pressure fun for us.'

Graham Hopkins, a twenty-year-old drummer born in Dublin, was in the crowd, having just finished recording an album in Los Angeles with Kilkenny five-piece My Little Funhouse. 'I wasn't happy in My Little Funhouse, and I wanted out,' says Graham. 'Myself and the lads in Kerbdog were close friends back then, and indeed still are. Darragh [Butler, Kerbdog drummer] and I were at Phil Lynott tribute gig, which

Andy and Michael were playing at, in January 1996. Darragh talked to Michael about the drummer situation and found out they were going to have auditions.'

Those auditions took place in Dublin and London over the course of a few days. The band had a North American tour booked for April, to support the US release of *Infernal Love*, which would be released on January 30, so time was of the essence.

'We met some brilliant players but they just weren't right for the band,' says Michael. 'There was this session guy whose gear was actually at the Dublin place. He'd brought a lot of drums, and Andy jokingly said to him, "Did you forget your gong?" He actually had one and asked if we could help him up the steps with it. We said it was fine. Some people asked how "Screamager" went, and there were people who just wanted to jam with us, which was a waste of time.'

Following the auditions, Andy drew up a shortlist of prospective players. 'Because of the whole Fyfe situation, I wanted someone the opposite,' says Andy. 'One of the people I was thinking of was Ross Neville, who played drums in Tension, a punk band from Dublin. He was incredible, but temperamentally he was quite similar to Fyfe. Then Graham Hopkins came in and was like a breath of fresh air. He was very eager, very positive, and knew the songs. He had a certain brio which would have been infectious for the whole band.'

'Graham was very chatty and had a sense of humour, which was important,' agrees Michael. 'He was quite at ease with the whole thing and wouldn't shit his pants when we would rock up to a Belgian festival and play in front of sixty thousand people.'

The night before the band made a final decision on their new drummer, Andy and Michael had a meeting with touring musician Martin McCarrick, offering him the chance to join Therapy? on a full-time basis. 'He'd been playing with us on tour for a while, and he was up for it,' says Andy. 'We all decided that Graham would be good for the band.'

'I can't say I was lucky, because I don't like using that word,' says Graham. 'I believe you make your own luck. But on the day, there was an issue with one of Andy's guitars. While there was a bit of a run-around to get it fixed, I was hanging around with the guys for a good while. Then we played a few songs and had a laugh. They called me to meet up on the Friday night, and then asked me to join the band, I was like, *Fuck yeah, lads. Thank you!* We went to see glam rock legends Sweet in Dublin's Olympia Theatre and got pretty pissed drunk. All of a sudden, I was in this big band that I highly, highly admired.'

Shortly after the band's line-up was solidified, the four band members went to Morocco for ten days. 'The camaraderie started straight away,' remembers Graham. 'We had a laugh, just eating, drinking, hiring bikes and cars. It was a fantastic getaway, and we got to know each other really well. There was absolutely no musical instruments. It certainly was an interesting adventure.'

Following their trip to Morocco, the band booked time at the Factory studio in Barrow Street, Dublin, to rehearse ahead of their forthcoming tour of North America, where they'd be sharing bills with You Am I and Girls Against Boys. Andy had moved to Dún Laoghaire, a town along the coast from Dublin, and welcomed his bandmates to stay with him while they rehearsed. 'It was a great bonding session,' he remembers. 'We'd go through the set and have a drink and sit up and chat. Things were going so well, we thought we'd work on a couple of covers we'd been invited to do.'

At the Factory, the new-look line-up recorded a pair of covers: 'Vicar In A Tutu' for the album *The Smiths Is Dead*, and 'Where Eagles Dare' for *Violent World: A Tribute To The Misfits*. They then played their first show together at a fan club gig at the Attic in Dublin on April 10, followed by two more intimate warm-ups at the Lomax in Liverpool on April 23 and Newport's TJ's two nights later.

'I felt honoured to do my first show with Therapy? at the Attic,' remembers Graham. 'They played it numerous times before they signed with A&M. They'd packed the place then, so this gig was really special. We had to stop at one point because the ceiling in the bar downstairs was hopping. It might have collapsed.'

Five days later, Therapy? were supporting You Am I in North America for a week, before joining Girls Against Boys for the rest of May. 'Girls Against Boys had released *House Of GVSB* on Touch And Go, and there was a fair amount of hype around our US tour, so we'd decided to invite some European bands, as well as many others, to support in the US,' says Girls Against Boys frontman Scott McCloud. 'The reasoning behind this was our view that it was harder for European bands to make a dent in the US than the other way around.

'The first show I remember doing together was in Salt Lake City, though they may have started with us earlier,' he adds. 'I remember this because they were really shocked by the idea that Utah is a pretty dry state, meaning there aren't any bars open late—it's a very Mormon state—and they were amazed by this.'

'To be honest, we were a bit in awe of Girls Against Boys,' says Andy. '*Venus Luxure No. 1 Baby* and *Cruise Yourself* were such big records for us. They were all handsome, skinny dudes, very composed, and their shows were mind-blowing. Everything fell into place during those shows.'

'Having played ninety-minute sets for most of the previous year, it was really nice to play shorter sets,' says Michael. 'We were like, *Forty-five minutes? Fan-fucking-tastic! Let's just go in and blitz the place and get the fuck off the stage!* It was a no-pressure scenario, and the clubs were packed. Touring was a lot more fun.'

Shortly after returning home, the band played three high-profile European festivals: Pinkpop at Landgraaf in Holland on May 27, and Rock Werchter in Torhout and Werchter, Belgium, on July 6 and 7. At Rock Werchter, the band were second on the bill, sandwiched between Foo Fighters and the main attraction: David Bowie. Something struck Andy as he noticed the headliner watching the band intently from behind the monitor desk. Therapy? were about to play 'Turn', and in a moment of brief panic, Andy wondered what Bowie might say after hearing the opening line, '*Turn and face the strange*', which he'd originally seen used as a chapter title in Jay Stevens's book *Storming Heaven: LSD & The American Dream* a few years earlier.

'Martin was a huge Bowie fan,' winces Andy. 'He went to speak to him afterwards, and I was going, *Oh fuck!* When he came back, I asked if he said anything. He said our set had a "great energy", and that was it. I mean, god bless David Bowie, he could have turned up and said, "Excuse me, I want a word." I didn't realise what I'd done until I heard "Changes" on the radio a year after *Troublegum* was released.'

A week later, the four were back on a flight back to North America to support Ozzy Osbourne in amphitheatres on his Retirement Sucks Tour. 'I think that tour happened because of the "Iron Man" cover we'd done with Ozzy,' says Michael. 'That tour was the first time I saw an ice sculpture, which was of the Ozzy logo. It was nuts. We were treated really well, and we knew his drummer, Mike Bordin from Faith No More, and Rob Trujillo from Infectious Grooves and Suicidal Tendencies. We did that a lot of that tour in two vans, which was maybe a bit ambitious, because of the distance between each show. His guitarist Joe Holmes and Mike would give us a case of their beer every night. We tried to drink it all, but it got to the point where we had to sit on the beer in the van because there was so much of it. We had to leave some of it on the side of the road. We finished that tour in a bus.'

'We had to switch over to the bus,' adds Graham. 'I think a degree of cabin fever was starting to kick in. I was so happy, because I had spent the previous three years touring the US in a Ford Econoline. It was the height of summer, and those shows were a sweat-fest. It was such a fucking brilliant tour.'

The band's new mobile home could comfortably store their free cases of beer, and the darkened highways quickly dissolved into a woozy haze.

To express their gratitude for inviting them onto the Retirement Sucks tour, the band decided to buy a gift for Ozzy and his wife, Sharon. But, as Ozzy wasn't drinking, bottles of whisky or champagne were out of the question. A massive bouquet it was, then.

'Our tour manager organised this delivery of an ostentatious arrangement of flowers,' remembers Andy. 'We didn't realise Sharon had gone home by that point, and Ozzy was standing there, laughing, "Why'd you send me flowers? I'm not dead yet!" We ended up using that exchange on the song "Little Tongues First" on *Suicide Pact—You First* a few years later.'

Next was another stint with You Am I during August, which drew many familiar faces, kicking off with a date at Moe's Mo' Roc'N Café in Seattle on July 30. 'That was a venue owned by [R.E.M. guitarist] Peter Buck,' remembers Michael. 'He came down with his wife. Patty [Schemel] and Melissa [Auf der Maur] would have been there, too. We actually saw a lot of people we'd met on the Helmet and Jesus Lizard run. There was a good vibe on that tour.'

The next month saw an extensive cross-Canada trek with Doughboys, who they'd taken out on a German tour two years previously. 'We'd played places we'd never been to before, like Kitchener and Churchill,' remembers Andy. 'When we stayed in Banff we saw moose, and we were told by the hotel staff to keep the ground floor windows shut in case a bear tried to get in. I think those few months were something of a trial by fire for Graham, but it was a memorable few months.'

'Nothing really prepares you for playing an out-of-season ski lodge in Whistler,' laughs Michael. 'That tour reminded me of when we'd play in Ireland during the early days; if there was a corner of a room which could facilitate a band and a PA, then we'd play it. Wiz, God rest his soul, from Mega City Four was playing guitar for them, so it was a lot of fun. It was chaotic in many ways. We'd play, pack down our gear and find ourselves in these small towns and go, *Right, what trouble can we get into?*'

With their touring commitments over for the year, the band spent much of the autumn writing and demoing ideas for the follow-up to *Infernal Love*. 'With four people in the band, we'd relaxed the rules a little bit, and all four of us were trying to write songs,' says Andy. 'Graham and Martin were very, very forthright in their opinions, so we'd write a song and someone wouldn't like a part, so we'd start again. We'd played "Stay Happy" on the Canadian tour, and we'd more or less written "Church Of Noise", "Black Eye Purple Sky", and "Born Too Soon".'

After a shaky start to the year, things were finally back on an even keel.

YEAR 1997
EIGHT/welcome to the church of noise

The four continued work on *Semi-Detached* at Ritz Studios in Putney after the New Year. It was during these writing sessions that Andy suggested that the band simply record a lo-fi album, possibly as a reaction to the high production values of *Infernal Love*. 'I think we'd had a run through of "Church Of Noise" and wanted to get an 8-track and record it there and then,' says Andy.

The band took a break in February to perform at the Heineken Hot Press Rock Awards at the BBC Blackstaff Studios in Belfast. It was at this ceremony that the band debuted 'Don't Expect Roses'. In an interview with *Kerrang!* writer Paul Brannigan, Andy revealed the song was about the Labour party's 1997 election victory, and 'how people shouldn't expect things to change overnight'.

'That was one of the first songs we wrote for the album,' he says. 'Normally, our songs would have a melancholy streak running through the chord progressions, like a sense of resignation and sadness. When Graham joined, he was so outgoing, so it fed into the songwriting. The main riff on "Don't Expect Roses" is quite brash and uplifting—a real bolshie bruiser. The chorus is, I suppose, about not getting your hopes up.'

The band were invited to perform at Dublin's Red Box on March 17 as part of MTV's *Live 'N' Direct* series. Their eighteen-song set featured four brand new songs: 'Tightrope Walker', 'Black Eye Purple Sky', 'Church Of Noise', and 'Don't Expect Roses'. Soon after, they made final preparations for their new album, joining forces once again with *Troublegum* producer Chris Sheldon.

'We'd heard one of the *Troublegum* singles on the radio when we were driving somewhere, and we were like, "This sounds fucking great!"' remembers Michael. 'We thought the new songs would suit his production style.'

Initial recordings for *Semi-Detached* took place at Chipping Norton Recording Studios in Oxfordshire. The bulk of the album was recorded in March and April, with 'Church Of Noise' being one of the first tracks to be committed to tape.

'We were listening to a lot of Rocket From The Crypt, and "Church Of Noise" was originally a very heavy garage-rock song, before we added that clean riff at the beginning,' says Andy. 'There was a lot of talk about there being a proper possibility of peace in Northern Ireland,' he adds. 'It was a year before the Good Friday Agreement was reached. Me and Michael were talking about writing a song about what unites us and the feeling of community that music brought about.'

'Straight Life' was another song written early on at Ritz Studios, inspired by their early dance-orientated songs 'Teethgrinder' and 'Neck Freak'.

'We wanted something that had an almost techno-like groove,' says Andy. 'I had the guitar riff and the harmonics on the chorus was like Big Black. For the lyrics, it was a nod to *Troublegum*. When we would go home, people would be like, "You're back in the real world now." People I grew up with seemed to stop listening to music when they became an adult. They'd get a job and be thinking about paying their car insurance, getting a mortgage, and playing darts in the pub. I'd be with friends who wondered why I'd listen to bands like Drive Like Jehu and Big Black and say, "Aren't you a bit old for that?" I'd be completely frustrated. I didn't want to be told I had to fit in. Someone who starts fights in a kebab shop on a Saturday night must be fucked off with his life at home.'

The title was taken from *Straight Life: The Story Of Art Pepper*, the autobiography of a jazz star with a troubled past. 'He had a lot of problems with drugs,' explains Andy. 'He hadn't touched his saxophone in a long time, but then he got a call from Miles Davis. I think he'd been doing smack all night, and his agent was like, "Hey man, you're a fucking genius, you'll be all right," so he talked himself into doing the gig. He would look in the mirror and tell himself that. It became an in-joke on tour. We'd be like, "I wish I hadn't drank ten pints last night, we're on stage soon … I'm a genius!"'

A boozy night in Randalstown inspired the song 'Black Eye Purple Sky', with Andy waking up with no recollection of the previous night's events. 'I don't get blackout drunk, but the next day I was with the person I'd been out with, trying to piece together what had happened,' he explains. 'There's something about hangovers, too. They can have this feeling of crushing grief, where you need some sort of reassurance. It feels like someone's standing on your chest, and this song is trying to capture that feeling.'

Andy cites his marriage to his wife Kris as the catalyst to a change in lifestyle, as detailed in 'Tightrope Walker'. 'My wife never asked me to stop drinking or doing drugs, but because I now had a responsibility, I found I was doing it a hell of a lot less,' he admits. 'When I first got married, I didn't touch anything or drink for four or five months. The lyric "*every movement, every vibration*" is the fear that comes with sobriety. Everyone thinks that drugs and alcohol amplify everything, but I found it to be the other way round. I was more receptive to music that I loved, rather than thinking I liked stuff because I was out of my mind on coke.'

The title 'Born Too Soon' relates to a discussion about a friend's premature birth, with music inspired by Milwaukee emo four-piece The Promise Ring, who'd released their Jade Tree debut *30° Everywhere* the previous year. 'I thought that was a beautiful title for a song,' says Andy. 'I was listening to them a lot while we were writing. It initially had a lot of clean chords, which they use, but obviously with us being Therapy?, we added a lot more distortion. It's a strange one, that. I think we played it on the next tour but I don't think we've played it since.'

The album's final track, 'The Boy's Asleep', is one of its highlights: a brooding swell of guitars with quiet vocals and no drums. 'Graham was asleep in the control room when we recorded it,' says Andy. 'He slept all the way through.'

'I've always been one for naps,' Graham admits.

'The chorus came from Michael, who's also a good guitar player,' Andy continues. 'Because of his metal background, he'd tune the bottom string to D. Martin had this almost Pink Floyd line for the verse, and we played around with it for ages.

'When I was writing the lyrics, I wanted something that was a bit like "Good Night" by The Beatles. When I mentioned *The White Album* to Chris, he knew that I was going to say that we should get an orchestra in. He calmed me down and said it would sound better if we kept it stripped back. It's one of my favourite songs on the album, but I wish I'd taken a bit more time and properly nailed down the verses better. I was just improvising a conversation in the background through a little cheap microphone. It turned out really well and we used to end the gig on that song.'

Shortly after the Chipping Norton sessions, the band returned to Homestead Studios in Randalstown to record overdubs. Late one night, Andy was inspired to spontaneously record 'Lonely, Cryin, Only'. 'One of the tape ops had shown me how to record something if I had an idea,' he remembers. 'The title came first, then I had this kind of Roy Orbison vocal melody and chorus. I did the guitars, vocals, and bass. Graham played drums. What I didn't realise was that the bass wasn't tuned,' he adds. 'It was in tune with itself, something ludicrous, like in F-sharp or F. So the next day, whenever we tried to play along with it, we had to retune our guitars. When I conceived the track, I was hearing something like "Screamager" or "Nowhere", almost like a Misfits song.'

'I seem to remember it came together so quickly that I wasn't even in the studio with them when the recording started,' Chris adds. 'It was my engineer, Matt Sime, who started the tape rolling. I came in and heard what they were doing and just loved it! We finished the recording very quickly and everyone was just delighted with it. Martin's backing vocals on that song are excellent. It remains one of my favourite Therapy? tunes.'

For a band who'd worked relentlessly since their formation, 1997 was a year with a fairly sparse gig schedule. Apart from the *Hot Press* and MTV bookings, the band performed sporadically throughout the summer, appearing at Finland's Ilosaarirock festival and Austria's Forestglade festival. The following month, they played sets at Denmark's Smukfest (aka Skanderborg), Switzerland's Festival du Gampel, and Slovenia's Hoska Prebuja.

In September, the band decamped to Moles Recording Studio in Bath. Producer Chris had booked in another job, so it was up to engineer Matt to man the production desk during these sessions, which yielded 'Heaven's Gate', 'Safe', and 'Tramline', as well as future B-sides '60 Watt Bulb' and 'Suing God'.

Andy describes 'Safe' as one of his favourite tracks on the record. 'When we were in the studio, I asked Martin what prepared piano was,' he recalls. 'He showed me a few tricks, like putting paper clips on the wires, and getting a coin to scrape along the strings. Michael started playing along with this percussive scraping sound that worked on the song. It was quite like a Faith No More track, and we ended up with a piece of music we all really, really liked.'

Andy's sobriety informed the lyrics to the song. 'When I was in my bedroom above the studio, I'd sit at my desk and look at this huge apartment block,' he explains. 'There were probably thirty-six rooms, and, after a while, you get to know people's routines. The verses were a dialogue of what I'd imagined people were doing in their homes. What kind of relationships they were in, that kind of thing. I was hyper aware of these things, because I wasn't drinking alcohol. I'd have otherwise been in the pub or sparked out on the duvet asleep. I wouldn't have taken any of this in.'

'Tramline', meanwhile, is a song that Andy regrets including in the album's final track listing. 'That was a bizarre one,' he says. 'At the time, The Prodigy were getting really big, and we're all massive fans. When we toured *Infernal Love*, we'd play "Teethgrinder", and people thought it was a cover of theirs. Martin had written a demo with a drum machine and we built the song around it. It was very much manufactured in the studio, and I dug out the "rock-star bullshit" lyrics from my notebooks. It wasn't Therapy? and it wasn't like The Prodigy. It sort of fell between two stools, and I never thought it was that great. We tried playing it live once to a backing track, and it sounded fucking terrible.'

That autumn saw the band play their first-ever shows in Turkey, at Saklkent in Ankara on October 3, followed by a set at the Bostanci Gosteri Merkezi in Istanbul. 'Those shows were brilliant,' says Michael. 'The Ankara venue was absolutely rammed. When we played Instanbul, it was like an arena. I wondered if it was a little ambitious for our first time here, so I talked to the promoter and asked how many tickets we'd sold. He said, We've sold no tickets. He explained that in Turkey, no one really bought tickets in advance, because so many bands seemed to cancel at the last minute. But, sure enough, it was full, and people were going nuts. It was one of my favourite shows because it was such a wild card.'

November and December were spent at Metropolis Studios in London, with Michael flying in from Belfast to record extra bass on 'Lonely, Cryin',

Only'. 'It was an expensive folly to come all that way when we realised Andy's 3am recording at Homestead was perfect,' he remembers.

Over two decades on, Andy has reservations about what the band set out to achieve in the studio. 'The album took way too long to make,' he says. 'We had four different opinions going in four different ways. Looking back, I think that's part of why the four-piece experiment didn't really work out. You had Graham and Martin who'd joined a very successful rock band who were still playing high up on bills in Europe and were on the covers of magazines. They didn't want that to end, and they were pushing for this album to be a success, too. They hadn't signed up to be in a band to make a lo-fi experiment, which was suggested at the beginning of the year.

'I think the songs were good, but the really strong songs were over-embellished,' he adds. 'I really like songs like "Straight Life", and "Heaven's Gate", but there's too much going on. "Lonely, Cryin', Only", for me, is too poppy, as in the arrangements are too light,' he adds. 'Some of the songs weren't quite up to scratch. We'd spent so much time on the album that we got into a terrible mindset of, rather than scrapping songs that weren't good enough, we would add more parts, more guitars, and harmonies, in the hope it would somehow make them sound better.'

'The album was certainly difficult to make, mainly because of the time it took,' remembers Chris. 'Maintaining focus and enthusiasm over such a long period is tough. Graham nailed his drums quickly, and Michael put the bass lines to bed in his usual fast, furious, and ridiculously accurate manner. I'm not sure I've ever worked with a bass player who can deliver as consistently as Michael. Andy and Martin recorded their guitar parts separately, but because this time we didn't have all the songs finished before we started recording, there was still a fair amount of experimentation going on, and this takes time.

'There's no doubt that having two extra opinions made some decisions more lengthy,' he adds. 'My feeling is the new band didn't gel quite as well as they had done as a three-piece. This is certainly no slur on Martin and Graham, who were and are fantastic musicians and people; their contributions to the album are wonderful. For me, having the extra musicality of Martin's made adding extra parts here and there a breeze, like the odd keyboard part at the beginning of "Straight Life". But I take what Andy has said. I still love *Semi-Detached* as an album, and I wish it had been better served by the record company, but it was not to be, as there were all sorts of changes going on at A&M, and the album promotion suffered as a result.'

YEAR NINE/'no fucking egos, no rock-star bullshit ...'

With *Semi-Detached* complete, the four-piece chalked up their first show of the year on January 20, as surprise guests at an *NME*-sponsored event at London's Astoria. Sandwiched between fledgling Scottish indie-rockers Idlewild and headliners Deftones, Therapy?'s ten-song set featured three songs from their forthcoming album: 'Tightrope Walker', 'Lonely, Cryin', Only', and 'Church Of Noise'.

In a four-star review for *Kerrang!*, Paul Rees wrote, '"Tightrope Walker", an ebony-tinged stomp, is more rounded and evolved than anything the band have tried their hand at before—taking the darker parts of the *Infernal Love* album and running with them. "Church Of Noise" ... isn't to be sniffed at, but the incessant four-part squawking of the title sounds like a quartet of men catching their todgers in their flies at the same time.'

'That show was a no-brainer to do,' remembers Michael. 'It was a good to come back with a bang after not playing in the UK the year before. Me, Graham, and Martin went to see Mogwai at the Astoria a couple of days later. It was one of the best gigs I'd seen at that point. They blew my head off.'

February brought another opportunity to perform new material. This time it was by invitation of BBC Radio 1 DJ Steve Lamacq, for his *Evening Session* show. Their set, recorded at London's legendary Maida Vale studios, included 'Church Of Noise', 'Black Eye Purple Sky', 'Tightrope Walker', 'Teethgrinder', and a cover of DJ Shadow's 1997 single 'High Noon'.

March 2 saw the release of 'Church Of Noise', which reached no. 29 in the UK singles chart. The song was originally set to include a sample of Dr Ian Paisley describing his favourite music to BBC Radio Ulster presenter Stuart Bailie: 'Good Christian music. Music with the gospel in it.' The idea was nixed by A&M's legal department, however. Or, as Andy puts it, 'They shat their pants.'

Despite *Kerrang!* writer Paul Rees's initial reservations earlier in the year, 'Church Of Noise' was duly awarded the magazine's 'Single Of The Week' by Ray Zell, who wrote, 'No pissin' about here, mate. "Church Of Noise" is your actual, bona fide, clever, rock-cred, radio-friendly 45. In fact, there's at least three hit single ideas at work in one song here.'

The day the single was released, Therapy? kicked off a six-date UK club tour at Portsmouth's Wedgewood Rooms, followed by dates in Galway, Limerick, and Cork. 'They were great shows,' says Michael. 'The way of working seemed to have changed in the year we'd spent in the studio, so touring was more staggered around the release of the album.'

The band completed their Irish dates with a performance on Raidió Teilifís Éireann's Kenny Live, a Saturday-night talk show hosted by Pat Kenny. You can find a YouTube clip of them tearing through 'Black Eye Purple Sky' before a new, silvery demographic. 'I can't think of anything more incongruous than Therapy? playing to a bunch of pensioners, but there you go,' reads one comment below the video. Fair point, well made.

Semi-Detached was finally released on March 30, boasting a surreal cover image of a couple buried up to their necks in sand, inspired by Samuel Beckett's play *Happy Days*. The critical reception was largely positive. '*Semi-Detached* is the sound of a band with 20/20 vision, a band who know exactly what they're doing, why they're doing it and who they're doing it for,' wrote Ben Myers in a four-out-of-five review for *Melody Maker*. 'That's why, as an album, it's completely self-contained and provides a seatbelts-off ride from beginning to end. ... Therapy? are a true rock band with the looks, the lifestyle and, most importantly, the timeless, deafening songs. Just intelligent pop'n'roll played by a bunch of charming beer-drinking bastards.'

'There might be less in the way of satanically bad "Screamager"-type puns, messy brain-splatter, and Norman Bates chic, yet the same twin engines of self-loathing and testosterone power the record,' wrote *NME*'s Victoria Segal in a six-out-of-ten review. 'They haven't slathered the songs with orchestral pomp to give them the stamp of maturity (there is a cellist but that's always a good thing) or proudly returned with an embarrassingly out-of-touch electronica set, but they have other, more familiar ways of texturing their music.'

Kerrang!'s Paul Elliott expressed some doubts as to whether the band could scale the same heights as *Troublegum*, yet awarded the release a four-star review. 'It's crunch time for Therapy?,' he wrote. 'Three years have passed since they last released an album, the chart-topping *Infernal Love*. Since then, the face of rock music has changed. Massively. In this business, you're soon forgotten. Therapy? ... have taken a huge risk in spending so much time making this album. It has to be great, if not a classic. Is *Semi-Detached* as good as Therapy? need it to be? Yes. Just. It's a fascinating record. Overall, it's not as boisterous as *Troublegum* ... but in time, *Semi-Detached* may prove better than either *Troublegum* or *Infernal Love*.'

Three years previously, *Infernal Love* had been given an absolute kicking by *Metal Hammer*'s Pippa Lang. *Semi-Detached*, however, struck a chord with writer Essi Berelian, who awarded it nine out of ten. 'This is a loud, obnoxious, abrasive blast of an album,' he wrote. 'Herein lies the Therapy? paradox: we are presented with Cairns's darkest musings once again, yet they are robed in rich layers of memorable and affecting melody—the man simply can't help penning great anthemic choruses.'

Hot Press writer Patrick Brennan praised the depth of *Semi-Detached*, noting, 'Therapy? have proved they can progress beyond the adrenaline rush of the mosh crowd. Listen carefully and you'll hear how unique and truly uncategorisable they are. Welcome, indeed, to the "Church Of Noise". Worship at this angst-ridden altar.'

'Maybe *Semi-Detached* got a good reception because it was similar to *Troublegum*, more straight down the line,' muses Michael. 'I think people were quite glad that we were playing to our strengths.'

Following a month-long tour of Europe, Therapy? went out on a five-date UK tour with support from Groop Dogdrill, a Doncaster trio who'd built something of a tough reputation both on and off the stage. 'We had toured with the likes of Cable, A, Foil, and The Wildhearts, and it was always a scream from start to finish,' says Dogdrill drummer Hugh 'Hug' Kelly. 'We had just finished a tour with another band and their egos were off the fucking scale, so much so that I couldn't grasp why going out and playing had become cold all of a sudden. We were on the last date of the tour in Glasgow and I was totally fed up, and the call came through—I think Damo [Fowkes, bassist], as he was the only one with a mobile at that time—that we had got the support slot with Therapy?, and instantly everything changed. Foil had said it was just like being with mates: no fucking egos, no rock-star bullshit. I knew everything would be OK again.'

The first stop was at Sheffield's Leadmill, where, after the show, there was an altercation between Graham and Dogdrill frontman Pete Spiby. 'That was a weird night,' remembers Andy. 'I adore the Leadmill, and it was a sold-out show. A lot of their friends were there and had commandeered our dressing room. Pete's really nice but can be a smart arse at times! A friend of his was wearing Martin's coat, and she giggled. Pete said something sarcastic to Graham, and he decked Pete. It was completely out of character, but it did get quite heated.'

'It wasn't a punch, but the whole evening is slightly hazy,' explains Pete. 'I'd jumped on Graham's back and was holding on to that giant of a man for dear life. We were in a stairwell outside of the dressing room, and he somehow threw me over his shoulders and body-slammed me onto the floor. I was probably being over-playful, and might have pissed him off by jumping on him.'

According to Pete, he stayed on the floor and noticed that Graham began to panic, thinking he might have knocked him out cold. 'I must have thought this was a hilarious situation and decided to play up to it,' Pete continues. 'I gave Damo a cheeky wink to let him in on the wind-up, and he put pressure on Graham with a line of *what-the-fuck-have-you-done?* questions. Unfortunately, our drummer, Hug, who's also known as a bit of a panic merchant, started to openly fluster. The two of them were like Godfrey and Jonesy from *Dad's Army*, and the situation was too funny not to laugh and fess up that I was OK. Whether there was any damage to my head is another story.'

'They were laughing about it the next day,' says Andy. 'It was all water under the bridge. We're also big enough to know that if you're on tour with someone, holding a grudge poisons everything. The tour was a lot of fun.'

On May 18, 'Lonely, Cryin', Only' was released as a single, backed with the band's cover of 'High Noon', new song 'Kid's Stuff', and fresh recordings of 'Diane', 'Teethgrinder', 'Disgracelands', and 'Skyward' spread across its CD, vinyl, and cassette formats. It reached no. 32 in the UK. The video was directed by John Hillcoat, whose previous credits included *Ghosts … Of The Civil Dead*—the film from which the band had sampled Nick Cave for the beginning of 1992's 'Nausea'.

'John Hillcoat is an absolute legend,' Andy told *Team Rock* editor Paul Brannigan in 2014. 'When we met John to talk about making this video, Martin McCarrick and I had breakfast with him in a cafe in King's Cross, and we chatted about movies for two hours before we'd even mentioned the video. To this day, this was the most fun I've ever had on a video shoot.'

On June 19, the band were invited to perform as last-minute replacements for Korn at Ozzfest at the Milton Keynes Bowl. The American band's guitarist, Brian 'Head' Welch, had chosen to stay in the USA as he and his then-wife, Rebekah, were expecting a child; a press statement explained that the couple had been told the birthdate would be in July, which goes some length to explain the Bakersfield nu-metallers' eleventh-hour decision to drop off the bill.

'Sharon Osbourne completely got us that gig,' remembers Andy. 'We were staying at a hotel in London because we were rehearsing. Dave Grohl had expressed an interest because Foo Fighters were on a bill with all these heavy bands, like Pantera, Slayer, and Black Sabbath, obviously. We agreed to it immediately, and we were in Milton Keynes the following day.'

Kerrang!'s Paul Rees reviewed the Ozzfest show and noted the band's super-charged performance: 'Therapy? go about their business with a fire that had been absent from their most recent showings. Top marks, too, to Cairns and McKeegan's Laurel-and-Hardy-esque banter, and some top guitar smashing at the end of a fine "Screamager".'

By now, the band had begun to sense that all was not well at A&M, as promotion for *Semi-Detached* was scarce. Shortly after their Ozzfest appearance, it was confirmed in the press that the label would indeed be closing down. The Polygram corporation, which owned A&M, was being taken over by Seagrams, and it was understood that the band's new home would be on the Mercury label. They even went as far as to record a video message for the staff of Mercury, saying that they were looking forward to working with them in the future.

'We know the label's managing director, Howard Berman, because he was at A&M when we first got signed,' manager Gerry Harford told *Kerrang!*. 'And Mercury have shown that they can sell a few records in the past. We're just looking forward to working closely with them.'

That business partnership did not come to fruition. The four-piece discovered that they did not figure in the label's future plans, and *Semi-Detached* would not be released in North America. Without a label, they were still committed to an autumn tour of the UK and Europe that would last for almost two months.

'Originally, we were told to sit tight, but no one knew what was going on,' says Michael. 'It was a weird old time for everyone because people didn't know if they were going to have a job. We were in a bit of flap because we had this fucking long haul trek planned for the end of the year.'

'Around the end of the festival season, Gerry called me up and said, "We need to meet in a hotel tomorrow, can you turn up for it? Martin is flying over as well,"' adds Andy. 'I knew something was up. He explained that the label had looked at the figures and didn't want to pursue any further stuff with Therapy?. In all honesty, it's a knock to your pride—a real kick in the balls. When you find out something like that, it dawns on you that there's going to be no money to record or pay for tour adverts.'

Gerry's plan for the band was simple. They would continue to promote *Semi-Detached* and look for a new deal. 'I didn't want to end our A&M days with an album that would be quickly forgotten and be seen as a failure,' he says. 'It wasn't a failure, and, had the label not imploded, we would have gone on to make the album more successful.'

'We found quite a few labels and two good labels who were very interested,' he adds. 'It was positive; labels didn't see us as a dropped act looking for a new home. They saw us as victims of circumstances, and I don't think that they would have viewed us in that light had we lain down moaning after A&M fell apart. Continuing to work showed interested labels that we had a strong fan base.'

So, for the foreseeable future, Andy and Michael would have to foot Graham and Martin's wages, pay the crew's wages, and pony up cash for the tour buses. It was going to cost thousands of pounds. 'We had to dip into all the money we'd made on *Nurse*, *Troublegum*, and *Infernal Love* and pay for everything until we found a new deal,' explains Michael. 'Touring can be quite a money pit, so it hit the band's coffers quite hard. We'd been strongly advised to cancel the tour, but as far as we were concerned, people had bought their tickets, so we decided to do it.'

The band were quickly approached by a slew of record labels. Some suggested they adopt a nu-metal sound to fit in with the current crop of bands filling the pages of the rock and metal press. 'The landscape had changed somewhat,' says Andy. 'We had a presence in Europe, and we had a presence in some places in South America and Canada. We were still a draw for record labels, and we had a number of meetings. There'd be labels who'd say they loved the band and we could do what we wanted, but we'd get peanuts for it. Someone, who'll remain nameless, suggested we get a girl in the band. He'd pointed out one band in a magazine and actually said, "Bird in the band, 75 percent of the sales." Unbelievable. My big thing was that I didn't want us to sign with someone for the sake of getting a deal. Luckily, we had all these shows coming up, and that took our minds off it all until we found a label we felt comfortable with.'

The band took Groop Dogdrill out with them once again for the two-month trek, which began with five UK dates before heading into Europe. 'We had a lot of fun with them on the last tour,' remembers Andy. 'They reminded us of a lot of old Dischord bands and stuff like that. They were suitably noisy, and Damo in particular had a brilliantly dark sense of humour. Nothing fazed him at all.'

The bands were getting along famously during the tour, and following a show in Fribourg, Switzerland, Andy and Pete ended up at a karaoke bar, singing a few Elvis numbers in front of a bemused crowd. 'We had an incredible time,' says Pete. 'We did the tour in an old water-board van and stayed in roach motels. They toured in a Nightliner bus and "declined" sharing a bus with us idiots. I wonder why?'

On December 14, Therapy? played their final show of the year at JB's in Dudley. 'It was shoehorned onto the end of the tour,' explains Michael.

'It was apparently the venue's Christmas do. We thought it would be a fun way to end the run, because it had been a long old tour; everyone was ill, tired, and skint. We asked if they could organise Christmas dinner, so we had this horrendous microwaved meal served up, and then we did the gig. Apart from a few hundred diehards, everyone was just there to get pissed at the club night and listen to "The Final Countdown".

'Two guys got on stage and knocked the mic into Andy's face a few times,' he adds. 'His mouth was bleeding. Someone stole two of Martin's pedals mid-song as well—just pocketed them and jumped back into the crowd. Afterwards, we just sat in this freezing cold dressing room, just grateful that the year was over.'

YEAR 1999
TEN/gringo and the speedo menace

Without a label, and with considerably diminished bank accounts after bankrolling their previous tour, the band's woes were further compounded when Graham broke his arm days before they were due to begin writing and demoing new songs. After watching a show by Garbage at the Point in Dublin on January 14, he and writer Paul Brannigan had found themselves drinking with Bono at U2's hotel, the Clarence, in the Temple Bar district. In the early hours of the following morning, the drummer slipped and fractured his arm.

'It was a night of absolute chaos,' remembers Graham. 'I was in a *Big Lebowski* phase at the time and was drinking White Russians. I suppose I had one too many, and I slipped when I was running for a taxi. It was a rainy night. I didn't feel anything, but Darragh [Butler], who was staying at mine, saw my swollen arm as soon as I got in the front door, and he took me to the hospital straight away. I'd broken my elbow and was out of action for three months.'

'It really didn't fill us with much hope,' says Andy. 'We'd been dropped and people's perception of us had changed and we'd effectively lost a member of the band as we were getting ready to write an album.'

Undeterred, Andy, Michael, and Martin went to Ritz Rehearsal Studios in Putney, London. Armed with an Alesis SR-16 drum machine, which they nicknamed Gringo, they began to work on the follow-up to *Semi-Detached* while speaking to potential labels. 'It was pretty grim with no drummer, to be honest,' says Michael. 'We did our best with Gringo, but it was a soul-destroying period.'

Rough demos were sent to prospective producers and labels, but the feedback was not favourable. 'Record labels were signing nu-metal bands left, right, and centre, and we were recording demos with a rudimentary drum machine,' explains Andy. 'The first question labels would ask was, "Will it sound like *Troublegum?*" and we knew it wouldn't. Joe Barresi and Dave Sardy weren't interested. Terry Date, who we'd worked with on the Black Sabbath tribute, said it'd cost $275,000.

'At this point, our confidence hadn't turned into defiance, it had turned into despair,' he adds. 'We were beginning to pick fights with each other, and I think it was the closest we'd ever been to splitting up.'

Someone suggested the producer Head, who'd worked with PJ Harvey on her 1992 debut, *Dry*. Head—real name Howard Bullivant—arrived at the Putney rehearsal space with no preconceptions. He listened to the band play, with Gringo keeping time with robotic precision. 'The only record he said he really knew was *Babyteeth*,' says Andy. 'We played what we had and he said he was on board. Our self-worth and confidence took a turn upwards.'

More label meetings followed, and it dawned on the band that the industry's landscape had shifted drastically during their seven-year tenure with A&M. 'Grunge and the new punk thing had come and gone,' remembers Michael. 'Everything had changed. We heard people talk about USP [unique selling propositions] and product and units.'

The band signed with Ark 21, a forward-thinking label set up by Miles Copeland and his brother, The Police's drummer, Stewart Copeland, in 1977. On a roster that included Belinda Carlisle, Alannah Myles, and Chris De Burgh, Therapy? stood out like a goth on a beach. What caught the band's attention, though, was the assurance that there'd be no interference and no pressure to create a carbon copy of *Troublegum*.

'Someone at Ark 21 had worked with us behind the scenes at A&M,' says Andy. 'We had a few meetings with them, and the stuff we played them was raw as fuck, like a black metal band recording in a watery basement. They just wanted us to make a record we wanted to make.'

'Ark 21 was ironically part of Universal,' adds Michael. 'So it was like we were sneaking in through the back door.'

While the band were courting labels, *Suicide Pact—You First* (its title taken from a t-shirt description in Rupert Thomson's 1991 book *The Five Gates Of Hell*) began to take shape. They were given a creative boost when Gringo was given a break and drum tech Jon Odgers—also the drummer in The Men They Couldn't Hang—breathed new life into the demos.

'Using the drum machine was excruciating—like water torture,' says Andy. 'We asked Jon to sit in. Not only was he a great drummer, he was a great lad. He came up with that brilliant drum pattern on "He's Not That Kind Of Girl" and gave it a pseudo-jazz swing.'

The band had two live bookings in May. Michael's brother Charlie sat in for Graham at Queima Das Fitas in Coimbra, Portugal, on May 7, and two weeks later at Balalec Festival in Lausanne, Switzerland. 'Charlie was quite nervous, but he'd really learned the set well,' says Michael. 'We had a laugh and he managed to play while Graham was sat behind him, heckling him with his arm in a cast.'

After Graham's arm had fully healed, the band rehearsed the album and recorded one final batch of demos before traveling to Great Linford Manor, the Milton Keynes studio where they'd previously tracked drums for *Infernal Love*. 'There were so many things we had to go through to get to this point,' says Michael. 'It felt really good to let rip and record new music.'

During their time at Great Linford Manor, the band shunned the distractions of Milton Keynes and rarely set foot outside of the studio, save for the morning of August 11, when the UK experienced a total solar eclipse. 'That was a surreal moment,' says Michael. 'My memories of recording *Suicide Pact* revolve around watching *Saving Private Ryan* a lot. It felt like it was every day. We'd blast it through this amazing sound system, and then we'd record. We were a bit socially backward, coming out of that session. It was all whisky, fried chicken, and the sound of gunfire.'

'We didn't really see the outside world, and that added to the claustrophobic feel of the album,' adds Andy. 'We lived and breathed music. When we stopped playing, we'd go into the lounge and just blast albums by Atari Teenage Riot, Godspeed You! Black Emperor, Mogwai, and The Stooges.'

Working with Head allowed the four to indulge their more leftfield creative ideas, too. 'God Kicks', a haunting acoustic anti-ballad, was recorded outside in the early hours after a night spent drinking a popular Tennessee whiskey. 'Great Linford Manor had a driveway that was open to the public, so lads would come over in their cars and do donuts,' says Andy. 'We had to wait until they'd went home before recording. Normally, if it was one in the morning and someone said, "Wouldn't it be amazing to record outside?" 95 percent of producers would suggest we try it tomorrow. What was brilliant about Head is that he'd be into doing it straight away.'

The resultant album was perhaps Therapy?'s most creatively unrestrained work to date. 'We were frustrated and angry and we got our mojo back,' says Michael. 'It was almost like a lock-in, which allowed us to just focus on the music.'

The opening track, 'He's Not That Kind Of Girl', retains the jazz swing from the Putney rehearsals, while also being propelled by riffs in a Ministry, Birthday Party, and twisted psychobilly vein. In turn, Andy found inspiration in James St. James's memoir, *Disco Bloodbath: A Fabulous But True Tale Of Murder In Clubland*. 'It's all about the club kids in New York, and a drug dealer's murder,' he says. 'When you read it, you feel dirty, crusty, and uneasy.'

The Stooges' 1970 classic *Funhouse* and The Jesus Lizard were the reference points for the chaotic, disorientating 'Wall Of Mouths'. The title popped into Andy's head after learning to scuba dive on holiday with his wife, Kris. 'There was a school of fish in front of me, clacking their mouths open and shut,' he remembers. 'The phrase could relate to the static ambience of life, too.'

'Jam Jar Jail'—named after a Dublin punk band—emerged from a bass line by Michael, and inspired Andy and Martin to layer his 'sleazy Am-Rep' groove with 'fucked-up Hellacopters and Stooges' riffs. The flapping sound at the beginning of the track was courtesy of a frantic moth that was trapped in the studio, but is uncredited in the album artwork. An unsung session hero, if you like. 'That song's about trapped in your own sense of development and how you let the outside world see you,' explains Andy. 'Head trapped the moth in a jar, recorded it, and let it go.'

'Hate Kill Destroy' begins with a sample from Volker Schlöndorff's 1979 film *Die Blechtrommel* , aka *The Tin Drum*—'*Was, meint Ihr, wird aus diesem Kindlein werden? Gutes oder Böses?*' or 'What do you think will become of this little child? Good or bad?'—that sets up a Sabbath-like riff that's backed by Graham's thundering drum pattern. 'I think the working title was "Sabbath Song", actually,' says Andy, 'until I saw this kid wandering around a shopping centre in Milton Keynes with "Hate Kill Destroy" written on his t-shirt with a marker. The lyrics came from watching *Fight Club* when we were working in Putney earlier in the year.'

There's an interesting side-note to this particular track in that the band recorded it naked as the day they were born. 'It was a hot, sticky night,' laughs Michael. 'We were all tired and a bit burned out, so we got stark bollock naked—Head as well, on his leather chair—and played it through. Me, Andy, and Martin were OK, as we had our bass and guitars to hide behind, but Graham? One missed snare beat and he could have ended up in hospital.'

The title for 'Big Cave In', *Suicide Pact*'s monstrous mid-album instrumental, came courtesy of Head. 'We ditched the Marshalls for this record, and used some old Fenders, which I hadn't done since *Babyteeth*,' says Andy. 'A lot of the traditional rock armoury was gone and Head kept saying that our equipment always sounded like it was on the verge of collapse. We wrote this together when Graham came back as we couldn't have written this with a drum machine. The initial riff was me trying to write something like Rapeman—a terrible, terrible name for a band—and we spent a day or two writing the song.'

Things change pace for 'Six Mile Water', which was named after the river in County Antrim that connects the towns of Larne and Ballyclare. 'It's completely autobiographical,' says Andy song. 'It's about taking acid and thinking the city hall was burning as the sun rose.'

The song also refers to the band's regular drinking sessions during the early days, which they named 'Bukowski Day' in honour of the novelist *Time* magazine once described as a 'laureate of American lowlife'. 'When we rehearsed, we didn't really touch alcohol,' he explains, 'but we'd go out once a month and drink. One time, Michael fell asleep in the train station toilets at Larne; Fyfe and I nearly had to kick the door in to get him out.'

In hindsight, Andy notes the opening distorted riff in 'Little Tongues First' accidentally echoes Madonna's 'La Isla Bonita', but its frantic pace owes much to *Semi-Detached*'s 'Tightrope Walker' and *Babyteeth*'s 'Loser Cop'. 'It's got an absurd sense of carnival,' the frontman notes.

The idea for 'Ten Year Plan' was sparked by a conversation with Manic Street Preachers frontman James Dean Bradfield, backed with a riff inspired by the *Top Of The Pops* theme. Or if you're really pedantic, Led Zeppelin's 'Whole Lotta Love'.

'We were talking about careerism in music, and he mentioned all these young bands with ten-year plans,' says Andy. 'Being from Ballyclare, I wasn't sure what he meant. He explained it was a strategy and some musicians map out their lives, like they were working in the stock exchange. We had a crewmember who jumped ship to work for a bigger band. It sounds better to say you're working with a big important band than those has-beens Therapy?, so he gave us this speech like he was in [HBO drama] *Succession*, about how he was looking at the bigger picture and wanted so much more for himself: *So much for the ten year plan, you're just another company man.*'

'God Kicks', recorded drunk in a field under the stars, is a look at sectarian allegiances. In Northern Ireland, you might be asked which foot you kick with; Protestants kick with the right, while Catholics use the left. 'Someone like me or Michael would never ask that, because we don't give a fuck, but some of the more ardent followers of religion would,' says Andy. 'We had to be careful, because the line goes, "*God kicks with both feet and keeps his shoes clean*"—as in, he kicks both of us in equal ways and walks away unscathed while we're left to pick up the pieces. We also had to be careful not to come across like [Paul McCartney and Stevie Wonder's 1982 single] "Ebony And Ivory"! The fact we recorded it drunk in a field meant it wouldn't be cheesy.'

'Other People's Misery', on the other hand, is a high-octane blast with a punk-metal feel. 'The original version had an industrial four-on-the-floor feel, because of the drum machine,' says Andy. 'Whenever we played it in rehearsal, it sounded like a Primark version of Nine Inch Nails or White Zombie. So, to amuse ourselves, we played it in the style of Motörhead and thought there was something in it. It's a lot more deconstructed and less clinical.'

The album's closing track—if you discount the disorienting freeform experimental piece, 'Whilst I Pursue My Way Unharmed', hidden away at the end of the album—is 'Sister', a song based on a childhood memory

Andy had while in hospital. 'This is one I wrote on the acoustic guitar—a three-chord trick—and is actually one of my favourite tracks on the record,' he says. 'I have a vivid memory of my father, who wasn't the most sympathetic of men, shouting at me for the misery I put my mother through for ending up in hospital. At certain times over the years, I'll get these bouts of synaesthesia where I'll see a bright, white light and remember exactly how I felt in hospital, and asking the nurse why I was there.'

During their time at Great Linford Manor, the band spent their downtime making a thirty-minute horror film called 'The Speedo Menace'. '*The Blair Witch Project* had come out around that time, and we made our own version around the studio,' says Graham. 'It was hilarious. Andy was funny and Martin was made to be a theatrical actor. Diamond Dave was quite obviously the one and only Speedo Menace. Head had several different roles; he was a very eclectic actor. I have it somewhere in a box on VHS. I'll come across it one of these days, I hope.'

In the weeks leading up to the release of *Suicide Pact—You First*, Therapy? embarked on a small-scale, five-date UK tour, with Glasgow electro-industrialist Rico as support. 'We deliberately booked smaller venues because we wanted them to sell out rather than have the usual places be three-quarter full,' says Andy. 'The first gig was in Bristol, and the place went nuts.'

'It was a bit of a *fuck-you* tour, and quite cathartic,' adds Michael. 'It was great for the band, who were sat in a damp room six months earlier with no shows booked. We have that mentality to that day—it could be our last show, so let's go for it. There's no point keeping a bit in the tank. It felt like we put in a proper shift every night.'

Two days after the tour finished, *Suicide Pact—You First* was released. The band were pleased with the results. Just ten months ago, their future had been uncertain; now they were back on their own terms. 'Up until that point, I think *Suicide Pact—You First* was the biggest wild card,' says Michael. 'It's quite a bolshie album. It's not trying to hug you—it wants to give you a dead arm. We took risks, and I think they worked.'

'It's my favourite Therapy? album that I recorded with the band, without a doubt,' adds Graham. 'We went in and we fucking grabbed the bull by the horns and just rocked out. It kicked arse. I really loved was working with the producer, Head. He certainly brought out a certain side of Therapy? that had never been there before.'

The album found favour with critics at home and in Europe; in Germany, it was ranked as one of *Vision* magazine's top albums of the twentieth century. 'This, then, is not so much a comeback, but more of a *fuck-you* record to the paymasters who dumped Therapy?,' wrote Ben Myers in a four-star *Kerrang!* review. 'In doing so, they inadvertently inspired an album that is patently not designed for chart action, but is perhaps their greatest work yet. Not since the raw hardcore sounds of 1991's *Babyteeth* have Therapy? sounded so pumped up, twisted and ready to fire on all cylinders once again.'

'*Suicide Pact* takes a few listens to get into,' thought *Metal Hammer*'s Valerie Potter, who dished out an eight-out-of-ten rating. 'I suspect the songs will gain even more potency when played live, but fair play to Therapy? for once again spitting in the face of the easy option.'

'They've resurfaced in a fresher, more jubilant era, free from the poppy commercialism of earlier successes like *Troublegum*,' wrote *Rock Sound*'s Bethan Williams in a four-star review, pointing out the references to Nietzsche and James St. James's *Disco Bloodbath*. 'Therapy? are back, pinning victims to their couch, ready to pick brains apart.'

'*Suicide Pact* covers a lot of territory: grizzled punk, desert rock, math-y noise rock and whiskey-soaked, Tom Waits-ish homages to all that Prozac cannot cure,' wrote Kevin Stewart-Panko from the Canadian magazine *Exclaim!*. 'It's a good sign that Andy Cairns is back to his old cynical, dysfunctional self—cue "He's Not That Kind Of Girl" for some of the most biting Therapy? lyrics ever, and, coincidentally, one of their best songs in years.'

'A lot of people got what we were doing,' says Andy. 'It wasn't all lovely, though. Magazines like *Select* were scathing about it, and a lot of people were vocal about how much they hated the record. People who were fans of the band weren't shy about telling me they thought the record was shit.'

One publication in particular, *NME*, missed the point somewhat, referencing Scorpions, Alice Cooper, and The Cult in its two-and-a-half star review. 'At their best, Therapy? sounded like techno played with guitars that ate people, plus tunes. So why, six years later, do they seem like a relic from a bygone age?' it read. 'Elsewhere, though, the would-be-shocking song titles, and the over-stylised mummy-it's-a-nasty-man voices, reek of a band trying too hard to find a new identity.'

BBC Radio 1's *Rock Show* presenter Mary Anne Hobbs had her own take on the album. 'She said all copies of the records should be destroyed, live on air,' remembers Andy. 'That was kind of the reaction we wanted— if you don't like *Suicide Pact*, then you should really hate it. Michael and I wanted to return to our roots with this album, and we felt so vindicated when it was released.'

GOING NOWHERE?

YEAR ELEVEN/so much for the 10 year plan

On February 8, three months and twenty-one days after its UK release, *Suicide Pact—You First* was made available in North America. Back home, the band embarked on a month-long tour of the UK and Europe, for which they were joined by the Maryland quartet Clutch.

'I remember being on tour in America in 1993 and watching *Alternative Nation* in a hotel room,' says Andy. 'They played "A Shogun Named Marcus" from *Transnational Speedway League: Anthems, Anecdotes, And Undeniable Truths*. I bought that album the next day. When we got home, no one had really heard of them. It was Michael's idea to invite them on tour. They were one of those bands that, from day one, they were easy to get along with, and we'd watch them every night. They really made us up our game. They had a euphoric sense of the absurd running through their music. It was almost like watching jazz poetry over these stone-cold, amazing riffs.'

'When we toured America in 1993, we listened to them constantly on the bus,' Michael adds. 'We were massive fans, and, through a friend of a friend, we'd heard they wanted to come to the UK. So we got in contact and said, "So, what's the craic?" They were sweethearts—on the level— and I watched them every single night on that tour.'

Before their show at the Belfast Empire Hall on Match 9, Clutch expressed an interest in testing out the local liquor. After a phone call, Andy procured a bottle of *poitín*—an exceptionally strong distilled beverage first made by Irish monks in the sixth century—and presented it to their new friends. 'I told them it was Ulster moonshine,' he laughs. 'After we played that night, they said, "What was in that bottle?"'

Within days of the tour finishing, Therapy? headed to Austin, Texas, for the annual SXSW industry showcase. On March 16, they performed at the Lombardi Lounge, sharing a bill with Chicago industrial-rock band Sister Machine Gun. 'We played one show in America, which is nuts,' says Michael. 'We could have done a ten-date tour for the same money. But the SXSW show was a way of telling North America we still existed.'

'I remember it being the only gig that sold out that weekend,' adds Andy. 'We'd not been there for four years, and the night before we went to the venue and found out that it had sold out already. [Supersuckers frontman] Eddie Spaghetti loved *Suicide Pact*. Henry Rollins liked the guitar tones. [Nirvana producer] Jack Endino bought the album on the back of the reviews. It was one of the records that seemed to get us back on board with American bands and critics—and we did one show there.'

In May, the band returned to Great Linford Manor in Milton Keynes with producer Head. Over the course of five days, they recorded new tracks including 'Fat Camp' and 'Bad Karma Follows You Around' for *So Much For The Ten Year Plan*, an eighteen-track retrospective album that would fulfil their contractual obligation to Universal Records.

'That was less crazy than the *Suicide Pact* sessions,' remembers Michael. 'Up until that point, we weren't a band for standing on ceremony, so it was nice to put the brakes on for a minute. The label let us pick the track listing. It was more of an overview of the band, rather than single, single, single.'

'Bad Karma Follows You Around' has a distinctly Sub Pop feel, combining classic rock riffs with a hardcore attack. 'It was a comedy mixture of Status Quo and *Loose Nut*-era Black Flag,' Andy explains. 'The lyrics are about a conversation we'd had backstage in Southampton about a mutual acquaintance, and someone said, "Bad karma follows them around." The song is directed at the people in the business who'd hang around us when we were good for something and dropped us like a ton of shit when we weren't flavour of the month.'

'Fat Camp' was an unfinished song from the *Suicide Pact* sessions.

Informed by Cologne Krautrock legends Can, it's propelled by a hypnotic, fuzzed-up riff, backed by a thunderous drum pattern. 'At the time, I'd been reading about fat camps for people who wanted to lose weight,' says Andy, 'and a story about the world's first head transplant. I merged the two stories together to make a body-horror song!'

That summer, the band were a near-permanent fixture on the European festival circuit, performing at Finland's Nummirock, Germany's Hurricane Festival, the Lost Weekend at London's Dockland's Arena, a Motörhead all-dayer at Swansea's Singleton Park, the Bulldog Bash at Long Marston Airfield in Stratford-upon-Avon, and Belgium's Pukkelpop Festival. *So Much For The Ten Year Plan: A Retrospective 1990–2000* was released on October 2.

'Just when everyone is catching up with the electronica/rock sound Therapy? pioneered a decade ago, they're turning to the classic rock of the Stooges,' wrote *DotMusic*'s Graham Waveney in an eight-out-of-ten review. 'Bloody-minded brilliance! This compilation is a perfect introduction.'

'I'm usually apprehensive about greatest hits albums, because more often than not it's a road sign that the band in question has passed its creative zenith and is relying on a back catalogue to pay for green fees at the local golf course,' wrote Craig Young for *Ear Pollution*. 'But in the case of Therapy?, who are still fighting the good fight ten years on from the start of the race, *So Much For The Ten Year Plan* ain't so bad. For a band who over the years had claims against them for changing their musical approach on each album (like change is wrong and should be discouraged), the songs on this retrospective flow rather seamlessly when taken as a whole. This further reminds you why you should have their entire back catalogue in your collection.'

On the day of the album's release, the band embarked on a month-long tour of Europe, beginning with a free in-store show at the Virgin Megastore on London's Oxford Street. They played extensively across the Netherlands, Belgium, and Germany before returning to the UK for a twelve-date club run, including a three-night stand at the Underworld in Camden, London, in early November.

'Those Underworld ten-year anniversary shows were fun and felt good,' says Michael. 'We're not the kind of band to pat ourselves on the back but I remember thinking, *Fuck me, ten years? That's insane.*'

From late November until early December, the band decamped to Ritz Studios in Putney to begin work on their follow-up to *Suicide Pact—You First*. Early on, it appeared that the album would take on a distinct garage-rock feel, the roots of which could be traced back to their brief trip to Texas in March. 'After SXSW, me and Martin stayed over a couple of days to see The Yo-Yos, because we knew [frontman] Danny McCormack really well,' says Andy. 'They were playing with Zen Guerrilla, The Black Halos, and The Murder City Devils. We had a day off in Chicago on the way back, and bought The Murder City Devils' self-titled debut and *Empty Bottles, Broken Hearts*. I got totally into the super-charged modern take on rock'n'roll.'

'I was a fan of the band since the *Troublegum* days,' says Black Halos guitarist Rich Jones. 'I was living in Vancouver at the time, but I devoured the British rock press and listened to anything I could get my hands on. So, I was aware of Therapy?, but we'd never met. The Black Halos played a SXSW show at Emo's on a ridiculously stacked bill, and apparently Andy was in the audience with our A&R guy at Sub Pop, Dana Sims. After the show, Dana told me that he was watching with Andy, and Andy was in tears—of joy, thankfully. Andy later told me that he'd really felt despair at the state of music around that time, and that show had restored his faith and given him a kick up the arse to make a new record. Which, for us, was a pretty incredible thing to hear.'

'We'd done *Semi-Detached* and *Suicide Pact*, and people were telling me what we were doing was old-fashioned,' explains Andy. 'It was all Deftones and Korn. People would talk to me like I was a child and explain how they'd mixed dance rhythms with rock, even though we'd recorded "Teethgrinder", and done "Come And Die" with Fatal on the *Judgment*

Night soundtrack! I think Graham and Martin thought we should be going down the Deftones route, but I couldn't be told—I just wanted to do a fucked-up rock'n'roll record. With "Bad Karma Follows You Around", you could tell things were moving that way already.'

For their next album, the band booked time in Seattle with Sub Pop's go-to producer, Jack Endino, who'd worked with Mudhoney, L7, and The Murder City Devils, among others. He was championed by Wilt frontman Cormac Battle, whose band Kerbdog had recorded their 1994 self-titled debut at Rockfield Studios in Monmouthshire, Wales. Perfect, then, for Andy's vision of a fucked-up rock'n'roll record.

'His name had been bandied around when we were about to do *Nurse*, but it would have been the most obvious thing for a rock band to do at that time,' he says. 'Jack's name was on the records I was buying, and Cormac urged us to work with him. We were really excited to go and record in Seattle—we'd been in our own bubble, and I was interested to see what we could create while we were there.'

YEAR TWELVE/shameless
in seattle

Work on *Shameless* began on January 20 at Private Radio Studio in Seattle. The band spent five days in pre-production with Jack Endino, running through the material to iron out any kinks before recording the album proper. On the first day, they quickly learned one of the producer's house rules. 'We'd brought beers with us,' remembers Andy. 'Jack said that, in his experience, there's only one way a session goes when people start drinking—and that was downhill. We didn't drink while we recorded the album.'

The band then decamped to Robert Lang Studios in Shoreline, eleven miles north of Seattle. This state-of-the-art recording facility, cut into the hillside behind Robert's home overlooking the Puget Sound, has seen the likes of Heart, Foo Fighters, Minutemen bassist Mike Watt, and Alice In Chains pass through its doors. Nirvana had recorded their last ever studio session there, seven years previously, with the resulting track, 'You Know You're Right', eventually emerging in 2002 as part of their eponymous best-of collection. And, as with any studio worth its salt, a ghost was said to roam the facility, but the sheer volume being produced inside the live room most likely kept any apparitions at bay.

'I'm not sure if a spirit can haunt what was a big chunk of rock,' says Michael. 'It was a classy studio, with a brilliant live room. Jack was super into what he was doing and focussed on tiny details, but he was still a rock'n'roll producer. It took a while for us to get the northwest sense of humour, though. You'd be recording a take and he'd be like, "You're rockin' pretty hard there …" or "Well, that didn't suck." I couldn't tell if he was being sarcastic, but it was very low-key humour.'

During the three-week recording sessions, the producer's Seattle connections came in handy if ever the band needed equipment. 'Whenever we needed something, Jack said we could just go to Soundgarden's lockup, which was a big place down by the river,' Andy explains. 'They were super-nice, and they helped us out a lot while we there.'

'They were on hiatus,' adds Michael. 'In fact, [Soundgarden bassist] Ben Shepherd told us one night in the pub that Chris Cornell had been jamming with Rage Against The Machine members for some "supergroup". Jack also asked Matt Cameron, who was in Pearl Jam at the time, if we could borrow stuff from them. He checked with the other lads and gave Jack the access codes to their storage. It was a treasure trove of amazing gear.'

Respecting the producer's 'no drinking in the studio' rule, the four took advantage of Seattle's live scene and caught shows by Mudhoney, Supersuckers, Melvins, Tad Doyle's new band Hog Molly, The Catheters,

Clutch, and Nebula. 'There was this post-grunge, post-heroin hangover in the whole city,' says Michael. 'People seemed fragile. Everyone who'd been in a rock band or worked with a rock band had been through the wringer and had lost somebody close to them. There was a real sense of community, and people were very generous towards us.'

This became further apparent when Therapy? were joined by Screaming Trees drummer Barrett Martin, who added percussion to 'I Am The Money', 'Wicked Man', 'Theme From DeLorean', and 'Tango Romeo'. The Black Halos' Rich Jones and Rob Zgaljic visited the band, too, to see how the album was progressing: Rich added a guitar solo to 'This One's For You' and some handclaps on 'Endless Psychology'; Rob added cowbell to 'Gimme Back My Brain'.

'I showed up with no real idea of what they wanted me to do, but I was young and full of confidence, so I was up for anything!' says Rich. 'I think it was mostly spontaneous; backing vocals and handclaps, and basically whatever anyone could think that was needed. I think Jack might have suggested I do the solo on that one, so it was all kind of improvised on the spot. I love that song as well, and I was pretty happy with how it all came out. It was a pretty fun and relaxed vibe in the studio—everyone seemed to be really happy with where it was all going.'

The album's lead single, 'Gimme Back My Brain', was strongly influenced by the armfuls of albums that Andy had purchased during the band's SXSW trip the previous year. 'The title comes from from when we were in the studio,' he says. 'After a few days, he asked how it was going, and, because we'd not been drinking, I said, "Thanks for giving me back my brain."'

The album's second track, 'Dance', boasts a languid guitar line. 'That started out like a sleazy Jesus Lizard or Laughing Hyenas riff,' explains Andy, who adds that the next track, 'This One's For You', changed quite a lot in the studio, taking on echoes of Gluecifer and The Misfits on the way to becoming 'a 50s rock'n'roll song with a darker shade of guitar'.

'I Am The Money', he continues, 'went wrong'; it was, he says, a prime example of the phrase 'a camel is a horse designed by committee'. When the band played the song in rehearsals, Graham voiced concerns about how it sounded like 'Expedestrians' from Wilt's 2000 debut, *Bastinado*, and as a result it became something else entirely. 'He played us the song, and that sounded a bit like our own song, "Disgracelands", so we completely changed the riff. There was a Destiny's Child track we were all listening to at the time, so we tried to incorporate that into it. The title came from [Doug Liman's cult classic film] *Swingers*. I think from Graham's point of view, he wanted to make it more like Deftones, and I wanted to make it more absurd.'

The spiralling riff on 'Theme From Delorean' was written after Andy bought himself a Mosrite guitar. 'It was a model used by Johnny Ramone,' he says. 'I was playing around with it and came up with a surf-y riff. The title refers to the car that was built in Northern Ireland and is synonymous with the *Back To The Future* films.'

In keeping with a vehicular theme, the next track, 'Joey', is a high-octane tribute to Ballymoney motorcyclist Joey Dunlop that also name-checks Northern Irish football hero George Best and snooker legend Alex 'Hurricane' Higgins. Clutch frontman Neil Fallon makes an appearance on the track as the gruff-voiced compere, while guitarist Tim Sult provides some revving noises. 'That was quite a good track,' Andy brightens. 'That was inspired by the band Zeke, who come from Seattle.'

'Endless Psychology' was Andy's attempt to write a louche riff in the style that informed much of Queens Of The Stone Age's *Rated R*, with a noise solo by Tim. As for the lyrics, Andy's guess is good as anyone's: they speak of seeing the world through abstract expressionist Jackson Pollock's eyes, 'tree people', Carl Jung, and Oscar Wilde.

'I have no idea what that song was about,' says Andy, who admits there are a number of creative duds on *Shameless*. 'Wicked Man' and 'Alrite' were his attempts to write a Murder City Devils song ('I was in thrall of that band') and a Zen Guerrilla soul stomper, respectively. 'They both backfired,' he says, citing 'Stalk & Slash' as another song that 'didn't work'. 'When we were writing the album, we were talking about Nirvana's album *Bleach*. I thought that was our idea of writing a song like "Mr. Moustache", but it didn't really pay off. We didn't quite get there with the songwriting.'

The languid shuffle of 'Body Bag Girl' was inspired by a previous visit to Seattle, when the band played a show with Hammerbox in 1995. 'After the show, there were ten people in our hotel room and there was a girl who asked if anyone wanted some "body bag", which was a type of heroin,' says Andy. 'We all declined and asked her to leave. When she left, we were like, "Who the fuck would take a drug called that?" That's where the lyric "*Her eyes are sunk so deep / She's on the verge of sleep*" comes from.'

'Tango Romeo' is a story about a group of friends who were pulled over by the Royal Ulster Constabulary. 'It's about Northern Ireland told through metaphors,' says Andy. 'It's about some people we knew who were lifted by the police and taken to Castlereagh and strip-searched. That's where the "*Don't sneak in my underpants, you only had to ask*" comes from. I thought it sounded like a fucked-up version of Sparks.'

With the album completed, the band also recorded a glut of songs that would appear on various other releases over the coming year. In addition to the original experimental composition 'Valentine's Day 2001', there was a cover of 'Denim Demon' for the Turbonegro tribute album, *Alpha Motherfuckers*, released in June of that year, and a cover of The Black Halos' 'Blood Sucking Freaks' was recorded for a Sub Pop split single that never materialised.

'Funnily enough, we were just rehearsing that song for some Black Halos reunion shows, and the Therapy? version was brought up at rehearsal,' says Rich Jones. 'I have a cassette of the monitor mix of it that they gave me at the studio, and I'd transferred it to digital, so we were all just listening to it again the other week. I love what they did with it; I'd say they vastly improved on what was a real kind of Neanderthal bit of riff-rock *stoopidity*. And obviously it was very flattering for this kid at the time. We ended up covering "Lonely, Cryin', Only"—a song I'd always loved—and we turned it into a big, hammering anthem. Unfortunately, we never actually did a final vocal or mix on it though, so, like their cover, I don't believe it's ever been released. Maybe we should do that split single this year, finally?'

Therapy? also found time for a cover of 'Big Time', originally recorded by Andy's heroes Rudi, a punk band from Belfast. However, he and Martin butted heads during the recording of the track over their differing opinions about how the riff should be played. The eventual recording would later feature on the Japanese release of *Shameless*. 'I'd been playing that song since I was a kid,' Andy explains. 'Martin said I was playing the wrong note. I was so broken by the end of it that I did it his way. A few months later, I got an email from their guitarist, Brian Young, and it said, "We're made up that you did a Rudi cover, but the next time I see you, I'll show you how to do the riff properly." This was a guy I'd idolised since I was a teenager, and I will never forgive Martin for that.'

After mixing *Shameless* at Hanzek Studios in Seattle—where Neil and Tim from Clutch added their parts to 'Joey'—the band planned to round off their North American visit with two low-key shows at the Graceland venue in Seattle and the Satyricon in Portland. They were forced to cancel the gigs after Graham sprained his fingers during an argument with Andy, then flew home.

The band returned to North America for an eight-date, DIY tour that started at Pittsburgh's Club Laga on May 4 and ended nine days later with a set at Boston's Bill's Bar. 'We did that tour with just a tour manager,' says Michael. 'We sold the merch ourselves, lugged the gear—we were keen to show we could tour America and didn't have to do it on a level the agents and label thought we had to be on. It was good fun.'

On June 21, the band performed at a party at Soundgarden in Dortmund, at the request of the German magazine *Visions*. The next day, they were back in the UK to record a clutch of B-sides for future single 'Gimme Back My Brain' at John Henry's in Islington, London. The plan was simple enough: they would spend the day recording six songs that featured 'gimme' in the title: 'Gimme! Gimme! Gimme! (A Man After Midnight)' by ABBA, 'Gimme Danger' by The Stooges, 'Gimme Nyquil All Night Long' by German digital hardcore duo EC8OR, 'Gimme Gimme Shock Treatment' by the Ramones, and 'Gimme Gimme Gimme' by Black Flag, plus their own composition, 'Gimme Therapy'.

'That was a tough session,' laughs Andy. My favourite cover was the ABBA song. I think Steve Lamacq played that at the Reading Festival that year. The Black Flag and Stooges songs were obvious ones to do, but we didn't do [ZZ Top's] "Gimme All Your Loving". I think Graham played the drumbeat a few times, though.'

The single was released on August 6, but because it contained seven songs it was ineligible for the UK's singles chart. It charted at no. 6 on the 'Budget Albums' chart instead. Thankfully, *Kerrang!* did not follow such rules, duly awarding the track 'Single Of The Week'. Prior to that, the band made several appearances on the European circuit, playing Austria's Forestglade Festival and Rock Zottegem and Dour Festival in Belgium.

Shameless was released on September 3, to mixed reviews. '*Shameless* is, for the first few songs, one of the finest Britrock albums ever made,' wrote *Drowned In Sound*'s Graham Reed in a three-out-of-ten review. '[But] it's painful to listen to, if only for the fact it'll be compared to classics of their past and found to be a shallow, pale photocopy by a band that's but a shadow of its former self.'

Harry Guerin at Ireland's RTÉ awarded the album three out of five: 'Having reinvented and resurrected themselves with their 1999 album *Suicide Pact—You First*, Therapy? have returned with the album they should have made six years ago when basking in the afterglow of their Mercury-nominated *Troublegum*. If *Suicide Pact* was the quartet's broody, staying-in record, then *Shameless* is best seen as their jukebox collection, the type of album you want blaring in the background when you're out way past bedtime.'

The album earned another three-out-of-five review from *AllMusic*'s Jason Anderson, who wrote, 'A slight return to punk and hard rock form, *Shameless* records a Therapy? intent on capturing its own late-80s/early 90s rock underground aesthetic with just a bit more melodic shimmer. This is probably for the better, but not in time to reclaim any mid-90s commercial momentum.'

Reviewing the album for *Kerrang!*, I found the band's turbo-charged take on garage rock a thrilling listen and gave the album a four-*K* rating: 'On the whole, *Shameless* is a no-frills affair which embodies everything that rock should be: loud, sweaty, obnoxious and at times a little paranoid. Hey, it worked for Black Sabbath.'

Two decades on, Andy has many reservations about many aspects of the record. 'What we should have done was built on the template of *Suicide Pact* and taken six months off before deciding where we wanted to go,' he says. 'I love the sound of the record but not the songs. We had a good time making the record, but some of the songs sound half-finished. When I listen to songs like "Gimme Back My Brain", it's a pastiche of a rock'n'roll band. I like "This One's For You", but some of it's shite. I think *Shameless* was a failure, and part of it was because I wouldn't listen to anyone else.'

'I Am The Money' followed the album on September 17, reaching no. 84 in the UK singles chart. The band had been scheduled to appear a couple of days earlier at Tattoo The Planet at London's Wembley Arena, but the event was postponed, with many of the acts on the bill finding it impossible to travel in the wake of the 9/11 terror attacks. Pantera, who had been due to co-headline with Slayer, issued a statement to explain the situation: 'We apologise to our international friends and fans that we planned on jamming and partying with, but there is absolutely nothing in the world worth compromising their safety or ours.'

The rearranged date fell before Therapy?'s headline tour of the UK and Europe, with support on the majority of dates coming from Kettering nu-metal act Defenestration. Two weeks after the last date, at Dublin's Ambassador Theatre, Graham announced that he was quitting the band. Then came the news that their tenure with Ark 21 was at an end.

'He was really enthusiastic when he joined,' Andy says of Graham. 'But around *Shameless*, his mood completely changed. He was always complaining about stuff.'

'I found the *Shameless* recording frustrating, because I shared a room with Graham in Seattle,' Michael adds. 'I'd have to hassle him to get out of bed, hassle him to get dressed, hassle him to get out to be where we needed to be on time. I felt like his mum. It began to become reminiscent of how it was with Fyfe, with me and Andy pulling it along. He'd become a bit detached. It was a tiny surprise when he left, but a bit of a relief, too. He had his reasons. It was all done and dusted by Christmas.'

Today, Graham admits that he hadn't been totally on board with the new garage-rock direction Therapy? had taken during the recording sessions. 'I just wasn't feeling it,' he says. 'I listened back to the album a couple of months ago, and there are certainly some brilliant bits. But, at that time, I was writing my own songs constantly, and they were more in the shape of things that were influencing me. When the band and crew were in the back lounge of the tour bus, listening to Turbonegro, The Stooges, Misfits, or whatever hardcore punk you could possibly think of, I'd be going to sleep in my bunk listening to Elliott Smith, Nick Cave, or Scott Walker, that kind of vibe. I had nothing at all against rocking out. Jesus, I'd be still getting up on stage for ninety minutes every night and giving it fucking *socks*, you know?'

It was the death of his friend, New York-born musician Mic Christopher, in November 2001 that led Graham to reassess his role in the band. 'He was on tour, opening for The Waterboys in Europe,' he explains. 'He had a fall and was put on life support. I got a train to Groningen to visit him

ABOVE LEFT ANDY CAIRNS IN HIS
'POUNDLAND RORY GALLAGHER' PHASE,
1983. **ABOVE** MICHAEL MCKEEGAN
REHEARSES HIS STAGE MOVES IN
LARNE, 1982. **LEFT** NEIL COOPER
CELEBRATES HIS BIRTHDAY WITH A
SNARE-THEMED CAKE, 1977.
(UNLESS OTHERWISE NOTED, ALL OF
THE PHOTOGRAPHS IN THIS BOOK ARE
FROM THE BAND'S ARCHIVES.)

DRILLING OF HANDS AND FEET.

LISTEN YOU FUCKERS

Late shows:
Blue Velvet

THERAPY?
LMs
+DISCO
CONOR HALL
FRI 22 FEB
7·30-12·00

Let the experts move your treasured trees

AMPUTATION OF LIMBS.

OPPOSITE THE BAND'S FIRST PROMO SHOT, BELFAST, 1990. **THIS PAGE** A SELECTION OF FLYERS, INCLUDING ONE FROM THE BAND'S FIRST EVER GIG (*ABOVE, COURTESY OF PAUL CHAPMAN; ALL OTHERS COURTESY OF GEORGE SMYTH*). **BELOW RIGHT** ANDY AT THE ERRIGLE INN, BELFAST, FEBRUARY 28 1990.

THE SAUSAGE MACHINE
PLAYS DISGUSTING MUSIC
AT THE MOONLIGHT CLUB WEST HAMPSTEAD TUBE
APRIL 26TH FRIDAY
THERAPY +MIDWAY STILL
THURSDAY 2ND MAY +SLEEP+
MAJORITY OF ONE (USA) JUICE
FRIDAY 3rd MAY
DRIVE + JAILCELL RECIPES
FRIDAY 31st MAY
FUDGE TUNNEL + SUPPORT
THURSDAY 6TH JUNE
GO! +DECLINE (USA)

ABOVE AN ALTERNATIVE PAINTING FOR *PLEASURE DEATH* BY GEORGE SMYTH (*COURTESY OF GEORGE SMYTH*). **BELOW** PREPARING TO HIT THE ROAD, DUBLIN, APRIL 1991. **RIGHT** FLYERS FOR A LONDON SHOW IN 1991 (NOTE MISSING QUESTION MARK) AND A 1990 TOUR WITH THE BEYOND, FEATURING A CERTAIN NEIL COOPER. **OPPOSITE** DESERT SESSIONS: THE BAND IN LAS VEGAS, MAY 10 1993.

The BeYoND

12" 4 track "MANIC SOUND PANIC" out now
Big Cat Records through Rough Trade

+Junderfunk,
& THERAPY
THE VENUE, EDINBURGH
SUN 15th JULY

TOP A PROMO SHOT FROM 1993.
ABOVE MICHAEL AND ANDY RECORDING
THE *SHORTSHARPSHOCK* EP AT BLACK
BARN STUDIOS, SURREY, JANUARY 1993
(*BOTH PHOTOS BY CHRIS SHELDON*).
LEFT WITH OZZY OSBOURNE, RECORDING
VOCALS FOR 'IRON MAN', LOS ANGELES,
APRIL 25 1994. **OPPOSITE** *TROUBLEGUM*
PROMO SHOT, 1994.

THIS PAGE A SELECTION OF MAGAZINE COVERS FROM 1994, AND A 'KRITICS' CHOICE' AWARD FOR *TROUBLEGUM*. **OPPOSITE** TAKING A BREAK FROM INTERVIEWS, BRUSSELS, BELGIUM, 1995.

VOL 18 NO 4 • 9 MARCH 1994
PRICE £1.36 (INCLUDING TAXES)

HOT PRESS

CONTROVERSY 1 • NIALL STOKES AND EOGHAN HARRIS:
the article the SUNDAY TIMES refused to print

CONTROVERSY 2: THE SMITHWICKS/HOT PRESS AWARDS
not a turkey in sight (and that's official!)

THERAPY?
young gums go for it

By Gerry McGovern

darlings! it's mr. pussy • interview liam fay
the edge • daniel day-lewis • the sultans of ping

KERRANG!

KRITICS' CHOICE ALBUM OF THE YEAR!

1 TROUBLEGUM Therapy? (A&M) "The most perfect collision of Punk and Metal you will hear this year... This is Therapy? turning their previous threats into actual aural Meggary... Take the rampant riffsmate of the likes of Metallica, Megadeth or even Priest, and Stiff Little Fingers' ability to write gigantic Power-Punk and the pant-shipping directness of Sugar and you're close... Sheer gale-driving intensity.
KKKK. Phil Alexander (£1,450).

So what do Punk Metal kings Therapy? reckon of the splendid accolade of being voted the Kerrang! Critics' Number One album of 1994?
The top-smart hide trio had this to say: "Obviously we're absolutely knocked out. It's been a brilliant year, in no small way thanks to the tremendous support we've had from Kerrang! readers and writers. There is no way we could have done it without you. Thanks! Look forward to seeing you in 1995." Andy, Fyfe and Michael.

VISIONS

Ausgabe 1994
DM 4,80

Therapy?
IRISH BLEND

2 BAD
S.S.L.
PRONG
FREAKY FUKIN WEIRDOZ
GEORGE CLINTON
VOODOOCULT
KING'S X
GREEN DAY
DAS EFX
MINK STOLE
FLAMING LIPS
KRISTIN HERSCH

FREE INSIDE! 32-PAGE FESTIVAL GUIDE

MELODY·MAKER
MUSCLE POWER FOR NOWT   JUNE 11, 1994 75p

Tattoo's company!
THERAPY? & ROLLINS
Radiohead ★ NIN ★ Underworld ★ Lush ★ Gary Numan ★ Anti-Nazi Rally ★ Creation Discography

ABOVE LEFT AN AD FOR METALLICA'S 'ESCAPE FROM THE STUDIO' SHOW AT CASTLE DONINGTON, 1995. **ABOVE** ANDY FINDS A QUIET SPACE TO WORK ON SOME GUITAR DURING THE *INFERNAL LOVE* SESSIONS AT REAL WORLD STUDIOS, BOX, WILTSHIRE, 1995. **LEFT** AN *NME* COVER FROM 1995.

ABOVE MUCKING AROUND DURING
A PHOTOSHOOT WITH ANTON
CORBIJN IN PORTUGAL, 1995.
LEFT ANDY ON STAGE AT THE
MONSTERS OF ROCK SHOW AT
PACAEMBU STADIUM, SAO PAULO,
BRAZIL, SEPTEMBER 2 1995

TOP MICHAEL AND ANDY BACKSTAGE IN RIO DE JANEIRO, BRAZIL, SEPTEMBER 5 1995. **ABOVE AND LEFT** THREE *KERRANG!* COVERS FROM 1994–95 (*COURTESY OF KERRANG!*). **OPPOSITE** AND THEN THERE WERE FOUR: THE NEW THERAPY? LINE-UP AT THE FACTORY, DUBLIN, IRELAND, 1997.

ABOVE *SUICIDE PACT—YOU FIRST*
PROMO SHOT, 1999. **RIGHT** MIXING
SHAMELESS WITH JACK ENDINO,
HANZSEK STUDIOS, SEATTLE, 2001.
OPPOSITE TAKING A BREAK FROM
THE *HIGH ANXIETY* SESSIONS, 2002;
ANDY OUTSIDE JACOBS STUDIO,
SURREY, JANUARY 2006; WORKING
ON *ONE CURE FITS ALL* AT JACOBS.

ABOVE *CROOKED TIMBER* PROMO SHOT, DURHAM, ENGLAND, 2009 (*PHOTO BY TOM HOAD*). **RIGHT** NEIL ON STAGE AT LINZER STADION IN LINZ, AUSTRIA, JULY 4 2009.

ABOVE ON THE COVER OF THE UKRANIAN MAGAZINE *GHEЙ* IN 2007. **ABOVE RIGHT** ACES HIGH: TAKING A PRIVATE JET TO THE PENINSULA FESTIVAL IN TARGU MURES, ROMANIA, AUGUST 26 2010. **RIGHT** WITH LAFARO FOLLOWING A 20TH ANNIVERSARY SHOW AT VICAR STREET, DUBLIN, NOVEMBER 5 2010.

ABOVE *DISQUIET* PROMO SHOT,
MARSDEN BAY, TYNE & WEAR, 2015
(*PHOTO BY TOM HOAD*).
RIGHT ANDY SUITED UP ON TOUR
IN 2012. **OPPOSITE** *A BRIEF CRACK
OF LIGHT* PROMO SHOT, SALFORD,
2012 (*PHOTO BY TOM HOAD*).

LEFT *WOOD & WIRE* PROMO SHOT,
STEPNEY BANK, NEWCASTLE, 2016.
ABOVE *DISQUIET* PROMO SHOT,
SANDHAVEN BEACH, TYNE & WEAR,
2015 (*BOTH PHOTOS BY TOM HOAD*).

ABOVE AND LEFT PORTRAITS OF NEIL, ANDY, AND MICHAEL, TAKEN IN REDCAR DURING A PROMO SHOOT FOR *CLEAVE*, 2018 (*ALL PHOTOS BY TOM HOAD*).

ABOVE RECORDING *GREATEST HITS
(2020 VERSIONS)* AT ABBEY ROAD,
LONDON, NOVEMBER 8 2019
(*PHOTO BY PETER CAPSTICK*).

on the day of a gig in the Netherlands. Mic died on the day of our London show [at Ocean, on November 29], and then I decided it had to be time [to quit the band].

'I suppose the sudden and shocking death of Mic made me realise how short life is, and how I needed to be true to myself in many ways. His funeral was in Dublin, on the last day of the tour. I knew in my mind it was going to be the last gig for me, but I didn't want to make things sour for the guys on that day [by] telling them as much. I rang all the lads individually, as everyone was living in completely different localities and countries. I genuinely found it difficult, but they were all very understanding.'

YEAR THIRTEEN/the derby demon

For the second time in thirteen years, Therapy? began a new year without a drummer. They were also without a record deal. But with no live dates looming until a three-week tour of Scandinavia booked for April, followed by a number of summer festival appearances, the three remaining members had some breathing space and a chance to collect their thoughts before embarking on the now-familiar audition process.

At the end of 2001, Therapy? were being tour-managed by John Adkins, who also worked with the San Diego band Rocket From The Crypt and the London-based four-piece 3 Colours Red. The latter had parted ways in 1999, and it was suggested that Therapy? consider recruiting their drummer, Keith Baxter—formerly of folk-metal pioneers Skyclad—to fill in for the time being.

'Having bankrolled Graham and Martin's wages from 1998 onwards, myself and Michael felt we needed to do these shows,' says Andy. 'More importantly, we didn't want to let down the fans who'd already bought tickets. And when John heard Graham had left, he mentioned Keith was a Therapy? fan and a really good drummer. We called Keith, then met up with him at rehearsals in London a few weeks later. Impressively, he'd done his homework and knew all the tunes; he was easygoing, hard-working, and got on well with everybody.'

On March 20, Andy went to see Rival Schools, the New York four-piece led by Quicksand frontman Walter Schreifels, at the Garage in London. There, he bumped into Neil Cooper; the pair had not seen each other since Neil's band The Beyond played the Stick Of Rock in Bethnal Green almost twelve years previously.

'I'd travelled down from Derby to see the gig,' Neil remembers. 'By the time I met Andy, I think I'd had a few too many beers, and I may have been sliding down the bar. We caught up, and he mentioned that they were looking for a drummer—and did I fancy it? It's mad looking back and how randomly it came about. If I hadn't got the train that day, I wouldn't be in the band.'

The Beyond had gone on hiatus in 1994, which led to Neil joining Cable and playing on their mini-album *Down-Lift The Up-Trodden* the following year. He was also performing with Gorilla, a band featuring his old Beyond bandmates John Whitby and Andy Gatford. 'It got to the point where I'd come off tour with Cable then go back out with Gorilla the next day,' he explains. 'It was nuts. There was someone called Roland Oliver, who was doing monitors for Therapy? on the *Infernal Love* tour, and was doing front of house sound for Gorilla. In 1996, he'd mentioned in passing that Fyfe had left the band and that I should go for it. I was so frazzled and freaking out with what I had going on anyway, and I didn't want to drop two bands in it, because I'm loyal—if I'm in a band, I don't want to dick people about. And to jump into Fyfe's shoes at the time was a big thing.'

'That was the annoying thing!' Andy laughs. 'If he'd joined the band then, it could have been so, so different. His style was beyond a perfect fit for us—and with me and Michael, temperament-wise.'

The following day, Andy rang Michael in Belfast to tell him about his chance encounter. 'We hadn't seen Neil properly for years, but him joining the band seemed like a good idea,' says Michael. 'He was into the same music and was an incredible drummer.'

Andy immediately called Neil; during the conversation, he laid out the band's plans for the year and told Neil to begin learning their set. 'He explained that Keith was going to do the dates in Europe, and then I'd play at a festival in Portugal in August,' says Neil. 'The way Andy put it was, "Let's do that and see how we get on." I was over the moon.'

The Scandinavian tour kicked off in Denmark on April 4, with a show at the Tobakken in Esbjerg—one of Denmark's largest indoor concert halls. Shows followed in Aalborg, Aarhus, and Copenhagen, before the band crossed the Skagerrak to perform in Norway, Sweden, and Finland.

'3 Colours Red weren't doing anything,' Michael recalls, 'and Keith really wanted to go out and play. He came from a thrash background, so he could play fast and tight. We always half-jokily talked about forming a Slayer tribute band. He was quite shy but brilliant to be around. I don't think he was in a good place with his drinking, but we didn't realise that at the time. I don't think it would be out of place to say he was a functioning alcoholic then, but it never, ever affected his playing.'

During the summer, Therapy? began their run of European festival appearances at Dauwpop in Holland on May 9, followed by Ozzfest at Punchestown Racecourse in County Kildare on May 26. The headliner, Ozzy Osbourne, had to pull out at the last moment due to a throat infection, but the show went ahead without him. (Ticket holders were offered a refund or a free pass to see Santana, UB40, Meatloaf, Bryan Adams, and Paul Weller at Marley Park later that summer.)

In the run-up to their appearance at Belgium's Lokerse Feesten on August 8, the band booked in some rehearsals at John Henry's in North

London. 'I had learned sixteen or seventeen songs by the time we got to London,' says Neil. 'The rehearsal time became shorter and shorter. In the end, it was literally one run-through of the set, then we were off to Europe.'

Luckily, Neil's debut went off without a hitch. The following gig, five days later at Marktrock Festival in Belgium, was also a success. The sighs of relief could be heard from far afield. 'We knew straight away he was the man for the job,' says Andy. 'By the end of the summer, we felt that it was going to be amazing. He slotted into the band perfectly.'

'To do one rehearsal showed they had faith that I could do it,' adds Neil. 'I had bits of paper with song parts on everywhere, but I'm a big believer in saying yes to things and just going for it. But I could have completely bottled it.'

Soon after the summer shows, the band found a new home when they signed a worldwide deal with Spitfire Records, a subsidiary of Eagle Rock Entertainment that had released albums by Napalm Death, Dio, Danzig, and Black Label Society.

'I would frequently bump into Diamond Dave at gigs, or when he was presenting his show on Total Rock Radio, which was based in Putney at the time,' says Spitfire Records' former label manager, Darren Edwards. 'I had been a fan of Therapy? for quite some time. I managed to see them when they toured Australia and quite a few times in the UK. I can't quite remember if I asked Dave what they were up to, or if he had just mentioned that they were label-free and looking for a new home. Either way, I instantly told him that we'd be interested in talking to them about signing with Spitfire Records, and he connected me with their manager, Gerry. Signing the band remains one of the biggest highlights of my career.'

Over the autumn, Andy travelled regularly to Derby's Hive studios to run through new song ideas with Neil, prior to sending recordings to Michael and Martin. 'Martin didn't go to any of those rehearsals because he was adamant he wasn't going to Derby,' says Andy. 'Michael couldn't really come over from Northern Ireland so much, as we were being really careful with money in the band bank account—we hadn't any money through from the label at that point. So I took songs like "Who Knows", "Stand In Line", "If It Kills Me", and "Limbo" and worked on them with Neil. Neil came up with an amazing drum hook for what became "Rust". I thought it could be something off a Shellac record.'

Some older tracks were dusted off and reworked: 'Hey Satan—You Rock' was originally called 'High Anxiety', while 'Nobody Here But Us' dates back to the *Semi-Detached* sessions with Chris Sheldon. 'We were watching Nirvana's *MTV Unplugged*, and the next day I'd recorded the chords,' says Andy. 'Chris said we didn't have time to start writing new material, so it was put on the back burner.'

'My Voodoo Doll' was originally called 'Armageddon Checklist', and was initially performed at a deathly slow tempo—like 'The House Of Love meets The Jesus & Mary Chain', as Andy puts it. 'Last Blast' was written later, after Martin joined the band. 'I'd say three-quarters of the album was written before we actually got together,' says Andy, 'and the rest was bits and pieces of older material.'

In December, the band entered Parkgate Studios, a residential studio located in Catsfield, near the historic town of Battle in East Sussex. It was decided that the band's live sound engineer, Pete Bartlett, who'd recorded the 'Gimme Back My Brain' B-sides in 2001, would produce the new album. 'He knew how to get our live sound,' says Michael, 'and we wanted it to be really punchy.'

'Pete didn't suffer any bullshit,' Andy adds. 'He doesn't tart things up in any way, or pull any punches. I knew I'd really enjoy working with him.' At Pete's suggestion, Andy took the bedroom above the studio so he could record vocals late into the night.

Suffolk extreme-metal band Cradle Of Filth had just recorded *Damnation And A Day* at Parkgate, and word got back that a resident of a local mental-health facility had been found 'giggling' at the foot of one of the band members' beds. Neil, whose chalet door had a faulty lock, took to barricading the door each night before going to sleep.

Martin was absent at the beginning of the album sessions, opting instead to do some session work, playing cello on Biffy Clyro's *The Vertigo Of Bliss*, which incidentally was produced by Chris Sheldon. He and his wife, Kimberley, can be heard performing on the tracks 'Bodies In Flight', 'With Aplomb', and 'Now The Action Is On Fire!'.

'We'd been massive fans of Biffy for a long time,' says Andy, 'but this was news to us. We'd just got a new deal and were about to record a new album with a new drummer, and he decided to go off and play with somebody else. That was a red flag.'

'I remember Andy, Neil, and myself were loading the gear in, and I remember thinking, *Where's the team spirit?*' adds Michael. 'We'd tracked the drums, and I think I was almost finished playing bass by the time he rocked up.'

When it came to adding guitar parts to the album, something was clearly amiss. 'It was obvious that Martin hadn't done anything since the rehearsal,' says Michael. 'Pete was pulling his hair out, because nothing was right; a lot of the parts that we'd done in the demos, Martin had either forgotten or didn't want to play or had changed. It was just a real mess.'

'One morning, when we were having breakfast, Pete played Devil's advocate and asked Martin whether it would be better to play lots of guitar and not have as good an album, or play less guitar and have a better album,' he continues. 'Martin was of the opinion that he'd stick with playing all of his guitar parts. I remember being really hacked off about that.'

'I did see arguments between Martin and Pete about where the album was going, and they weren't on the same page,' says Neil. 'Pete just wanted to get the best out of us.'

Spitfire were delighted with the way their new signings' material was taking shape. 'We didn't have any preconceived ideas for what we wanted from the band,' Darren explains. 'We just wanted them to make the album they wanted to make. A co-worker and I visited the band at Parkgate Studios and tried to play it a little cool in the studio. I told the guys that we liked what they were doing, and although I really wanted to stay longer, we kept the visit short so as not to interfere with their creativity. When we started driving back to London, I was on such a natural high from what I'd heard, I clearly remember bellowing in the car, "THAT SOUNDED FUCKING AMAZING!"'

The band eventually wrapped up recording just before Christmas, and the four members went back home for the holidays. Back home, Andy's phone rang. 'Pete had listened back to the album, and he called to say that Martin's parts were all over the place,' he says. 'His guitar parts didn't really gel, and his singing style didn't really sit right. Michael and I decided to go back into the studio in January to fix it.'

YEAR FOURTEEN/tension
in the ranks

Shortly after the New Year, Andy and Michael returned to Parkgate to add the finishing touches to the new album. 'Pete managed to get the label to pay for some more studio time,' says Michael. 'Andy sat and redid all of Martin's guitar parts in a few days—and I think Martin doesn't know about that to this day. When we came to rehearse for the tour, Martin mentioned to Andy that he couldn't remember who played what on the album.'

'It was a pain in the arse to do,' adds Andy. 'That's what it was. A pain in the arse.' He also added vocals to the song 'Not In Any Name' while Chris Sheldon was mixing the album. 'We'd recorded the music but didn't have the lyrics finished, and it was destined to end up on the cutting-room floor,' he explains. 'I came up with the lyrics one night, about 9/11 and

Tony Blair's incursion into Iraq to appease the Americans. My grandfather died in the Second World War, and within five days his brother had died. The first time I ever saw my father cry was whenever we went to visit my grandfather's grave. My dad was only five or six when his dad died. There's the line "*My granddad was cannon fodder / To think he died for the likes of you*"—this is what happens with young men who go to war. The games are played by somebody else, and the people that pay the price are just pawns.'

Chris Sheldon completed mixing the album, and the mood in the Therapy? camp was decidedly buoyant, despite the obstacles they'd faced in Catsfield. 'The label loved the album, we were happy, and everyone was in a good mood,' says Michael. 'At that point in time, it was easy to brush everything under the carpet. The main thing was that the album was done.'

The album was titled *High Anxiety*, after the 1977 Mel Brooks film. It was only while the album was being prepared for release that Andy had the sudden realisation that his friends and label signings Pet Lamb had an album of the same name on Roadrunner. 'I had this cold shiver go up my spine,' he remembers. 'I called Dylan [Philips, the band's guitarist and vocalist] to explain. We went back a long way. He said I didn't need to worry—he gave me his blessing, and we kept the title.'

Compared to *Shameless*, *High Anxiety* had the energy, focus, and feel of the band's earlier releases. Opener 'Hey Satan—You Rock' began life as an acoustic song in the vein of Johnny Cash, about the 'commercialisation of evil. We were guilty of this as much as the next band,' says Andy, 'but at the time, there were so many T-shirts which had pentagrams on them. In the 70s, the first time you heard Black Sabbath's first album, it was—and it still is—genuinely creepy. The commodification of metal and things dark has kind of taken the shock value out of it since then. I regret the almost comedy value in the lyrics, and I think the title and chorus could have handled them better. I still like the tune.'

Next was 'Who Knows', which boasts a frantic metal riff with an earworm of a chorus, sparked by Pink's 2001 single 'Get The Party Started', while the lyrics were partly inspired by John Niven's novel *Kill Your Friends*. 'I've always been a sucker for pop music,' says Andy. 'There's a line that goes, *"You're a model, actress, anything / You're a fucked up loser nobody."* There was a phrase that started coming up called the Triple Threat: *I dance, I sing, I act*. We used joke about people that would walk over their grandmothers to get success, and there's a line in John Niven's book that a certain pop star of the time "would have risen at the crack of dawn every morning for a year and swum naked through a river of shark-infested semen—cutting the throats of children, OAPs and cancer patients and throwing them behind her as she went". That's what inspired the song. The book is about someone who works in the music industry and it's exactly what it was like. At this point in time, I didn't really do coke, but reading *Kill Your Friends* made me break out in a sweat.'

'Stand In Line' sees the band revisit the slow, hypnotic riffs that had informed the likes of 'Lunacy Booth' and 'Neck Freak'. 'That's about consumerism, and how people can placate themselves as long as they've got bread and circuses,' Andy explains. 'We wanted the song to feel as if someone was almost singing this to themselves while they were sleepwalking.'

'Nobody Here But Us' was written in a Vancouver hotel room in early 1996 while the band were celebrating Michael's birthday. 'It was four in the morning and I had my acoustic guitar,' says Andy. 'We all took turns to ad-lib the vocals until the concierge came to the room and told us to shut the fuck up. It's about people and liggers that I've known, and just sticking to a small circle of friends that you trust.'

'Watch You Go' was intended to be a mid-paced Misfits style song, like 'This One's For You' or 'Lonely, Cryin', Only'. 'This and "My Voodoo Doll" are the two tracks I regret recording for *High Anxiety*,' says Andy. 'The way that we executed this is really simplistic, and it just sounds so throwaway.'

'If It Kills Me', on the other hand, has been a staple of the band's set as recently as 2018. 'I remember writing this on a really hot night in 2002,' says Andy. 'My wife and son had gone to her parents' for a weekend, and I'd been left at home with the intention of writing new material. I'd gone to a football game and met up with some friends in the pub. I'd come home feeling like the king of the world with all these ideas. I set up my guitar and mic and belted out a rough version and woke up the next day to clear away all the empty beer cans before my wife got home. I went out to the bin and my neighbour was smiling: "Big night, then?" I realised I'd got all the windows in the house open. His house was just directly across, and he'd heard every fucking thing. From the arrangement to Neil's drumming, it's one of my favourite songs on the album.'

'Limbo' was one of the first songs that Andy and Neil worked on together in Derby. 'I listened to loads of the band Love and tried to write a song like "A House Is Not a Motel",' says Andy. 'There's a line that says *"on the eve of my release"*. Neil started laughing and asked if I'd put that there because it was the name of a song by The Beyond. It must have been subliminal.'

'Last Blast' was pieced together towards the end of the writing sessions. 'I don't remember anything about this song,' Andy admits.

'Rust', one of the album's highlights, begins with a thunderous drum intro, punctuated by Andy repeatedly snarling about *'the letching corpse of rock'n'roll'*. 'I had this song as a four-track demo which was a bit like something off Big Black's *Atomizer* album,' he says. 'Neil added the drum hook, and it sounded massive. It was a real calling card for Neil, and I think having that track on the album gave him a great deal of confidence, too.'

In March, the band were booked to shoot a video for 'If It Kills Me', which would be released as a single the following month, but complications arose a few days beforehand when Neil felt his arm crack during a game of football. 'There was this netting around the pitch,' he remembers, 'and I grabbed it as I went in for the ball. My arm twisted and it cracked. I went home, and my girlfriend—who's now my wife—said that I'd gone grey. I couldn't move my arm, so I went to A&E. The ball in my shoulder socket had split in two. The doctor said the ligaments were stronger than normal because I was a drummer. They'd normally just tear, but this meant the recovery time would be much quicker. I had painkillers and put my arm in a sling. The director filmed me from the opposite side. If I held my arm against my side, I could move my hand. Watch the video and you'll see a man who's in absolute pieces. They said it would take six weeks, and the tour started in six weeks to the day. The NHS were bloody brilliant, and I've not had a problem with it since.'

Before their main tour in support of the new album kicked off in May, the band had another couple of bookings to honour. On April 6, they performed at the Hard Rock Magazine Awards in Paris, with Michael's brother, Charlie, standing in for Neil. Two weeks later, they did a live radio session at Studio Brussel in Brussels before an audience of competition winners. The call this time went out to Keith Baxter.

'We played "If It Kills Me", and Keith had demoed that track with us,' explains Michael. 'But when it came to recording it for *High Anxiety*, we'd changed it up, and Keith had to relearn it. He took it all in good humour, and the session went well.'

Reviews started to roll in for *High Anxiety*, and the album was noticeably better received than *Shameless*. *Classic Rock's* Ian Fortnam awarded it four out of five: 'It's the closing section of the album that probes the deepest into Andy Cairns's inner psyche. If this record does ultimately prove to be Therapy?'s final shot at immortality, then he wants to go out with a bang. And here it comes. If "Last Blast" is the setup, then the truly ferocious "Rust" is the ultimate teeth-rattling sucker punch. An immense track, it is very probably the first true grunge classic in ten years. *High Anxiety* is proof positive that Therapy? are a necessary evil once more.'

Hot Press's Colin Carberry gave the album a score of eight and a half out of ten, describing it as a 'clean-shaven and grown-up record. ... *High*

Anxiety is like welcoming home a much loved and entertainingly errant friend. Honestly, you'll be glad to have Therapy? back on your couch.'

Mick Stingley, writing for the website of now-defunct Los Angeles metal radio station KNAC, praised Therapy?'s return to the sound of their earlier work in a three-star review. 'Ten years into the game haven't mellowed this fighting Irish group: "Hey Satan—You Rock", the poppy lead track, starts the punk-rocking and neck-snapping fun, which grooves along and tells St. Peter to "park my car" while storming through the gates of Heaven,' he wrote. '*High Anxiety* is an aptly-titled album that cooks with speed and harmony: the gap between Nirvana and Motörhead can be bridged with this kind of Therapy?.'

On May 13, the band kicked off a short run of UK headline shows, with support from Groop Dogdrill bassist Damo Fowkes's new hardcore band 3 Stages Of Pain, and Suffolk punks Miss Black America. 'Getting Damo's new band on the bill was a no-brainer,' says Andy. 'Our management had just started looking after Miss Black America. Their shows were really good fun, and it had sold out. I remember talking to someone about the "If It Kills Me" single, and they'd mentioned how many it needed to sell to go into the Top 40—something like 1,200 copies. I looked at our tour dates and worked out that if one in five people at our shows had bought that single, we would have had another Top 40 song.' The single ended up at no. 76. 'I realised then that people were coming to our shows, but they weren't necessarily buying our records.'

The press response to the new-look Therapy? line-up was positive. In a review of the band's show at London's Mean Fiddler, *Classic Rock*'s Jerry Ewing noted that the band had played with a sense of invigoration. 'Therapy? seem to have rekindled their creative fires and are clearly having as much fun as the sweaty audience,' he wrote. 'New drummer Neil Cooper, ironically once of early Therapy? touring partners The Beyond, provides one almighty solid backbone to the band's gritty sound. The punk aggression is still there, but they've seemingly regained the knack of writing hugely enjoyable catchy tunes. Keep that up, and play with the kind of vigour they showed tonight, and Therapy? are likely to be with us for quite some time to come'.

On June 6, the band filmed a homecoming show at Belfast's Mandela Hall for future DVD release. 'We hadn't played Belfast in a while, and it sold out in advance,' remembers Andy. 'This was at the point when, critically, our currency was at an all-time low. *High Anxiety* did a little bit to repair that damage, but, after *Shameless*, it was difficult. Basically, every review of Therapy?, if they weren't going on about the beard, it was questioning our relevance. The gig itself was fantastic and one of the best nights of my life.'

'The gig was amazing, and we'd played "Teethgrinder" for the first time on that tour,' says Neil. 'We ran through it in the dressing room with guitars but no amps, and me drumming on a table. If you watch the *Scopophobia* DVD, you can see Michael shake my hand at the end of the song! That recording is the first time we'd ever played the song on our equipment together.'

The band once again spent the summer touring the European festival circuit, and then, on September 7, they were invited to support The Rolling Stones at Werchter Park in Belgium, as part of the Licks World Tour. Simple Minds, Clouseau, and De Mens were also on the bill. 'A lot of family came out to that one,' remembers Michael. 'It's one thing to be on *Top Of The Pops*, but to play with Rolling Stones is another thing entirely.

'That show went a lot better than I thought it would,' he adds. 'One of the coolest things that happened was that when we came to set our gear up, they had this huge ego ramp. It must have been about fifty metres long, going out into the crowd. I joked with one of the Stones crew and said, "For the exclusive use of Mick Jagger?" And he said, "You can go on that. It's your stage, so knock yourselves out."'

In late October, the four-piece headed out to Europe for an extensive tour that would take them around the Netherlands, Germany, Denmark,

Finland, Norway, Italy, Belgium, and the Czech Republic, before returning to the UK for further dates. The band's Belfast set from June was released on DVD on October 27. Directed by Perry Joseph, *Scopophobia*—meaning an irrational fear of being looked at—featured the band's full nineteen-song set in front of a sold-out hometown crowd.

'Mandela Hall seethes and moshes as the band play a triumphant set, comprising convincing performances of both fresh material … [and] old hits,' wrote *Classic Rock*'s Grant Moon. 'The sweaty vibe of the venue is captured well, but the crystal-clear sound like it was taken direct from the mixing desk: the unforgiving feed means that while you can hear just how tight Andy Cairns's four-piece has become, it's missing that "live" element, and isn't a very faithful representation of the in-yer-face Therapy? experience.'

'The gig, like most Therapy? gigs, is superb,' wrote *Drowned In Sound*'s Christopher Lloyd. 'In this time of hyped-up cod-rock bands (hello, Linkin Park), who seem to be in it for the quick buck, this is what we really need. Anyone willing to part with fifteen quid to own it is in for an aural treat.'

Towards the end of the year, things took a distinct left turn. In late November, Martin became ill after contracting an ear infection following the band's show at the London Astoria. 'I woke up the next day and noticed I had a slightly blocked ear,' he subsequent recalled, in an interview for the BBC Radio 3 documentary *Between The Ears*. 'It wasn't painful or anything. I saw my doctor and he poked around inside my ear and said I had an ear infection and gave me some antibiotic drops.

'When I was in Glasgow, my ear started to get quite painful; I ended up seeing an ear specialist who got quite angry with me and told me I shouldn't have been putting these antibiotic ear drops in, because I had a perforated ear drum. It was on a journey from Glasgow overnight to Nottingham where the real problems kicked in. I started to find myself going almost deaf in my left ear, and my right ear seemed to be losing some of its function.

'The pain started off as a mild ache, like a dull toothache, and after an hour it turned into what felt like a gradual, buzzing of electricity in my ear which exploded. It happened every ten minutes, to the point where I could hardly move or speak. Someone on the bus suggested it was a migraine, and I thought that was perfectly reasonable. I got to Nottingham and couldn't stand up properly.'

Martin was hospitalised and eventually diagnosed with a rare neurological disorder called Ramsay Hunt Syndrome. 'The virus not only left me deaf but paralysed the left side of my face and devoured my senses of taste and smell—not to mention giving me the feeling that I was being repeatedly hit on the head with a baseball bat,' he later revealed in a Q&A for a Siouxsie & The Banshees fan site. 'Luckily, I have fully recovered, aside from slight hearing loss and no sense of smell in my left nostril.'

So, back to Nottingham Rock City. With Martin resting at a nearby hotel, the band were faced with a dilemma: they could either pull the show or go on stage and play one man down. 'We were all really worried about Martin,' says Andy. 'The tour manager made the call—we did the gig and adjusted the set accordingly.'

Following the show, the mood in the dressing room was a mixture of relief and jubilation. 'I'll be blunt, but when I was sat there playing, the whole set just pinged to me,' says Neil. 'It felt that the three of us were on the same page. Suddenly, it felt more focussed and powerful. All I remember was Pete Bartlett coming into the dressing room after we played and saying, "You guys should be a three-piece again."'

Eight shows later, after finishing the tour, the band took the decision to continue as a three-piece. 'We felt awful, because Martin was so bloody ill, but with the way things were going, I think we realised that it would be a lot easier if it was just the three of us,' admits Andy. 'I loved the guy's company. He was really witty and really good fun to be around, but within the band it just became impossible.'

In early January, a meeting was called in London. Andy, Michael, and Neil informed Martin that his services were no longer required.

'Don't get me wrong, Martin's a brilliant guy, but, musically, we didn't click, and that became more apparent the longer he was in the band,' says Michael. 'The last studio session was kind of a fiasco, and, performance-wise, he'd tailed off quite a bit. But fair play to him, he said they were all fair comments and that he'd been feeling that he wanted to move on and try different things. I think he was even talking about moving back to North America at that stage.'

'It was sad,' adds Andy. 'I think that for a while, because of the way things were going with the band, and that he was a classically trained musician, people thought that he'd left us, rather than the other way round. We did what we had to do, and we were ready to move onto the next stage.'

After nine years, Therapy? were officially a trio once more. The three remaining members vowed to make more of an effort to address any grievances head-on, rather than allow them to fester. 'We actually said, "Look, let's not mess around. If something's pissing someone off, let's just flag it up straight away,"' says Michael. 'If anyone had a problem, we agreed to flag it up rather than let it build up and have a meltdown in the middle of nowhere. A lot of that comes with being a bit older; it's just a basic life skill, isn't it? It's amazing how few life skills a lot of musicians have.'

In mid-February, Backyard Babies dropped out of a spring UK tour with The Wildhearts, and it was announced that Therapy? would take their place. 'If anyone thinks that this is not just as good, if not better, a bill, then I suggest instant medical attention,' Ginger Wildheart told fans via his band's official website on February 17. 'Therapy? are one of the greatest live bands to ever exist, and I, for one, am as excited as fuck to be playing with them as our very special guests, and presumably wiping the floor with us on some nights. This is going to be a tough one.'

In March, Michael travelled to Andy's home to work on song ideas before the pair headed to Derby's Hive studios to flesh out the songs with Neil. 'Whenever my wife went to work and my son was at primary school, we'd sit in the front room and work on songs,' says Andy. 'Things started coming together really quickly, and I remember feeling really excited about what the new album would sound like.'

One thing was apparent in the album's embryonic stages: a reduced line-up would force Andy and Michael to readapt their approach to their instruments. 'I became quite lazy when we were a four-piece,' admits Andy. 'As a three-piece, you have to think of chord voicings that make sense in that environment. It woke me up—it was a challenge, but in a good way.'

'For me, it was great,' adds Michael, 'because I'd learned to play a certain way with two guitarists. This time, I could play big grinding bass riffs in songs like "Polar Bear".'

At the beginning of April, Therapy? played their first ever shows in Russia—almost nine years to the day after cancelling several gigs there in order to complete *Infernal Love*. They played Saint Petersburg's Port Club on April 2, and Moscow's DK Gorbunova the following night. Next came the tour with The Wildhearts—who'd just released the B-sides collection *Coupled With*—and openers The Glitterati. Livers: brace, brace!

'When you see The Wildhearts and Therapy? on a tour poster, the first thing you think of is probably crazy, dipsomaniac nights, but there wasn't any carnage,' admits Andy, still with an air of surprise. 'Ginger wasn't drinking on that tour. It was good to be back out on the road, playing as a three-piece. I remember thinking that some of our stuff, like "Rise Up" and all that, didn't really go down too well with the Wildhearts crowd. When we played in London and opened with "Meat Abstract", I remember our sound man Pete telling us that a bunch of Wildhearts fans were stood near the desk shouting "fucking cunts" at their top of their voices.'

'What I liked about that tour was, we took one tech and Pete for front of house,' says Michael. 'We were pulling our gear off stage, packing it away. It was like a further bonding of the new mindset of the band, all hands on deck.'

In the middle of the run, the band shared a bill with Bridgend quintet Funeral For A Friend and Belfast four-piece The Dangerfields at Mandela Hall in the latter's home town. The show was part of an eleven-day *Music Live* festival, with Iron Maiden's Bruce Dickinson set to present a very special edition of his BBC 6 Music rock show from the venue. In addition to airing tracks from the show, the Maiden vocalist joined both bands for a cover version. He played Black Sabbath's ominous, eponymous classic with Funeral For A Friend before joining Therapy? for a run through Deep Purple's 'Black Night'.

'I'm obviously a huge Iron Maiden fan, so we were talking about what song we could do with Bruce ahead of the show,' remembers Michael. 'Something like "Run To The Hills" or "The Trooper". I was like, "Let's keep it straightforward, lads. We're not going to do 'Alexander The Great', are we?" The day before the show, we found out he wanted to do "Black Night", which I had to learn twenty minutes before soundcheck. We went through it once with him and he went, "That's great!" He's always been a real gent to us.'

'The first time I met Bruce was at Donington in 1994, when he came into the dressing room and we had a chat about the Marquis de Sade,' says Andy. 'I really liked him—he's really bright and funny. When we did "Black Night", I stressed that I was certainly no Ritchie Blackmore; there weren't any guitar gymnastics, but it was a lot of fun to do.'

The band returned to England to complete the remaining dates with The Wildhearts, including a memorable show at London's Hammersmith Palais on May 10. 'The filling of an extremely meaty sandwich indeed,

Therapy? are cocky, vulnerable and lovable all at once,' wrote *Classic Rock*'s Dave Ling. 'When Andy Cairns's guitar strap fails, he allows the instrument to crash to the floor, and struts around the stage like Freddie Starr on Viagra. Naturally, the *Troublegum*-era material is best-received, although "Teethgrinder", "Potato Junkie" and "Hey Satan—You Rock" help secure a rousing response.'

On June 1, the band decamped to Stanbridge Farm Studios in Hayward's Heath in West Sussex to demo the new album with soundman Pete Bartlett, producer of *High Anxiety*. 'Andy and Michael were very forward-thinking when it comes to the writing process,' says Neil. 'Very early on, I knew we'd be making an album we could be proud of. The songs were good and there was a great energy between the three of us, even on the demos.'

A week later, the band loaded their gear into the van and headed an hour east to Catsfield's Parkgate Studios, where they'd record *Never Apologise, Never Explain*. They gave themselves two weeks to record—no more, no less. It didn't help that the European Football Championships were in full swing in Portugal at the time, but the deadline was comfortably met. 'Hot, claustrophobic, men sweating,' remembers Michael. 'We didn't really leave Parkgate unless we needed toothpaste. I think we might have gone for a drink maybe once? How things change.'

The album's opener, 'Rise Up (Make Yourself Well)', is informed by the frantic, feral feel of their earlier releases. 'With this record and Martin gone, I was very self-conscious about getting back in touch with the music that meant a lot more to me,' says Andy. 'I started listening back to old post-punk records, back from when I was a kid: Joy Division, Public Image, Magazine, and all that. I started listening to Fugazi again. "Rise Up" is totally Fugazi; it's got that elasticated, almost African bass line, and a sort of excoriating guitar. Neil added a bit of jungle in there, too. There was a sense of taking back responsibility that I think we'd lost when Graham and Martin were in the band. We'd got this really hard work ethic back, which reminded very much of when the band formed in 1989.'

The pace is maintained with 'Die Like A Motherfucker', propelled by a buzz-saw, early industrial metal riff. 'That was a stomper,' says Andy. 'The title is a play on the "Like A Motherfucker" sticker Johnny Thunder used to have on his guitar. It's got some intricate guitar, too; I dipped into my Geordie Walker from Killing Joke bag to come up with that one.'

'Perish The Thought' was inspired by Don DeLillo's 1997 novel *Underworld*, with 'a bit of early twentieth-century philosophy thrown in for good measure', as Andy puts it. Music-wise, it's a grab bag of genres and ideas: Motown, lean riffing, and a groove reminiscent of Rapeman's version of 'Just Got Paid' by ZZ Top.

For Andy, 'Here Be Monsters' started as a title, sparked by an afternoon viewing *Pirates Of The Caribbean* with his young son. Inspired by a riff on one of Michael's demo CDs—named 'Rainbow Riff' in a nod to Ritchie Blackmore's band—Andy had the idea to write a simple garage-rock song. 'The initial vision of a three-chord trick, knuckle-dragging garage screamer has been honed into a head bobbing thing of fury,' Andy wrote in his diary on the band's website diary at the time, noting that The Constantines and Propellerheads also had a hand in shaping the finished song.

'So-Called Life' was written with Clutch in mind, while its title was inspired in part by the writer Chuck Palahniuk. 'There's a truthfulness in the way he describes things,' says Andy. 'I really regret the title, though. It was only that the song was done that I found out that *My So-Called Life* was a teen soap opera that starred Claire Danes.'

'Panic' was written quickly while the band were together in Derby. The two-minute song hurtles along at different tempos and creates a fitting sense of unease. 'The music sounds like it's hyperventilating,' suggests Andy. 'I think Neil asked if we'd ever played "Animal Bones" from *Babyteeth* much. I had a riff that had a similar feel. The track was based on a conversation that Neil and I were having about white-collar crime, and how come the people at the top always get away with it.'

'Polar Bear'—which was released as a download single with 'Rock You

Monkeys' on June 13—is built around a repetitive, Shellac-esque guitar line, propped up by Michael's stoic bass and Neil's inventive drumming. 'This song's about an anxiety attack and feeling like you're trapped in a room or your head is in a cage,' Andy explains. 'Neil gets full credit for making the song the way it is. I wanted the vocals to be deadpan, like someone who's completely beaten and had enough. I sang the song as if I was pacing around a room, completely driving myself nuts and wearing a trench in the ground with my footsteps.'

The main riff in 'Rock You Monkeys' recalls Turbonegro at their most grimy. In fact, the song itself sits well alongside the fuzzed-up garage rock of 2001's *Shameless*, and offers some respite from the claustrophobia of much of the rest of the album. 'We'd written songs like "Die Like A Motherfucker" and "Rise Up", and I think I'd panicked and felt like we needed some kind of pop song in there,' says Andy. 'It's about what can happen when you're in a band who've been around as long as Therapy?, where people want you to behave in a certain way and ask when you're writing the next *Troublegum*. People like that comfort, but it's not just in music. It's in everyday life; it's the certain buttons that people can press to make you almost dance as if you've got currents going through wires in your shoulders. It's a bit glam rock and has a nice hook.'

'Dead' is about severing links with the past, the words as spectacularly blunt as the riffs: '*Friends, who fuckin' needs 'em? / They only let you down / They take your time, they bleed you dry.*' 'This is about an old acquaintance of mine in Dublin,' Andy explains. 'We'd helped them out with money and getting started in the business, and it was like, almost as soon as the band were seen as completely uncool, he dropped us like a ton of shit. This song was written for him. It's quite blunt and to the point, and deliberately so; it's almost meant to be like the sound of someone cutting ties.'

When the album was released, Andy revealed that the guitar work in 'Long Distance' had reminded someone of early R.E.M. 'This got me thinking about how much I used to love that band,' he remembers.

'*Murmur* and *Reckoning* were big albums for me. *Reckoning* was beautiful, like someone half-whispering, half-crying secrets into your ear. "Long Distance" was one of the first songs we had. I was playing along with At The Drive-In's *Relationship Of Command*, and I really liked some of the chord shapes. I kept repeating this riff I'd written and it sounded like At The Drive-In playing "Every Breath You Take" by The Police.

'I didn't have the lyrics until I'd visited an acupuncturist,' he adds. 'I'd been having sinus trouble and headaches. While he was sticking needles in me, he hit me with some Zen philosophy. He said, "People get stuck in patterns and bogged down as if their feet are walking in molasses." He asked me when I took my dog for a walk, whether I turned left or right out of the front gate. He said I should go the opposite direction, things like that, and it would free you psychologically. It sounds absolutely ridiculous, but it did work. I came back from that session and wrote the lyrics in five minutes: "*I start today / I drive the other way.*"'

The chaotic Les Savy Fav-meets-The Jesus Lizard clatter of 'The Ship Is Sinking' takes a similar lyrical cue to 'Dead': who can you really trust? 'One of the good things about Neil joining the band was it made us realise who our true friends were in the business,' says Andy. 'It also got us thinking about how, in life, the easiest thing to do sometimes is to run away. I'd rather go down with an idea than settling or sell myself out instead of desperately grabbing the next lifeboat to drag me out of this shit. We'd rather just stick to our ideals.'

'Save The Sermon' builds on the late comedian Bill Hicks's philosophy that life is 'just a ride', backed with a riff down-tuned to C, with what Andy calls 'a South Of Heaven bit and a Helmet bit', including a spirited solo take on free jazz. 'I can't remember that much about the song, which probably tells you all you need to know,' he adds.

Album closer 'Last One To Heaven's A Loser' was partly written at a soundcheck in Italy—details are scant, but Andy recalls the dressing room being decked out with pornographic wallpaper—and the rest at his home, where the furnishings are infinitely more salubrious. The result? Revolting Cocks meets 'I Was Made For Loving You'-era KISS disco-rock, with an added 'Cossack' middle-eight and an auto-wah frenzy.

When the band were recording the demo at Stanbridge Farm, Pete suggested they play the song as fast as they could. 'It was one of those things where the title came first and the rest of the song was written around it,' says Andy. 'When I initially conceived the idea of the song, it was more mid-paced, like "Die Laughing". I think it's too fast. I sometimes wonder if we lost some of the power going down that route.'

Never Apologise, Never Explain was released on September 27. The monochromatic artwork centred on the number three: three wooden supports on the cover, three plugs in one adaptor on the back, three pylons. It gave the sense of unity and a strengthened purpose. Indivisible.

Although the album failed to chart, reviews were largely positive across the board. *Drowned In Sound*'s Christopher Lloyd awarded the album nine out of ten, noting that it 'visits the same territory as *Pleasure Death* and mixes it with the more melodic moments of *Troublegum* without looking too far back into the past'. RTÉ's Harry Guerin gave it three out of five: 'With the departure of cellist and second guitarist Martin McCarrick, Therapy? are back as a three-piece, but their snarl remains as loud as ever. With this album gruff from beginning to end, a return to Therapy?'s chart days seems a long way off. Then again, no one ever won money writing off this band.'

The album earned a three-star review from *Classic Rock*, too. 'After doing the rounds for years with less than gargantuan rewards, Therapy? could be forgiven for sounding a little world-weary by now,' wrote Carol Clerk. 'But following last year's *High Anxiety*, they're roaring in with no holds barred, and they're not bringing happiness and joy. Therapy? are especially compulsive when at their most malevolent. The prevailing mood is at least curmudgeonly and cynical and, at best, just screaming mad.'

Radio 1 Rock Show presenter Mary Anne Hobbs—who a few years earlier had declared on air that copies of *Suicide Pact—You First* should have been destroyed—had clearly forgiven the band (and vice versa), and now invited them to record a Maida Vale session on October 1. Over the course of a few hours, they recorded 'Up', 'Die Like A Motherfucker', 'So-Called Life', and 'Panic'. In the band's online diary, Andy, after a week of press and travel, noted, 'It all sounds live and energetic, though I'm so spaced out with tiredness I feel as though I'm doing the whole thing in a huge insulated suit.'

Following three days of rehearsals, the band kicked off a two-week tour of Europe with Amplifier in tow, followed by another fortnight in the UK and Ireland with Tokyo Dragons and Winnebago Deal in support. After clocking up thousands of miles, the band closed their 2004 account with a sweaty, packed show at Dublin's Ambassador Theatre on December 8.

Although they had had to navigate a tricky start to the year, Therapy? ended 2004 on an upswing. The next twelve months would prove to be just as busy.

YEAR 2005
SIXTEEN/no sleep 'til
castle donington

On January 23, Andy and Michael performed an acoustic set in Belfast as part of the One Day—Aid For Asia charity event. The benefit show featured forty acts across three venues—the Limelight, Katy Daly's, Spring & Airbrake—to raise money for victims of the Indian Ocean earthquake and tsunami, which had struck on December 26.

'The tsunami gig at the Limelight was fantastic,' remembers Andy. 'The crowd were brilliant, singing along and forgiving us various bum notes and forgotten lyrics. I also had a chance to catch up with a lot of old faces I hadn't seen in ages, and saw some good bands. My favourites were the Bete

Noires, Fighting With Wire, LaFaro, Just A Word, Corrigan, and Robyn G. Shiels, to name but a few. Most importantly, lots of cash was raised.'

Six days later, the band returned to Athens, Greece, for the first time since the *Troublegum* tour in 1994. 'The show at Gagarin 205 was incredible,' says Andy. 'We hadn't played there for nearly eleven years, but we still managed to get a large and enthusiastic crowd at the gig. There were way more people than we expected and everybody we met was friendly, helpful, and cool as fuck.'

During the winter, Andy recorded a vocal for Belgian experimentalists 48 Cameras, reciting a text by author Nicholas Royle for the album *After All, Isn't Tango The Dance Of The Drunk Man?*, which would be released the following year through the Interzone label. 'Nicholas is the author of two of our favourite books—*The Directors Cut* and *Antwerp*—and 48 Cameras make sometimes strange and often beautiful music,' he explains. 'Basically, I read a piece of Nicholas's text over the phone to Jean Marie's answering machine, and he added it to some music.'

On March 25, the band began a twenty-three-date tour of Europe and the UK at Paard van Troje in The Hague. 'I like this town and I like this venue,' remembers Andy. 'In 1999, I took acid after the Crossing Border Festival and went AWOL. They were marvellous psychedelic times, I can assure you.

'After the gig, John, our tour manager went missing,' he adds. 'He'd gone to pick up some excellent bottles of wine. He burst onto the bus at 4am with a bag of wine, exclaiming *Ta-da!* like the hero returning from battle, only to find us all fast asleep. Boring, boring bastards.'

The tour continued through Luxembourg, Belgium, Holland, Sweden, and France, where Therapy? were invited to record a session for Europe 2 Radio in Paris on April 12. 'We were doing a radio session for the *Arthur et les pirates* show, which would be broadcast live on the drive-time show at 4pm,' remembers Neil. 'We arrived to set up the equipment. The bass and guitar setups were normal, but what do I get? Yes, you guessed it, an

161

electronic drum kit. My favourite. It sounded pretty cool, actually, and the sound engineers and studio team were brilliant. We played "Nowhere" and "Polar Bear" for them. You get such a great buzz doing sessions that are going straight out to two million people. If I drop a stick, fall off my seat, or if one of the lads breaks a string, it could all be game over. Brilliant! You can't beat it.'

The band completed this leg of the tour with shows at Brighton's Concorde 2, Swindon's Furnace, and Nottingham's Rock City on April 21–23. The following months saw them return to Turkey to play shows at Izmir's Bornova Hayat Acikhava on May 13 and at Istanbul's Venue Maslak the following night. They had been due to play these two cities the previous year, until the promoters cancelled at the last minute.

'Our first surprise of the day came when we saw a Therapy? feature in the Turkish Airways in-flight magazine,' remembers Michael. 'It was very surreal and funny to see the other passengers doing a double-take when Andy boarded the aeroplane.'

In Izmir, the band took the opportunity to use their soundcheck to work on a new song called 'Passers By'. Much of the summer was punctuated by European festival appearances, including a headlining appearance on the Napster stage during the third day of Download at Donington. The stage opened early on Sunday morning, beginning with Henry Rollins performing a spoken-word 'Sunday Sermon'. The bill also featured The Dresden Dolls, Trivium, and Deftones vocalist Chino Moreno's side-project Team Sleep. Despite beginning the day with a 6am flight to Helsinki (having played Estonia's Rabarock Järvakandi the previous day) and on to Heathrow, the band's first Donington appearance since 1995 was a success.

On August 12, Therapy? played the Bulldog Bash at Shakespeare County Raceway in Stratford-upon-Avon, their second appearance at the biker-run festival in five years. 'I met Sonny Barger, who founded the Oakland charter of the Hells Angels,' says Michael. 'He'd just released his book *Freedom: Credos From The Road*, so I got that signed and had a chat. The festival was great; there was mayhem everywhere, but, in a weird way, it was still family friendly. I think if we sounded like Motörhead or ZZ Top, we might have had an easier time. We weren't going to bust out "Loser Cop" in the middle of the set.'

On September 22—Andy's fortieth birthday—the band learned that Spitfire Records had taken up the option of releasing a third Therapy? album. 'For a few months, I thought we might be looking for a new deal,' says Andy. 'I'd talked myself into thinking that we wouldn't have a label, so I didn't want to write a lot of stuff only for it not to be released. At my birthday party, Gerry told me the news, and I think that's when I really started writing for the next album.'

Save for an appearance at Belgium's Rock Ternat festival on October 8, the band spent the rest of the year focusing on their ninth full-length album. They reconvened at Derby's Hive Studio in early November to rehearse a batch of new songs: 'Sprung', 'Unconsoled', 'Something's Got To Happen', 'Rain Hits Concrete', 'Joe Blow', 'Passer By/Our White Noise', 'Overspill', and 'Fearless Leader Fails'.

'The first song we'd written was "Sprung", because Michael had sent the riff for that on a CD, along with the bass line for what became "Unconsoled",' remembers Andy. 'I was listening to so much Killing Joke at this point, especially the self-titled album which Andy Gill produced. If you listen to songs like "Into The Light" or "Rain Hits Concrete", I wouldn't be surprised if Geordie Walker got on the phone and asked for his riffs back.'

In November, the band met with several prospective producers, due to Pete Bartlett's unavailability due to touring commitments. They met with Pedro Ferreira, who produced The Darkness's 2003 debut, *Permission To Land*. 'We really clicked with Pedro,' says Michael. 'He was super-enthusiastic, a really nice guy, and had quite big plans, sonically, for the album. It was interesting to hear his different approach.'

On December 11, the band decamped to Pingle Barn, a holiday cottage in Doveridge, about twenty minutes' drive from Stoke-on-Trent. There, they would demo eighteen new songs over the course of five days. 'We wanted to go somewhere that wasn't rock'n'roll, so our manager found us a place in the middle of nowhere so we could set up our equipment and make as much noise as we wanted,' says Andy.

'It was a mammoth task,' Michael adds, 'least of all because we had to turn a converted farmhouse into a makeshift studio work twelve-to-fifteen-hour days to translate our music into cohesive demos. We arrived to find that this "isolated" house was right next to two family homes. Did they really want a noisy rock band disturbing the peace for the best part of the week?'

The living room furniture was moved out as the band set up their amps as though they were to play a gig. Mics were fed through a mixer and into an eight-track digital recorder hooked up to another mixer and laptop. After some trial and error, the instruments' levels were attained. 'We decided to go for it, and, fair play to the neighbours, we didn't get one word of complaint,' Michael smiles.

'Looking back on it now, it was insane,' Andy adds. 'I had two full 4x12 stacks, Michael had two Warwick bass rigs, Neil had his kit, and we had a PA system in this tiny living room. We'd get up in the morning and play all the songs from start to finish.'

By December 17, the band had demoed eighteen new songs ready for the new album. In three weeks time, they would start recording their ninth album at Jacobs Studios in Surrey. The following night, Andy joined This Is Menace on stage for the song 'F8' at London's Mean Fiddler.

'It was a great year,' says Michael. 'No one left the band or broke any bones, and we were going into the new year knowing that we had an album ready to make. Well done, everyone.'

YEAR SEVENTEEN/'all you optimists can kiss my ass!'

Recording of *One Cure Fits All* began at Jacobs Studios in Farnham, Surrey, on January 9. Set in a Georgian farmhouse, the facility was named after a breed of sheep who grazed in the countryside around the building, and had previously hosted the likes of The Cult, The Smiths, The Wedding Present, and The Beyond—basically any band with 'The' in their name, so it made perfect sense for Therapy? to join the illustrious list of acts.

At producer Pedro Ferreira's suggestion, the trio set up to play the songs together, hoping to capture the energy of a live performance. Neil's kit didn't sound as punchy as usual, so it was dismantled and set up in a different room. 'Andy and I stayed in the same room, but Neil was next door,' says Michael. 'We could see him on a screen, and we joked that he could have done his drums at home.'

'I was recording via satellite!' Neil adds. 'It was the weirdest thing, playing along with the lads with all communication through a video monitor and headphones. We were recording "live" takes, and in hindsight this defeated the whole object. For me, it was pretty disconnecting, recording like that.'

After setting up microphones and setting the levels again, they started recording the album, beginning with 'Deluded Son', before heading to bed. 'Someone in the building said that The Smiths recorded *The Queen Is Dead* here, so I asked which room Morrissey stayed in,' says Andy. 'He'd stayed in the room above the studio, so I stayed in there.'

Pedro advised Andy to take measures to look after his voice due to the wintry weather and long hours in the studio. 'Justin Hawkins [of The Darkness] has got an almost operatic vocal style, which meant he had to be very careful during recording,' Andy explains. 'Pedro had me doing warm-up exercises and taking hot showers, running the water on my throat so it would open up and all that. It was completely new to me, which is funny, considering how long we'd been making albums by that point.'

While the songs were initially recorded in a live setting, Pedro's method of capturing the vocals proved to be a source of frustration. 'We got on really well with Pedro, but it was painstaking recording each song line by line,' says Andy. 'It wasn't just for the vocals. It was with lead guitar, it was with the drum fills, and everything, but, then again, you know these things happen for a reason. That's the way Pedro works, and it's proved to be very successful. They call it "comping", but it doesn't work for Therapy?. I think you either do a good take or you try again.'

'We'd listen to each song, bar by bar, would discuss which take sounded best,' adds Michael. 'It sounded good, but I think the editing process afterwards kind of sucked the energy out of it. I'm not mad on the finished version, actually. I'm disappointed that this album one didn't have that grunt to it. We had a good time making the album, but the end result sounded quite safe. You live and learn.'

'I agree,' says Neil. 'Pedro's such a brilliant guy and talented producer. I can completely understand why his method works for certain bands, but it wasn't right for us. The idea was to create a near-perfect "live" take of each song—we would record six or seven versions all playing together, then sit and listen through each version, bar by bar, and rate which version felt the best. Piecing all the parts with the highest votes together afterwards. For a band like us, this ironed out so much sonic energy and focus.'

After the ambient opener, 'Outro', 'Sprung' features some thrilling drum work from Neil and one of the album's standout riffs. 'Michael sent me the riff, and I thought it was amazing,' says Andy. 'At this point, he had a digital recording setup at home, and he was good at programming the drum machine. It was far removed from the days of the Gringo drum machine we used in the past. I was listening to a lot of Killing Joke at the time, so the chorus and chiming arpeggios were definitely influenced by Geordie Walker.'

Next was 'Deluded Son', another song informed by Love and their 1967 album *Forever Changes*. 'It has this weird, heavy psychedelia,' says Andy. 'It's about people we've all hung about with who had an incredible sense of their own self-importance, and it has a Hüsker Dü feel.'

Like 'Sprung', 'Into The Light' was inspired by Killing Joke's 1994 album *Pandemonium*. 'I had a really good riff which was discordant and grinding,' explains Andy. 'I wanted to make it something like "Stand In Line" from *High Anxiety*. I like what Neil did with the drums, but I think the song is too simplistic. It's about dealing with surrender.'

'Lose It All', a song about someone having a breakdown and realising that everything could disappear from their grasp, was written from scratch while the band were working on demos at Pingle Barn the previous month. 'I think we had a little bit of Fugazi in mind for that one,' says Andy, 'but it wasn't as naked and as raw as we'd envisioned. Something was lost in translation in the arrangement, and it didn't really pay off, that one.'

'Dopamine, Serotonin And Adrenaline' was shaped by Milwaukee quartet Die Kreuzen's song 'Elizabeth', as featured on their 1988 album *Century Days*. 'Those are the three chemicals you need in your body to make sure you're level,' says Andy. 'There's an acoustic guitar on this song, but it's so low in the mix you can't hear it. I like the melody and feel of it, but I wish I hadn't used the three words as the chorus; it just sounds lazy.'

'Unconsoled' is underpinned by Michael's simple yet effective bass line and a jazzy drum pattern. According to Andy, the lyrics are 'a midlife crisis on tape'. 'I got the title from Kazuo Ishiguro's book *The Unconsoled*, which came out in 1995,' says Andy. 'I was having a phone conversation with Ricky Warwick in America. He said, "You know, I haven't seen you in years, but I think about you every day." I thought that was a beautiful thing to say, and it went into the song. Michael sent me the bass line and it was sounded really mournful. It was brilliant bass line, but I don't think we developed the song enough. I think we were so caught up in knowing that we had a new record deal that a lot of the ideas were actually rushed.'

Floral roadside tributes inspired 'Our White Noise', another album highlight, shaped by The Ruts and Empire, a band featuring Generation X's Bob 'Derwood' Andrews and Mark Laff. 'They were big in influencing the likes of Fugazi,' says Andy. 'I was trying to write something like that. The song follows a news story about two girls who were stabbed and left for dead in Reading. A lot of people had walked by and hadn't noticed they were there. People wondered if they didn't see or just didn't want to get involved. In the song, I repeated the same verse and chorus, which I hate to this day.'

Kurt Vonnegut's 1969 anti-war novel *Slaughterhouse-Five* inspired the song 'Private Nobody', which is centred on the book's kind-faced protagonist, Billy Pilgrim. And so it goes. 'There's just something about that book,' explains Andy. 'I even like the film of it as well. I saw it when I was ten years old, and I remember all the scenes on [planet] Tralfamadore. The science-fiction and war scenes are really well paced, and there's parts that wouldn't be out of place in a Spike Milligan movie as well. Just the sheer absurdity of it all. The book is incredible in the way it describes the bombing of Dresden, and the slang it uses. I thought I'd put myself in Billy Pilgrim's shoes when I wrote the lyrics.'

'Rain Hits Concrete' is equal parts piss and vinegar, held together by a chugging riff. 'I had the opening line, "*All you optimists can kiss my ass*", which was something like a Flann O'Brien book,' says Andy. 'I thought, *What more misery can I think of? Rain hitting concrete.* You know, it's a grey day in Northern Ireland and everything is horrible. I just thought if I hammered that point home enough, it might even become mantric. It's one of the songs I like on this album.'

'Fear Of God' has a hypnotic, heavy riff and an opening line about '*soldiers with nothing to kill but time*'. 'I remember lifting that line from the Joaquin Phoenix film *Buffalo Soldiers*,' admits Andy. 'It's a very mixed-up song—I don't like it.'

The discordant riff that informs 'Heartbeat Hits' was re-appropriated from an old, unreleased song called 'Eggs'. 'We wrote it when me and Fyfe were still getting on, maybe in the summer of 1994,' says Andy. 'We were talking about a band called Bastro, who had a great album called *Rode Hard And Put Up Wet*. It had all these great riffs, and I played a similar one for Fyfe. We had the music but we didn't put any lyrics over the top of it. It can't really decide if it's a post-punk pop song or a skronk song. It just falls between the two stools.'

The final song, 'Walk Through Darkness', was written in the vein of 'Nowhere', 'Screamager', and 'Lonely, Cryin', Only', but the end product is something quite different. 'The end section, where it goes a bit "Celtic string", is maybe ill-advised,' says Andy. 'I don't mind the song. It's about 75 percent there, but as a songwriter I'm very disappointed. A little more time could have been taken to make it better.'

Andy reveals that *One Cure Fits All* is, after *Shameless*, his least favourite Therapy? album. Despite the buoyant mood in the band, he admits that he felt he was going down a creative cul-de-sac when he started writing the material in late 2005.

'I think a lot of the songs were written for the sake of it,' he says. 'I like some of the songs on the album, like "Private Nobody" and "Deluded Son", but I think some of it sounds unfinished. I wasn't hearing any music that was moving me emotionally or wanted to challenge myself musically. The album I listened to most while making this record was *Forever Changes* by Love, an album from the 1960s. When I was writing songs for *Never Apologise, Never Explain*, I was excited. This time, there was always a nagging feeling of whether the songs could be better, if I was repeating myself, or whether a song sounded finished or not. I was never happy with what I'd done.'

'I think we collectively feel this album could've turned out much better,' adds Neil. 'Personally, I think there are some great songs on there, but the production and mix doesn't work for Therapy?. The album would be a different beast if we re-recorded or remixed it today.'

Despite Andy's concerns, the album was received positively by the press. I awarded it four *K*s in *Kerrang!*, noting, 'This album sounds like a band with fire in their bellies. Where as some bands who've endured a career as long this three-piece choose to settle into nauseating complacency, Therapy? have delivered an album which keeps you on your toes and does not disappoint.'

Classic Rock's Simon Williams was similarly impressed. In an eight-out-of-ten review, he wrote, 'Therapy? are taut and muscular on "Sprung", crunchy and melodic on "Deluded Son", and shouty and incessant on "Rain Hits Concrete". With nary a riff wasted or hook line tossed away, this is forty-five minutes of pure punk metal rock for everyone.'

'Therapy? are well and truly carving their own tributary away from the mainstream, but there are so many bands sailing on by, powerless in the current, who could learn a great deal from these three pairs of safe hands,' wrote *Pixelsurgeon*'s Sam Gilbey in a seven-out-of-ten review, while *Drowned In Sound*'s Ben Yates concluded, 'Many of the songs on the album are potentially radio friendly, but after the challenging depth of *Never Apologise, Never Explain*, some Therapy? fans may leave feeling slightly disappointed. One thing you can't accuse Therapy? of is making an album twice, and *One Cure Fits All* again delves into uncharted territory.'

The album was released on April 24, but despite the swell of positive press it reached only no. 152 in the UK chart. That said, it had fared better than *Never Apologise, Never Explain*, which had failed to chart at all.

'The reception was all right, but everything seemed to be staying in the same place,' Andy reflects. 'Nothing was going forward. We were getting good reviews, we were getting good attendances at club shows, and we were beginning to play bigger shows around Europe again, which was all really, really good. We were getting added to proper festival bills in mainland Europe, but things like the local festivals back home that had put us on so much in the 90s, they wouldn't touch us with a barge pole, so it was kind of frustrating.'

The band kicked off their touring schedule with an acoustic in-store appearance at HMV in Belfast on April 28 ('We sold a shit load of albums that day,' says Andy), before heading out to Europe for a headline gig at Winterhur's Gaswerk Kulturzentrum in Switzerland a week later. Next up was a live set and an acoustic performance at the London Guitar Show, held at the Wembley Conference Centre on May 6 and 7.

'There was a never-ending supply of ice-cold Becks, Jägermeister, and Jack Daniel's backstage,' says Michael. 'I remember bending [Living Colour bassist] Doug Wimbish's ear. He was very gracious. I can see why those events are popular, and you could get into trouble, stuck in those conference rooms with nothing to do and a company credit card in your pocket. It was a very surreal gig—almost like a weird showcase. I think, for the kind of crowd that goes to those events, we weren't really their cup of tea, but it was a good experience.'

'It was like playing in front of a snooker audience,' laughs Neil.

Following a headline tour of the UK and Ireland, the band spent the summer on the European festival circuit. Towards the end of their summer schedule, they offered fans the chance to vote for their three favourite Therapy? songs, with the twelve most popular selections captured for a privately recorded web gig. The set, which was released the following January, was recorded at the Snug in Derby (formerly known as the Hive) and featured the following setlist: 'Screamager', 'A Moment Of Clarity', 'Straight Life', 'Knives', 'Teethgrinder', 'Lonely, Cryin', Only', 'Die Laughing', 'Nowhere', 'Dancin' With Manson', 'Evil Elvis', 'If It Kills Me', and 'Suing God'.

In September, the band began to notice an upswing when they began a lengthy tour of France. 'Things really hit rock bottom in 2003,' says Andy. 'But on this tour we began to meet people in the music business who'd grown up with the band. They were in their early teens when *Troublegum* had been released, and they were actually on our side. Our French promoter, Dominic, was one of these people. We had used to do well in France. During *Troublegum* and *Infernal Love*, we played massive venues, soap stars would come to our gigs, we'd be on the cover of magazines, we played with

Sting on national TV. After *Semi-Detached* came out in 1998, everything went downhill. We meant nothing in France. Dominic booked shows in what we'd call "secondary territories", and it was fantastic. They wanted to hear the old stuff *and* the new stuff, so we played these really long sets.'

During this period, Therapy? appeared at Festival Froggle Rock in Verneuil sur Avre and Festival Polyrock in Landerneau, and played gigs in Vauréal, Périgueux, and Biarritz, plus a bigger club show in Paris. 'Quite a few of the local rugby stars came to the Biarritz show,' remembers Andy. 'After the show, Dominic took us to a very posh nightclub to celebrate. It was right on the coast and the water looked really inviting. We stripped completely naked and went for a swim at one in the morning. When we eventually went to the club, people were laughing. We'd realised that they could see us take our clothes off from behind the mirrored glass.'

The French tour ended on October 14 with a show with New Model Army at Montivilliers's Gymnase Christian Gand. Two weeks later, the band arrived in Dublin to play two shows on Halloween: an afternoon acoustic set at HMV, followed by gig supporting Motörhead at the Olympia Theatre.

'That was a day of extremes,' Michael laughs. 'We'd done a festival with Motörhead, but never done a proper club show with them, so that was a highlight for me. The funniest part of the night was when Lemmy came in asked us if we knew the words to "Rosalie" [a song by Bob Seger, later covered by Thin Lizzy]. Maybe he thought every Irish band learns them at school or something. It was so old-school. Instead of looking them up online, it was like, "I don't know the lyrics … I'll go and ask the lads." There were definitely cheat sheets on the stage, but he did a great job. It was a great night: we played a blinder, and, as a Motörhead fan, I love the Phil [Campbell] and Mikkey [Dee] line-up.'

The year ended with a run of shows across Germany, from Dresden to Hameln, with support from one-time skateboarder and former Thumb frontman Claus Grabke. Just like their recent shows in France, the band noticed a similar swell of fans at their German shows.

'There was a noticeably different spin on things,' says Michael. 'I think the older industry types had either moved on or disappeared. It was good for us. With this new breed of promoter, they understood that the music business was changing considerably. There were bands who couldn't be bothered with touring. They either didn't like it or were just lazy. All of a sudden, their accountants would ring them up and remind them that records weren't selling and they'd have to start playing shows again. I think it's because of that the whole touring side really picked up again.

'We've met a lot of bands backstage at festivals and stuff, going, "For fuck's sake, I thought I was set for life, and now I need to go and schlep round Europe again,"' he adds. 'That's quite grim, I think. Bands can't expect to live off their royalties anymore. We were quite lucky in that we always liked touring and always played shows. There's always a different way of doing things—it's about being flexible—so working with these younger promoters was really exciting for us. It really opened up the possibilities of what we could do in the future.'

YEAR EIGHTEEN/volcanoes, sharks, and boozy bribery

On February 26, Universal Records released a compilation of Therapy's BBC Radio sessions titled *Music Through A Cheap Transistor*. Taken from various sessions recorded between 1991 and 1998 for John Peel, *The Evening Session*, *Friday Rock Show*, and *The Rock Show*, the twenty-eight-track download collection featured live favourites and three brand new songs: 'Pile Of Bricks', 'The Sweeney', and 'Lost Highway', a cover of a 1948 country song made popular by Hank Williams.

'To be honest, "The Sweeney" was a bit of a piss take,' says Andy.

'At the time, Britpop was really in, and I was joking about how a lot of famous British records—from The Beatles to The Rolling Stones—use the same kind of progression, a descending bass line. You can hear it in "Dear Prudence", a lot of Cream records, and "Remember You're A Womble" by Mike Batt. This was recorded in August 1995—Fyfe had completely lost all interest by this point and would half-heartedly drum along. That had an effect on us, so I thought, *Fuck it, I'll just go for a Sex Pistols guitar sound.*'

For band archivist Michael, the *Music Through A Cheap Transistor* release was a particularly satisfying document of their many trips to the legendary Maida Vale recording studio. 'I had most of the songs on cassette, which I'd taped off the radio,' says Michael. 'You would never get a listening copy out of the BBC. Up to this point, we hadn't really done a lot of retrospective stuff. The idea of the release just came out of the blue, and it was nice to give all those alternative versions a legitimate release. Andy and I wrote some sleeve notes, and it was a nice wee package. People really dug it, and it brought back a lot of memories.'

Classic Rock's Henry Yates awarded the compilation five out of ten. 'This being the twenty-first century, where it's more socially acceptable to have herpes than to own a tape collection, the punk-metallers' raucous visits to the Beeb have been assembled as a glimmering digital download,' he wrote. 'Here, it generally results in a solid re-tread of the tunes with slightly muffled vocals. Unmissable for Therapy? completists, then, but optional for anyone else.'

This year saw little in the way of live engagements compared to previous years—Therapy? played eighteen shows over the course of twelve months—but the trio's agent booked shows in some weird and wonderful locations. On April 6 and 7, they performed shows in Saint Pierre and Saint Gilles on Ile de la Reunion, a small island located between Madagascar and Mauritius.

'Playing gigs on a volcanic island in the middle of the Indian Ocean was a new experience for all of us,' Michael laughs. 'The first gig almost didn't go ahead because the volcano was active, and it was all kicking off—there was a huge dust cloud coming towards Saint Pierre, and everything was locked down.'

'That first gig was very odd,' adds Neil. 'We were on this idyllic island, relaxing, and I was looking up and down the beach thinking, *Who, out of this lot, is going to come to see us?* I remember standing in the venue's car park about an hour before the gig, watching the glowing volcano in the distance, while the promoter made frantic calls to find out if there was going to be an evacuation. My wife laughs about that to this day: when we were out there, she was sat eating her cornflakes when the news came on the TV saying the eruption was likely and the authorities were on the verge of evacuating the island. Thankfully, nothing materialised.'

During their visit, Michael had a brush with death while swimming. 'I ended up on this weird tidal swell and got out of my depth,' he remembers. 'It was going to be a very bad rock'n'roll death. A little later, I was talking to the locals and they said not to go in there again, because there was apparently a coral wall in the bay. When the tide reaches a certain level, tiger sharks can pop over it. I was thinking someone could have told us that before suggesting it was a nice beach to visit. It was an anarchic trip, with the threat of certain death from the elements.'

'I remember that conversation,' laughs Neil. 'We'd been swimming and snorkelling all day, then one of the locals told us about the sharks getting into the bay. We asked them how would we know when they did, and they replied, "Oh, you'll know."'

A few days later, on April 10, the band began another run of shows in Europe, beginning with two in Austria—at Vienna's WUK (Werkstätten und Kulturhaus) and the Orpheum in Graz—followed by several in the Balkans, taking in Ljubljana, Zagreb, Belgrade, Bucharest, and Kiev, and finishing at SDK MAI in Moscow on the 20th. 'I liked playing the Balkans because people were so up for it,' remembers Andy. 'There was a veneer of organisation, but there was an underlying chaos. In Romania, the local promoter would tell us stories that some of the statues were paid for with Audi cars instead of money and things like that. After the Bucharest show, I was invited to go bear hunting in the summer, but I declined.

'I remember when we played in Serbia, the person looking after us was brilliant,' he adds. 'He turned up in a state-of-the-art American Jeep and a ton of gold chains. He warned us that if any members of state or police stopped us and asked where we were from, they said to tell them we were all Irish. He said, "Remember to say you're not English, because of Tony Blair's bombing of Serbia." They couldn't reiterate that enough.'

During an epic drive through Eastern Europe, the band discovered how useful their tour merchandise and the leftover booze from their rider could be. 'We quickly learned how to get on the right side of border security guards,' says Michael. 'We'd drink half the rider and keep some local hooch to bribe our way through. We gave away a number of T-shirts, too.'

'We had a translator with us on that tour,' adds Andy. 'I think she was from Serbia, but she knew enough Balkan languages to help us when we got to the borders. At one stop, they were looking around the bus and noticed a lorry delivering Milka chocolate pull up. Once they got our vodka and T-shirts, they dashed off to get some free sweets. I kid you not—it was like something from a *Carry On* movie.'

Following the band's show Moscow's SDK MAI on April 20, they were greeted with a hefty bill at the airport. 'They tried to charge us a ridiculously inflated price to fly our equipment home, knowing we had no choice, and they wanted paying in cash,' Neil explains. 'Our tour manager was frantically running around, saying, "I don't carry that amount of cash!" as he tried to find a bank. Our translator said, "Be quick, because the price is going up the longer you take!"

'That run of dates was a lot of fun, though,' he adds. 'The whole trip had an air of lawlessness about it. I love getting out to places you wouldn't normally see and meeting the people. The gigs were fantastic and the people were brilliant; the authorities were often the problem.'

Shows followed in Greece, Austria, Switzerland, Slovakia, the Czech Republic, and Lithuania. Once those dates were completed, it was time to hunt for another label, the band's three three-album contract with Eagle Rock and Spitfire Records having expired during the summer. Spitfire Records label manager Darren Edwards suggested they contact Demolition Records, a label based in Jarrow. Founded in 2000 by brothers Ged and Eric Cook, Demolition was home to David Lee Roth, WASP, Twisted Sister, and The Quireboys.

'We organised a meeting in Derby,' says Andy, 'and they were really decent people. They explained who was on the label, but they wanted to branch out and have a band like Therapy? on the label. They'd mentioned that they were looking into buying a recording studio—Blast Studios in Newcastle's Stepney Bank—and said that one of the perks would be having really cheap studio time. We came away from the meeting thinking that that's where we needed to be right now.'

'That's a total asset for any label to have, and it was very attractive to us,' Michael adds. 'The people who worked at the label were great, and the general vibe in Newcastle was appealing to us. It seemed to be its own entity, and there was a healthy enough music scene, too. It felt like a fresh start for us.'

The band ended the year with a show at the Palladium in Cologne on December 22. With no line-up changes looming, and a new deal in place, Therapy? were on a roll.

YEAR
NINETEEN/everything
went black

On January 4, Keith Baxter died from a gastro-intestinal haemorrhage, surrounded by his family and friends at Royal Lancaster Infirmary. He was just thirty-six years old. The news hit the band hard.

'It was bleak,' says Andy. 'We all went to his funeral and at the end of the evening, his family had set up musical equipment above a pub that they ran and various members of Therapy?, 3 Colours Red, and The Senseless Things got up on stage and drunkenly ran through some cover versions.

'He helped us out at a time when we were at our lowest and managed to inject a sense of brio back into the live shows,' he adds. 'My enduring image of him is after a sold-out gig in Tampere, Finland, standing in the dressing room, saying, "This is fucking brilliant!" We had been so caught up in what we perceived to be other peoples view of the band and the ramifications of not having a label or a drummer. That night, thousands of miles from home, in a packed gig with people singing back our lyrics at us in a foreign tongue, he made us open our eyes to what was really in front of us, to enjoy it and live in the moment.'

Andy's own health was on the wane, too. He'd been suffering from chest pains, and his asthma was becoming unmanageable. 'I thought I might have lung cancer,' he says quietly. 'I had to go for scans. They could see something on one of my lungs. My wife and I were braced for the worst, but it turned out to be scar tissue. The specialist said I must have had some kind of fall in my twenties. The time waiting for the results was awful.'

Around the same time, Andy moved house, and, when he did, his breathing eased, too. 'There were horses out the back of the house we used to live in,' he explains. 'I must have been allergic to them or their hay.'

Despite receiving a clean bill of health, Andy found the first few months of the year particularly tough. 'I'd developed this dreadful fear of death,' he says. 'I felt absolutely dreadful—I mean physically and mentally. It was crippling. The thought of it kept me awake every single night, and it wasn't something that I'd felt since I was probably thirteen or fourteen. It really coloured everything in my life. I was reading Samuel Beckett's work for comfort, to see if it could give me some kind of normalcy. I put everything I was feeling into the songs I was writing for the next record, to try and get it out of my system.'

The band started working on the follow-up to *One Cure Fits All* in Derby, their new songs driven by grinding guitars and dub sonics. They approached Gang Of Four guitarist Andy Gill to produce the new album. As a defining influence of Andy Cairns's guitar playing (listen to 'Deep Sleep' or 'Stories') and the man responsible for shaping the sound of The Jesus Lizard's 1998 album *Blue* and Killing Joke's 2003 self-titled full-length, he appeared to be a perfect match.

'I thought the conversation might have gone along the same lines as when I called Steve Albini all those years ago,' remembers Andy. 'But I thought that if he'd worked with a band like Killing Joke, he might be into the idea. I called him and he was really friendly. He said he liked the band and asked for some demos.'

Gill responded positively to the new demos the band recorded in January. However, he wouldn't be able to commit to working on the album until the summer. 'We really wanted to work with him, so were happy to hold off until then,' says Andy. 'Gang Of Four had released an album called *Return The Gift* a few years earlier. They'd re-recorded all their classic songs in the studio and the guitar sound was amazing. Andy rang me back and said that he thought the material was strong and had an idea in his head about how he wanted the album to sound. That phone call really lifted me my spirits.'

In early February, Biffy Clyro pulled out of a Jägermeister-sponsored tour of Germany and Therapy? stepped in, seeing the shows as a chance to road-test some of their new songs. 'We did this a bit before *Never Apologise, Never Explain*, where we did some one-offs and the Wildhearts tour,' says Michael. 'We found that really benefited the progress on that album.'

On July 29, the band entered Newcastle's Blast Studios, located near the banks of the river Tyne, with the aim of recording fourteen songs. 'It was refreshing working with Andy, but it could be quite frustrating, too,' admits Andy Cairns. 'He was very easygoing, you could say. People like Chris Sheldon would always be up and into the studio for ten in the morning, and would be at the desk waiting for the band. This time around, we'd be waiting for Andy. This isn't a criticism of him, he just worked a different way than we were used to.'

'There were a few times where people would be playing in the studio, and he'd have wandered out of the control room to watch the evening news,' Michael laughs. 'He was a law unto himself. Maybe it was a weird psychology, because when we did actually play, it was all quite ferocious, like he got us to boiling point then let us simmer until it was time to record. I think everyone played out of their skins on this album.'

This studio visit was particularly memorable for Neil. The day before the sessions, the drummer learned of Andy Gill's unorthodox recording methods. 'I was thrown in at the deep end,' he remembers. The night before we went into the studio, Michael and I went for a pint. Sam [Morton, Gill's engineer] arrived and we were chatting about how the following day was likely to unfold. He said, "Andy likes to record the drums for the album first." That's normal, and I expected him to say, "followed by the bass guitar," but he said, "followed by the cymbals." I thought he was joking. I had to quickly figure out how to record the full album—all the rhythms and drum fills—without cymbals. Then I had record cymbals over the top, so they'd sound in time and in the correct places. I find it funny that Andy didn't consider giving me any heads-up. He was bloody right, though. It took a while, but the drums sound amazing.'

With their producer sticking to what you might describe as 'office hours', the band made good use of their time in the evenings to explore the delights of the city. 'We'd rented a house in Chillingham Road, so we were right in the heart of studentsville,' says Michael. 'It was a nice time of year, so we'd walk down to the studios. There was a good vibe and I definitely felt there was a lot of energy and positivity in the whole project.'

'It was good to go into a town where everyone was helpful and friendly,' adds Andy. 'It helped that the label was based there, the studio was based there, and the engineers were local lads. This album was the start of our ongoing love affair with Newcastle.'

The band finished tracking their fourteen songs on August 24. Andy Cairns headed down to the Beauchamp Building, the producer's own recording studio in Holborn, to add overdubs and the like. 'We were listening to a lot of electronica, and I was into Burial, too,' he says. 'Andy [Gill] had a good ear for effects and liked things like delay, echo, and reverb, which really helped shape the overall sound of the album.

'Initially, I wondered whether I should travel home to Cambridge every night,' he adds. 'I thought I might get more done if I stayed in a hotel down the road from Holborn. I was working from lunchtime until about 6pm, and I had an awful lot of time to myself in London. The studio was where all the city boys work, so I found doing the last part of the album quite boring, but I was glad to be working with Andy. It was quite weird, actually, because I was sort of in awe of him. I have all his records, and I listened to Gang Of Four a lot as a kid. It was quite unusual be sitting at the mixing desk listening to a guitar part and looking up and thinking, *Oh god, there's Andy Gill!*'

The band weren't satisfied with the initial mixes of the album, but Andy Gill had another project coming up, so the band headed back into Newcastle during a very wintry December. It was so cold there were reports of a Geordie considering wearing long sleeves before heading into town for a pint.

'Bizarrely, for a guitarist, Andy Gill's mixes were very *guitar-light*,' remembers Michael. 'It didn't have that *oomph* we were expecting, especially from the guitars. Andy and Adam Sinclair remixed it at Blast, and now it sounded how we wanted it. I think that, after all this time, we were getting more confident and better at saying how we wanted to do things to make the record sound better. The label agreed and had our back with that side of things, even if it meant pushing the record back a few months.'

The album was titled *Crooked Timber*, inspired by a line by the German philosopher Immanuel Kant: 'From the crooked timber of humanity, no straight thing was ever made.'

'I was forty-four when this album was made,' says Andy. 'When I was writing the songs, I had this constant psychobabble—a constant conversation going on in my head. I just wanted it to stop, and the only time it could stop was when I was asleep, but even then I found it hard to rest. I think the term is *midlife crisis*, and I think that what a lot of it was, to a certain extent.'

To that end, *Crooked Timber* is one of the most personal albums in the Therapy? canon, shaped by thoughts of mortality and the notions of self-identity that can plague the thoughts of a fortysomething.

The album's opening song, 'The Head That Tried To Strangle Itself', is informed by a slow pace that echoes the early morning sludge of thoughts creeping through an insomniac's head—or, as Andy howls, '*the mad house of the shrieking skull*'. 'I actually wrote the song during a sleepless night,' he explains. 'I wrote the lyrics down on pieces of paper, and when I eventually woke up the next day, the lyrics still made sense. Normally, if I write something down in the middle of the night, I have to reinterpret it to make it fit.'

'Enjoy The Struggle' was informed by Andy's immersion in the world of Samuel Beckett while he tried to occupy his mind with something other the great beyond, while he was awaiting the results of his scans at the start of the year. 'I'd always liked Beckett, but I got really obsessed with him,' he says. 'So much so that I began to read the people that influenced Beckett himself: Dante Alighieri's *The Divine Comedy*, Arthur Schopenhauer. I read Jonathan Swift and Thomas Mann, too. I was trying to drown out the thoughts in my head by reading so much.

'The lyrics came from reading Albert Camus's *The Myth Of Sisyphus*,' he adds. 'I suppose a lot of it comes from the existentialist thought that we're all actually kind of living a pointless existence in a hideous void, and how we make sense of everything. There's a really great quote in *The Myth Of Sisyphus*, where Sisyphus is condemned to roll a rock up the hill for the rest for eternity. He looks at this as man's struggle, and Camus says that if you imagine Sisyphus being happy in his work, that can alleviate some of the pain.

'That's what I took from it as well: I thought, *This is a meaning*. I was well aware that I wasn't exactly a single mum, living in a flat in Skegness with no hot water. I didn't exactly have it really, really bad, but at the same time I had this kind of constant screeching in my own head that I couldn't switch off. Thankfully, I had the band to try and get some of that noise and alleviate it from inside my skull.'

'Clowns Galore' was originally written during the *One Cure Fits All* sessions, and was based on the Jonathan Swift short story *A Modest Proposal*. 'When the book was first printed in the 1700s, he wrote it about the population getting out of hand and suggested that maybe we eat people instead,' says Andy. 'It was satirical but written in a serious tone. We took that idea, and we mentioned it in the song a little bit about like eating each other and just fattening kids for later on. That's what the lyric "*Gorging on everything all of the time / Passing it on to the brood / Fattening kids for the future ahead / In case we run out of food*" comes from.'

'Exiles' was inspired by a stark photograph of Earth and the moon, taken by the astronaut William Anders in 1968 during the Apollo 8 mission. 'It's terrifying and beautiful at the same,' says Andy. 'I was reading something on Beckett, and it had mentioned Beckett's laughing into the void to try and fend off the despair. This photo makes you realise just how alone in the universe we are: *"These exiles that we are, isolated on a distant dying star."*

The song changes tack by employing reggae melodies—something that came at the suggestion of the album's producer. 'Andy [Gill] explained that reggae melodies jump from one octave to the other and cascade down,' says the frontman. 'The vocals are quite winsome; it took a while to get used to it, but it worked really well.'

The album's title track—propelled by a growling bass line, furious drumming, and chiming harmonics—summarises the dark overall tone. 'These days, everyone tries to fit it, instead of just being themselves,' he continues. 'It examines what it means to be human—to realise that we are the only living things on the planet aware of our own deaths.'

'I Told You I Was Ill' takes its title from the Gaelic epitaph engraved on the gravestone of the British-Irish humourist and *Goon Show* creator Spike Milligan in Winchelsea, East Sussex (*'Dúirt mé leat go raibh mé breoite'*). 'The title gives the wrong impression, because it's funny, and it's classic Milligan, but the song itself is quite bleak,' says Andy. 'It's about depression and feeling trapped within the confines of your own environment. It was one of those things where the title was added, I think, to give a bit of levity to it.'

'Somnambulist' is one of the more upbeat tracks on *Crooked Timber.* The lyrics, however, are not upbeat by any stretch of the imagination. 'That was written during my, ahem, midlife crisis,' says Andy. 'On the second verse, the opening two lines were from my wife. She's a very positive person, whereas I have a terrible habit of dwelling on the negatives. If things get bad, she's really good at finding a place to grab onto and pull herself up: *"You see the sun in everyone / Sometimes I wish I could."* During that time I was really, really down, my wife and my son were the two people who made me want to get out of bed in morning.'

The idea for 'Blacken The Page' was sparked by a 'Zen' conversation Andy had a friend about eastern philosophy after confiding in him that he was having trouble writing. 'He asked what my desk was like, and I admitted it was horrendous,' he laughs. 'He said, "Have you ever tried just sweeping your arm across the desk, and getting rid of everything?" It had to do with a blank surface can resonate with you and feel like rebirth. It reminded me of Beckett, because whenever he got frustrated, he wanted to use black ink on a white page and colour in every dot and gap between each letter until there was nothing left but a blackened page. I suppose that was me trying to get to the point where I could look at an empty page and see hope, not despair.'

The hypnotic instrumental 'Magic Mountain' clocks in at just over ten minutes. It was inspired by Krautrock icons Can and Neu!, with a chord progression borrowed from jazz master John Coltrane. 'The chords at the beginning of "Magic Mountain" are the same ones used in John Coltrane's 'Giant Steps'—only they're played at an Eyehategod or Melvins tempo. It's quite a trance-y track that I could imagine being in a David Lynch film; you'd see someone driving along a motorway in the dark, with the white lines illuminated only by the headlights of a car.'

The title for the album's closing song, 'Bad Excuse For Daylight', came from a passage in Gwendolene Riley's 2007 book *Joshua Spassky*: 'A bad excuse for daylight was filling up Deansgate, and there were the usual wet people walking around in it.'

'This is going to sound incredibly pretentious, but the music in the middle, the pacing of the verse, was inspired by Stravinsky's *The Rite Of Spring*,' says Andy. 'The song is about how nature looks after its own. I was trying to sing a folk melody that would be cross between Portishead's *Third* album and something from the *Wicker Man* soundtrack. We almost had it like something Slint would do, and that was the part where we thought, *OK, we can get away with doing this*.'

Crooked Timber would be released in 2009, and remains one of the band's most creative excursions, distilled from a bleak despair. 'I've always been able to deal with things in life with a great deal of levity, and I think my background in Northern Ireland has always given us that really pitch-black sense of dark irony and humour,' says Andy. 'But when I was writing songs, all I felt at this point in time was despair. I couldn't find any little kind of splashes of colour anywhere. It was all monochrome and horrendous. Once the album was complete, things seemed to be a little better.'

YEAR
TWENTY/a spectacularly blunt german review

In late February, Therapy? reconvened in Lancashire to film a promo for their new album's title track with a local production company called Sitcom Soldiers. Their performance is interspersed with footage of an agitated man collecting sticks and branches on a desolate moor. As it begins to snow, he emerges from a wood to witness villagers slowly levitating and remaining suspended in the air.

The day before filming took place, the band learned that their usual black attire would not be suitable for the shoot, prompting a last-minute dash to the nearest shopping centre to buy clothes of a more earthen bent. 'After the frantic shopping spree, we hit the road for Manchester, all of us having an eye on an early start for the video shoot the following morning,' says Neil. 'Andy suggested a quick nightcap at the hotel, and I woke up with a pounding head. Schoolboy error. Despite being head-to-toe in grey and slightly blurry-eyed, we were eager, and the filming went surprisingly well.' If you keep an eye on the drummer during the closing frames, there's a palpable sense of relief at the song coming to an end, while the icy blast of an off-camera cooling fan soothes his hangover.

On March 9, the band made an appearance at a special show celebrating the reopening of the Ulster Hall in Belfast. The evening, titled Do You Remember The First Time?, was organised by BBC Northern Ireland's *Across The Line* and featured a diverse range of local acts, including The Divine Comedy, Duke Special, Foy Vance, Iain Archer, Jetplane Landing, Fighting With Wire, LaFaro, Cashier No 9, Kowlaski, and Panama Kings. Therapy? performed 'Screamager' and two cover versions: Stiff Little Fingers' 'Alternative Ulster' and The Undertones' 'Teenage Kicks', the latter having appeared on their 'Have A Merry Fucking Christmas' seven-inch in 1992.

'That Ulster Hall show was such a lovely evening; there was no bickering, petty jealousies, or moaning about billing,' remembers Andy. 'It felt like a celebration. We shared a dressing room with Snow Patrol, and in an interview with the BBC, we heard Nathan [Connolly, guitarist] tell them that Therapy? were the first band he'd ever seen in the Ulster Hall. At this point, Snow Patrol were becoming one of the biggest bands in the world, and they didn't care what slot they had, they just wanted to be part of it. To be asked to close the show was an honour, and it's a gig I'll never forget, especially the closing version of "Teenage Kicks".

'The Ulster Hall has always been special to me,' Andy continues. 'The first proper gig I ever attended—i.e. not a youth club or church hall punk gig—was Siouxsie & The Banshees at that venue. I was very young, and my parents nervously dropped me off outside, which was lined with scary-looking punks drinking cans of Harp lager and play fighting. I'll never forget the feelings of terror and joy as I made my way as close to the front as I could. I stood staring at the glow of the small red and green lights on the amplifiers and had butterflies in my stomach with anticipation.

'The very first time Therapy? ever played the venue, in 1992, I was at soundcheck when I remembered that feeling of being near the front and looking up at the lights,' he continues. 'I promptly took off my guitar and jumped off the stage so that I could go to the barrier and stare up at our own lights, all the while thinking about how amazing it was that tonight somebody would be going through the same feelings for our band.'

In the weeks leading up to the release of *Crooked Timber* on March 23, the press response was largely positive. 'When the album rocks, it's fabulous,' wrote *Classic Rock*'s Neil Jeffries in a seven-out-of-ten review. 'Cairns mixes punk fury with classic metal riffs and Neil Cooper's drums throughout are fantastic, his snare ringing like an oil drum and driving the bedlam of opener "The Head That Tried To Strangle Itself", "Enjoy The Struggle" and "I Told You I Was Ill". Ill, possibly, sick even—but Therapy? are still a long way from dead.'

'*Crooked Timber* manages to be both accessible yet deliriously unsettling,' wrote *Kerrang!*'s Ian Winwood, who awarded the effort three *K*s. 'It's no small beer that more than a decade after their commercial heyday, Therapy? manage to fashion an album of song-based material that is entirely original … this is a proud and relevant collection from a sometimes weird, often wonderful, invariably talented group.'

Even the *NME* was impressed, giving the album a score of three-and-a-half out of five, with Martin Robinson noting that this release could turn the band's fortunes around: 'This Andy Gill-produced effort reconnects them with some of their old guile, with these Kant-quoting outsiders making a virtue of unpredictability. "Clowns Galore" is pure Hüsker Dü, "Blacken The Page" is evil Arctic Monkeys, and "I Told You I Was Ill" is like Joy Division starring in *Driller Killer*. The pretensions that have soaked in over the years frequently make the album ponderous, but with gloom-rock back, Therapy? could rise again like a nut-job Lazarus.'

Writing for the German edition of *Metal Hammer*, however, Tobias Gerber slated the album, beginning his critique by asking, 'Was zum Teufel ist denn hier passiert?' ('*What the hell happened here?*') Over the course of his review, it becomes clear that he was hoping for a cynical re-tread of *Troublegum*. 'The strengths of the Irish are simply moving melodies, catchy tunes, fresh energy ... the highlights—which are actually only less annoying moments—can be counted on one hand.'

Then again, the German rock press has a reputation for being spectacularly blunt. The UK's *Metal Hammer*, on the other hand, described *Crooked Timber* as 'the most startling album yet from the unpredictably fascinating band' in an eight-out-of-ten review.

'With some albums in the past, the more indie press would have loved it and the metal press would have been a bit cooler on it,' says Michael. 'Or if the rock and metal press loved an album, the indie mags might have been a bit sniffy about it. But with *Crooked Timber*, everyone seemed on board with what we were trying to do, more or less. I do think some of it was a big ask for some of the more metal mags, especially in Europe.'

There was much debate over the artistic direction of the *Crooked Timber* cover. In the end, the band settled on a simple, monochromatic sleeve featuring their logo, Andy's 'Gemil' doodle—more on that later—and the album title in scratchy handwriting. 'It's not even as stark as it could have been,' says Andy. 'We could have had everything embossed in black. I think we discussed doing the whole thing in black. It was like, *How much more black could this be?*' The answer, of course, is none.

On the day of the album's release, the band performed an acoustic show at the HMV in Belfast's city centre, playing 'Blacken The Page', 'Exiles', 'I Told You I Was Ill', and the title track, before signing copies until the store closed. They then headed to BBC Northern Ireland to record a live session comprised of 'I Told You I Was Ill', *Crooked Timber* B-side 'Don't Try', and a new instrumental tentatively called 'Treacle Feet' (it would resurface under the name 'Ecclesiastes' on the band's 2012 album, *A Brief Crack Of Light*). 'I suppose it might have made more sense to plug the album and do faithful versions of those songs, but we had been chatting about how bands—us included—used to use radio sessions to do "exclusive" stuff and try out new ideas,' says Michael. 'Remember all those great Peel Sessions with one-offs and alternate versions?'

THERAPY?

On May 3, Therapy? kicked off a UK headline tour with Geordie rock'n'soul four-piece The Sound Explosion as their main support band, plus local opening acts. They made the decision to play their new album in full each night, including the ten-minute instrumental 'Magic Mountain'.

'With the previous albums, you'd start the tour off by playing eight new songs in the set, and, by the end, you'd only play four,' says Michael. 'We'd decided that, in the spirit of a fresh start, we'd play everything from *Crooked Timber* as a statement of intent, peppered through the set. Once people got on board with that, the shows were really good. You need to do the new stuff to keep the band alive; you can't just keep on doing greatest hits sets for the rest of your career, because that peters out pretty quickly. Likewise, you can't *not* play "Screamager". It's playing one off the other, really, and they have to kind of coexist.'

During the tour, the band learned that the album—which charted at no. 197 in the UK—had sold thirty thousand copies in Europe during its first six weeks of released, and had been certified silver.

On June 14, the band returned to Donington to play Download's Tuborg stage, on a bill populated by classic-rock behemoths like Def Leppard, Whitesnake, and ZZ Top. 'That was a good, solid festival set,' remembers Michael. 'You know, Download is one of those festivals where you never really know what you're going to get or who's on the main stage at that time.

'In 2006, I'm not sure what happened, but for some reason Neil's drum tech had put down the previous day's day sheet as a setlist,' he laughs. 'About three songs in, he glanced down to check what was coming and saw that day's itinerary. He was sat there in front of however many thousand people, panicking and trying to catch my eye. So, this time around, there were many setlists taped around his drum riser.'

'As a local, playing Donington is always a big deal,' says Neil. 'My older brother first took me in 1985—I was fourteen. ZZ Top headlined, but I'd really badgered my brother to take me because I was unbelievably excited to see Metallica, who were touring *Ride The Lightning*. So, when I walked out [in 2006] and saw the day sheet instead of my setlist, let's just say I had a mini-meltdown!'

The following month was spent on the European festival circuit, with shows in Austria, the Czech Republic, Ireland, Belgium, and Switzerland. On July 24, the band performed at the Demo Festival in Banja Luka, the second largest city in Bosnia and Herzegovina. 'We knew a little bit of the history and the Bosnian war, but to go there and see buildings with bullet holes was an eye-opener,' says Michael. 'Huge parts of the town were still in the process of being rebuilt. From a personal point of view, it just reminded us of growing up in Northern Ireland and seeing shows; everyone was in the room for the same reason, regardless of their background or beliefs.'

On October 14, the band embarked on a more extensive tour of the UK before venturing back into Europe, where they would remain until December 6. They were supported throughout the entire trek by Ricky Warwick, the former frontman of The Almighty, who'd released a solo album, *Belfast Confetti*, on DR2 Records earlier that year.

'I'd known Ricky since 1993,' says Andy. 'I was introduced to him by Chris Sheldon, because he was producing The Almighty's album *Crank* [on which Andy also contributed guest vocals on several tracks]. He lived near me when I lived in Ireland in the early 90s. We saw each other on a regular basis and became really good friends. He'd signed to Demolition Records, and he stayed on our bus during that tour. We got on really well. If this had been five years earlier, we'd have been out every night raging, but I'd started exercising, and he's always kept fit. I hardly ever drank, and we'd get up and go and find a gym. We kept each other out of trouble.'

'It was a no-brainer for us,' Michael adds. 'Ricky was starting with his acoustic thing, and he became part of the team. It was a really good fit.'

The band continued to perform their latest album in full during the tour, which took them from the UK into Holland, Austria, Poland, and the Czech Republic. Towards the end of the run, a panicked promoter in Hamburg stopped the band before they returned to play an encore.

'We came off stage in Hamburg,' remembers Andy, 'we'd played the album in its entirety, and the promoter came running into the dressing room going, "Please tell me you're going to play 'Screamager', 'Nowhere', and 'Die Laughing'?" We said we weren't sure what we were going to do, but he was like, "No, no! You must, everyone's complaining, saying, 'Where's the old stuff?'"'

Maybe that particular crowd had read the *Metal Hammer Germany* review.

'I think at that point in time we'd got into our own little bubble, but in a good way,' says Andy. 'We were really enjoying playing *Crooked Timber*, because a lot of the arrangements and use of effects—all that reverb, delay, and looping—meant that we really had to concentrate. We could play the stuff from the early 90s with our eyes shut, because we'd been playing those songs for so long. I thought it made it more of an immersive experience, but *Crooked Timber* is one of those records that … if you didn't like it to start with, you were certainly going to find the live show challenging.'

RISE UP

YEAR
TWENTY-ONE/live and
dangerous

Prior to the band's autumn tour the previous year, Demolition Records had urged Therapy? to record a show, with a view to putting out a live album. 'We maybe got ahead of ourselves a little and started talking about the classic double live albums: Iron Maiden's *Live After Death*, Thin Lizzy's *Live And Dangerous*, KISS's *Alive!*,' says Michael. 'We wanted to make a definitive live statement.'

Their recording of London's Garage on October 19 was full of 'digital glitches', however, and, according to Andy, it wasn't a show to chalk up as a raging success, either. 'Most bands say London shows are really difficult because everyone's too cool,' he says. 'We've been really lucky— we've always had a great reception there, and the tour was going great, but there was something about that Garage show. The crowd didn't really go for it, and I remember thinking, *What the hell just happened?* I didn't enjoy that show, and it certainly didn't look like the audience were enjoying it, either.'

The band recorded another show, this time at 013 in Tilburg, Holland, but it lacked the required atmosphere and energy. 'It was a sold-out show, and we played well,' Michael remembers. 'The crowd was very appreciative, but there wasn't the mania or the vibe that we knew was present at 90 percent of our shows. We regrouped and discussed what we were going to do. It had been a *Crooked Timber*-heavy set by that point, so we thought we'd change tack and do a few shows, and structure it so that we'd play every song twice. That way, if one fucks up, we'd have another version we could probably use.'

Following two January shows in Greece, the band's manager and agent suggested a three-night residency at the two-hundred-capacity Water Rats in London's King's Cross—a venue Therapy? had not played since the summer of 1995. Oh, and it would take place in March.

After two days' rehearsal in London, the band kicked off the first of their three shows on March 29. Fans travelled in from all over the world—the USA, Chile, Brazil, Japan, Finland, Belgium, and Walthamstow—to see them perform a career-spanning set in a tiny London club.

'Looking back, I've no idea what we were playing at, doing forty different songs over three evenings,' says Andy. 'I think we got it into our heads that if we were going to do a live album, it had to be a double album, to give value for money.

'Neil deserves a medal, because there were a lot of songs he'd not played very much, or at all,' he adds. 'He'd rented out a rehearsal space and spent hours and hours learning the set. The album's a bit rough and ready, but we had a great time doing it.'

In May, the band returned to Blast Studios in Newcastle to begin the arduous task of going through the three sets and mixing the final album with Adam Sinclair. 'We had to go over those tracks again and again and again,' Andy laughs. 'It was quite painstaking. By the end of it, I didn't want to hear any of those songs again!'

Of the forty songs recorded in London, thirty-six were kept for the album, leaving just four that didn't sound right, according to Michael. 'We got so ahead of ourselves,' he says. 'We decided that we could maybe do a third disc and rework some of the older songs, like "Animal Bones" and "Prison Breaker". In the end, the label said that it would end up being a triple- or quadruple-disc release, and it would prove too expensive. We kept those songs for *The Gemil Box*, which we'd release a few years later. I was really pleased with the way the live album came out. We could have bunged out the Tilburg gig and regretted it, but we stuck to our guns.'

'I seem to remember the label trying to direct the approach on that extra disc,' adds Neil. 'Acoustic versions had been mentioned. I think we there was an element of *fuck that*, and we produced something from the opposite direction. The version of "Animal Bones" came out as a distorted, massive Shellac-style bass-and-drums groove, with Andy's vocal over the top. It sounds amazing.'

The band kicked off their summer itinerary on June 19 at the Sonisphere festival in Mimon in the Czech Republic. The bill featured the 'Big Four' of American thrash—Metallica, Slayer, Megadeth, and Anthrax—plus Alice In Chains, Stone Sour, Volbeat, and more. 'As a fan, I didn't think I'd get the chance to go to any of the Big Four shows,' says Michael. 'But because we were doing the Sonisphere show at Knebworth later in the summer, they asked us to come to the Czech Republic. It was absolutely brilliant.'

Michael was in his element. 'I've been going to Slayer shows since maybe 1987,' he says. 'It was a teenage dream come true, watching them from the side of the stage.' Slayer guitarist Jeff Hanneman was still performing with the band at this point; health issues would lead to his departure the following year. 'Hanneman had this look of disgust on his face during the gig, because he was playing this filthy, evil music. It looked like he was enjoying hurting the audience with his riffs.'

By the time Therapy? reached Forestglade Festival in Wiesen, Austria, on July 17, they'd decided to bolster their sound by adding tech Stevie Firth on second guitar. 'When we did *Crooked Timber*, Andy Gill would bring my effects pedals out and put them on our laps in front of the desk,' says Andy. 'With things like reverb and delay, he'd mix on the move. Now, when I'm playing guitar, I'm fretting the chords and singing—I can't twiddle a load of effects pedals at the same time. Stevie suggested working the pedals live while we played, and eventually he said he could add second guitar to certain songs, and do backing vocals, too—if there were three vocals on a song, Michael would do some of them and he'd do some of them, and it just went from there. If you go and see the Manics, Biffy Clyro, or Green Day, they've all got an extra guitarist on the stage. We didn't want to become a four-piece again, so this was the best of both worlds—we could add a little colour to the set without having to put it on a computer.'

On July 31, the band headlined the Bohemia Stage at the UK leg of Sonisphere at Knebworth, playing their *Troublegum* album in full. 'I think a big catalyst for doing that was Andy seeing Iggy & The Stooges at Hammersmith Apollo in May,' says Michael. 'He said they played all of *Raw Power* with Mike Watt on bass. We realised that it doesn't have to be nostalgia—it can be visceral and vital. Obviously, when you're debuting something like that at a festival, it can be a tiny bit risky.'

The band walked out to a packed tent, but soon things began to go awry: during the opener, 'Knives', the power failed twice, which put Andy on edge for the rest of the set. 'That was one of the worst gigs I've ever had,' he says. 'I hated the whole thing. We were playing the tent, and to be honest, I was a little bit pissed off. *Troublegum* had gone gold in the UK, and I thought, *Do we have to play this album to headline a fucking tent? Have we really sunk that low in the UK?* Then I stuck my head in, and the tent was absolutely heaving. My wife and son had come down. We all had friends and relatives there, and other bands were standing at the side of the stage to watch. Then everything kept breaking down. By the time we started properly, I was so embarrassed and angry. I just ploughed through it—I didn't enjoy one minute of it. We had a gig in Europe the next day, and I just wanted to get on the bus and go. I felt like it was supposed to be a bit of a triumph, but it ended up being such a damp squib. It was fucking horrendous.'

In hindsight, it was a good job Demolition wasn't documenting the show for a DVD release … oh, wait. 'I'm quite surprised the DVD came out great, and it sounded good as well,' says Michael. 'I think the beginning of the set could have derailed us massively, but I started to relax about halfway through. People were going nuts, and that gave us a lot of confidence.'

The band finished their run of summer festival appearances on September 10, at Fezen in Székesfehérvár, Hungary. 'That was a good summer,' remembers Michael. 'At Pinkpop Classic, I got to meet Gary Moore. He's obviously a bit of a local legend, but we'd never met him before. We'd heard that he could be a little grumpy sometimes, but he was lovely to us. I had a really nice chat with him and was genuinely gutted when he died the following year.'

Next on the itinerary was another '*Troublegum* + More' show at Belfast's Mandela Hall on October 15. 'Now that show was good, because we did two sets,' Andy explains. 'We played a sort of best-of set, then *Troublegum*. The place was rammed beyond absolute capacity. When we opened the door to walk out on stage, it was like someone had draped a huge, damp, hot blanket over our head. When you see people singing along to every word, you realise how much *Troublegum* meant to them. It was a brilliant show, and after Sonisphere I was expecting the worst. I thought, *Right, I'm going to go home now and play a show in Belfast, and if this is terrible I don't know what I'm going to do.* Belfast really saved my mood that night.'

'We quickly learned that we should have done the *Troublegum* set first that night,' Michael adds. 'The first set really kicked the fuck out of us. We'd already done an hour of screaming and ranting and raving; it was all quite frenetic stuff. But that was a brilliant night.'

Shortly after returning from a small tour of Russian club shows in late October, the band started their *Troublegum* tour at Dublin's Vicar Street on November 5. The same day, the band's first-ever live album, *We're Here To The End*, was released.

'There's something comforting about having Therapy? around after twenty years,' wrote *Classic Rock*'s Emma Johnston. 'Prime ministers have come and gone, we've had booms and busts, but throughout it all they've have been there to cheer us up with a whale-sized riff and a staggering live show. They go straight for the hits, starting with a still thrilling "Screamager" and dragging us through thirty-six endorphin-releasing rock classics until we land, breathless, at a furious "Teethgrinder". While live albums always preach to the converted, this one shines because the band sound so ridiculously happy to be on stage.'

The *Troublegum* tour took the band through Germany (no complaints this time from any Hamburg promoters, it must be noted), Belgium, and Holland, and then to the Forum in London's Kentish Town on November 19. 'That was one of the best shows we've ever played,' says Michael. 'The venue was rammed, and everyone was really up for it. After the show, Paul, our agent, said to me, "You were getting emotional on stage … you were going to cry." I can reveal that some water came out of my face. My wife Gabine was there, and she was pregnant expecting our first child, so that technically was his first ever live show.'

For Andy, the Forum set went some way to torching the bad memories lingering from the near-disaster of Knebworth. 'This is what I thought Sonisphere was going to be like,' he says. 'Like the Water Rats shows, people had come from all over for the show. They'd flown in from places like Germany, Holland, Austria, Brazil, and Chile. That place holds about 2,300 people, and they came to see *Troublegum* played in full.'

At the end of the show, a group of fans presented the band members with copies of a self-published book, *We're Here To The End Too*, containing photographs and comments about what the band meant to them, and how their music had saved their lives. 'We'd come off stage and were chatting to our families and friends, and then we were presented with a parcel,' says Andy. 'We sat in the backstage area reading it. I was in tears. It was really, really moving. It rounded off one of my favourite gigs.'

'I was incredibly moved by what they'd put together for us,' adds Neil. 'They'd communicated with each other away from our Wall Of Mouths message boards and socials, so we had absolutely no clue. It was so touching. The book's fantastic.'

The following month, work began on the band's thirteenth studio album at Blast in Newcastle. Local news outlets were warning locals to invest in a coat by the time Neil travelled up from Derby to track his drums with producer Adam Sinclair. 'The lads had recorded the new songs we'd finished, playing along to a click track in Derby,' he explains. 'I arrived in Newcastle, and the original plan was, I'd get started, and record my drums using the click tracks as a guide. Michael would arrive after a few days to record the bass. Due to horrendous weather conditions and cancelled flights, this didn't happen.'

Forging ahead with the drum tracks, Neil kept his bandmates updated with recordings via email. 'It was unconventional,' he says, 'but the recordings were sounding great. After a day in the studio, I found myself pottering around this empty property set up for the three of us. A friend had given me a copy of *Loonyology: In My Own Words* by Charles Bronson—"Britain's most violent prisoner", not the *Death Wish* one. He wrote about his long periods locked inside the prison's isolation unit. It was a couple of weeks before Christmas, and it seemed like everyone was getting into the festive spirit. I remember being sat one evening back at our digs after a day's recording, reading that book and admiring the half-heartedly decorated Christmas tree in the living room. I suddenly felt very isolated. Fun times.'

Shortly before Christmas, Neil completed his drum tracks and headed home to Derby without seeing either Andy or Michael. 'I clearly remember driving out of the city with an incoming snowstorm in my rear-view mirror,' he explains. 'If I'd left a couple of hours later, I'd have been completely snowed in.'

YEAR
TWENTY-TWO/none
more black

During the first week of January, Michael made a second attempt to reach Newcastle to begin recording his bass parts. 'I was supposed to join Neil in the studio just before Christmas, but there was a massive snowstorm just before I was due to fly out,' he recalls. 'Neil and Adam were entombed inside the studio, and by the time I could fly over, there'd have been no time to do anything, so I left it until January. Neil had dug himself out and was back in Derby with his family by then. Towards the end of my session, Andy was due to arrive and start doing guitar and the vocals, but he caught the flu and ended up coming up later in the month.'

Despite the Arctic conditions, the recording sessions advanced smoothly. 'It went really well, considering we were never in the same room at the same time,' Michael laughs. 'People have said to me they love the sound of the record and its energy. But we literally sat alone with Adam, tracking our parts, then headed back to a cold, empty flat in Gateshead to eat beans on toast. The thing was, word got back to the label that we'd all come in individually, and they thought we'd fallen out. They were kind of tiptoeing around us in case we'd had this massive falling out. But it was just all down to circumstance.'

The initial recordings were completed in February and mixed the following month. By this point, the band had completed eight songs.

'Living In The Shadow Of The Terrible Thing' is a taut, sinewy opener, informed by the work of Samuel Beckett and Portuguese poet Fernando Pessoa. 'It's about how anxiety can hold you back: "*With heavy tread and treacle feet, I drag my baggage behind me*",' says Andy. 'I was listening to quite a bit of dubstep and dub, so the main guitar riff started out like a bass line, and I played the main riff in a similar vein to Helmet.'

'Plague Bell' stutters with the type of discordant, jazz-inflected riff favoured by Rollins Band guitarist Chris Haskett on the albums *The End Of Silence* and *Weight*, with a delicate piano melody buried under the chaos. 'This was one of the most unusual songs I've ever written,' says Andy. 'When I was feeling really unwell, during the run up to *Crooked Timber*, I started to take piano lessons from someone who lived a few doors down the road from me. Over the next four or five years, I managed to get myself up to a Grade 5, and I wrote "Plague Bell" on the piano. I worked out a brief arrangement, and we turned it into a rock song in Derby. It was something that I had to try, but it didn't drift into a John Lennon direction.'

'Marlow' was inspired by a group of African street musicians Andy had seen playing in Cambridge town centre. The title refers to Charles Marlow, a character from Joseph Conrad's 1899 novel *Heart Of Darkness*, the book that inspired John Milius and Francis Ford Coppola's 1979 war epic *Apocalypse Now*.

'I was walking around town with my wife and saw these musicians playing thumb pianos and drums,' Andy explains. 'They were playing this really hypnotic rhythm and I recorded it on my phone. In Derby, I plugged my phone into the PA and we started playing along. I added all these harmonics, which reminded me of the band Battles.'

'Before You, With You, After You' begins with a cascading riff that echoes the guitar style of The Jesus Lizard's Duane Denison, with lyrics inspired by Samuel Beckett's 1961 book *Comment c'est* (republished three years later in English as *How It Is*). 'It's quite a difficult book to read, but it's divided into three parts: "Before Pim", "With Pim", and "After Pim",' says Andy. 'It's about struggle and a lot of it is influenced by Dante's *Inferno*, almost as if a human life is going through a marsh or a muddy field.

'The song addresses life itself, the band, and my life and my friends,' he adds. 'It was originally quite poppy—I think the chorus ended up too generically emo. We fucked about with it to make it sit more comfortably on the album.'

The idea for the unsettling dub of 'Get Your Dead Hand Off My Shoulder' came to Andy while he was driving back to the band's rented accommodation in Gateshead during the middle of the night. 'I was heading back towards the bridge before you go to Gateshead, and there was a really huge car park there,' he says. 'It was empty and echoing, like it was haunted. In the car, I was thinking about different people and thinking about how sometimes you can let the past dictate the future too much: *"Frequencies sing your ghost / We've had our time together / Now I've got to let you go."* I wrote the lyrics when I got back to our apartment and finished the song later that day.'

The title of 'Ghost Trio' comes from a short Samuel Beckett play that was filmed for BBC2 and broadcast in 1977. 'It was originally going to be an instrumental, but I ended up writing the lyrics in one afternoon after seeing a news story about the Arab Spring,' says Andy, referring to the anti-government protests that had recently begun in Tunisia and would spread across the region over the course of the next year. 'That's where the line *"chains will be broken"* came from.

'The music was inspired by a track called "Guitar Trio" by Rhys Chatham,' he adds. 'He takes a riff and gets a lot of guitarists to play it over and over again. Because the guitarists are slightly out of time with each other, you hear all these different harmonics and all these different phases and pulses. We started playing just this repetitive riff, over and over again and the song was written.'

The main riff of 'Why Turbulence?' tumbles like a brick in a dryer, aided and abetted by a distinct jazz swing under the lines *'Big black hooded perambulator / Running red lights to the cemetery.'* 'I've always had quite a love of obnoxious jazz, like Charles Mingus's "Haitian Fight Song" and Eric Dolphy's album *Out To Lunch!*' says Andy. 'Anything which is a bit kind of cheeky and petulant, really. I think the song was written after listening to loads of Mingus. I'm not really sure what the lyrics are about, actually.'

The final song to come from the winter sessions was the frantic clatter of 'Stark Raving Sane', the title of which was taken from Tom Stoppard's existential tragicomedy *Rosencrantz And Guildenstern Are Dead*. 'I think this is one of the songs on the album that falls flat,' says Andy. 'When we initially started writing, one of the records we went back to was *Bleach* by Nirvana. I get bored of rock music quite easily; I listen to electronic music and mad jazz. So, any time I think I'm getting bored of rock music, I stick on *Bleach*. I think I was trying to write something like that, but I'm not really happy with the way this one came out.'

The eight songs were completed in February and mixed the following month. The bad then returned to Blast in June to record two more tracks for the album. 'We talked to the label and mentioned that a lot of albums were around thirty minutes long these days,' says Andy. 'But they asked if we had anything else. We sent them demos of "The Buzzing" and "Ecclesiastes".'

'The Buzzing' is an abrasive, avant-garde piece that flits between washes of black metal and dub techno, with a fearful Andy flooding the verses with thoughts of being lost in the system. 'The main theme of the narrative came from hearing stories from my wife, Kris, who works with people in care,' he explains. 'Quite often, people get themselves into these situations which take on Kafkaesque proportions, where the paperwork becomes just absolutely absurd. I also saw the Beckett play *Not I*, starring Lisa Dwan. She talks about the buzzing, which I perceived to be about the peripheral static of existence, but also the constant nonstop babble and burbling in the head, which I touched on with *Crooked Timber*.

'For the music, we wanted to make a mini-suite of songs that flies by under four minutes, so it can capture a confused headspace,' he adds. 'I wanted it to be almost like how, whenever you're having a manic episode, you go through four different personalities at the same time; that's what it's about—the horrendous inability to be still. There had to be a certain amount of discordance to make it grate, to make it uncomfortable, so that took quite a bit of working. I really liked the end result, and I presumed wrongly that our fans would probably not like it. It's actually gone down quite well when we've played it live.'

Like 'The Buzzing' and 'Marlow' before it, album closer 'Ecclesiastes' throws another curveball. This is slow-burning, gentle, post-rock song with vocals sang through a vocoder. 'This used to be called "Treacle Feet", and it was like a slow-moving giant robot,' says Andy. '*Ecclesiastes* is a chapter from the Old Testament, and the word kept coming up whenever I read Albert Camus or Samuel Beckett. The Byrds' "Turn! Turn! Turn! (To Everything There Is A Season)" is about it.

'I tried to write a song like [something by] Will Oldham,' he continues, 'and it had a really nice melody. It was almost like a country-influenced post-rock song and I'm glad we did it. We've only tried to play it live once, and that was at the SO36 in Berlin. In a confined, controlled environment of a recording studio, the vocoder sounded amazing. With thousands of watts of amplification, let's just say it slightly more problematic. I sounded like Stephen Hawking.'

'I was chatting with Andy one night about "Ecclesiastes",' adds Neil, 'and I suggested the song had a bloated, slow-moving feel to it. That's when I had the idea for the groove. I recorded the drums for the song at twice the speed the song would finally be. When played back, the recorded drums were slowed down to the correct speed, giving a slow, sluggish, and flabby sound to the kit. It sounds great on the record, but without triggers, it would be a bloody nightmare to do live!'

With Therapy? focusing on the album, their touring itinerary was quite sparse. There were a handful of European festivals in the summer, including shows in Romania, Greece, Finland, Ireland, Austria, Belgium, Bulgaria, and Germany.

Their new album, titled *A Brief Crack Of Light*—a phrase taken from Vladimir Nabokov's 1951 memoir *Speak, Memory*, in which he cheerfully describes life as 'a brief crack of light between two eternities of darkness'—

was initially touted for October release, but then, following the addition of 'The Buzzing' and 'Ecclesiastes', it was pushed back to the following year. 'There was no point in just rushing it out,' Michael explains. 'It made sense to sit on it a little while longer.'

On November 4, the band played Belfast's Ulster Hall with County Down classic-rock revivalists The Answer and LaFaro as part of Belfast Music Week, which was in its second year. During The Answer's set, Andy and Michael joined the band for a cover of Stiff Little Fingers' 'Alternative Ulster'.

'Therapy? appear to punish our ear drums a little more. Dressed for the occasion in black shirts and suits, they look very much the part on the grand Ulster Hall stage,' wrote Carrie Davenport for the BBC's *Across The Line*. 'They're blessed with the classic dark sense of humour only us Norn Iron folk can do and as usual the set is littered with wise cracks. Andy jokes about the last time he played the Ulster Hall (for the glorious event that was Do You Remember The First Time?) and getting told off for swearing, so he makes the crowd sing the naughty bits for "Potato Junkie". Radio edit on stage it may be, but the crowd are certainly making up for it and when he asks them to shout the dirtiest word they can think of, we nearly die laughing when one particularly enthusiastic rocker screams "Carrickfergus" at the top of his lungs.' Absolute filth.

A month later, the band drew a line under their year's activity by pulling a double shift at the Hard Rock Hell V festival in Prestatyn the following month, where they performed acoustic and electric sets. Scream for us, Pontins! 'I wasn't sure what to expect,' says Michael, 'but the vibe was great. We hung out with Ginger Wildheart and Rich Jones, and the acoustic set was good, too.'

'A lot of the people in the audience looked like 80s metal fans,' says Andy, 'and I thought, *Right, this might be a bit weird for us*. But, you know, shame on me. It was a fun way to end the year, and, going into 2012, we had a lot to look forward to.'

YEAR
TWENTY-THREE/lucky number
thirteen

On January 23, in the run up to the release of *A Brief Crack Of Light*, Therapy? released 'Living In The Shadow Of The Terrible Thing' as a download-only single. It was accompanied by a suitably post-apocalyptic promo video, shot by Sitcom Soldiers the previous November. And, in the weeks leading up to the album's release on February 6—North America would have to wait until September 11—the press response to Therapy's thirteenth full-length was once again largely positive.

'"Living In The Shadow Of The Terrible Thing" and "Before You, With You, After You" are vicious, raw and strangely catchy as ever,' wrote *Rock Sound*'s Jen Walker in an eight-out-of-ten review. 'That's the beauty of Therapy?—how many other bands can write loud, bass-heavy, fuzzy, and aggressive songs that span all the alternative genres and appeal to rockers, grungers, metallers, punks and goths alike? This is Therapy? at their best in almost every sense of the word. Who said thirteen was unlucky?'

'A far more important band than they're given credit for, Therapy? took uncompromising indie post-punk noise to a metal audience and had chart hits into the bargain,' wrote *Louder Than War*'s Ged Babey. 'Twenty years in the business of rocking hard and dark, this is their thirteenth studio album and quite possibly their finest hour (forty-one and a half minutes to be precise). This really is a return to form, a career-best.'

Clash magazine awarded the release eight out of ten, noting, 'This latest album packs a similar punch to back then, full of raw grittiness and attitude to match. Guitars to the fore, Therapy? have always exuded a commercial undercurrent and it's that ingredient that makes them compelling—equally now as then.' *Metal Hammer* dished out four stars, describing the album as 'a potentially game-changing opus', while in a four-*K* review for *Kerrang!*, I wrote, 'Whereas most bands who've enjoyed a twenty-three-year career could be reluctantly forgiven for settling into a rut of tried and tested formulas, this trio continue to challenge even their most dyed-in-the-wool fans.'

The Danish blog *Metal Revolution* was also impressed, offering a scientific rating of 90 percent. 'Therapy? show absolutely no signs of stopping or even of slowing down, but even more importantly, they are at the place in their career where they feel absolutely comfortable,' wrote Zoran. 'Their albums and nonetheless live performances breathe of enjoyment and creativity. They have nothing to prove and so much to give. Unlike with so many other bands the comfort of their current situation results in exciting new material, some of the best of their career.'

However, while *Crooked Timber* had been warmly received by the *NME*, *A Brief Crack Of Light* was not to writer Noel Gardner's liking. 'Their stoicism and open ears are admirable, so it's a great shame that this album's component parts—vinegary noise-rock, cinematic grandeur and a game approximation of Battles entitled "Marlow"—don't raise the whole above "nice to know they're still around" status.'

Andy admits that he was surprised by the largely positive feedback to the album. 'After *Crooked Timber*, we started getting more of the indie press, like *Clash* and magazines like that,' he says. 'Before that, trendy hipster magazines had an awful misconception of the band. They hadn't a clue about us, and they got it into their minds that we were some really unfashionable, hoary old metal band. Someone once compared us to Anvil. Absolute bollocks.

'The fans have been brilliant,' he adds. 'After *One Cure Fits All*, I think we had to make albums like *Crooked Timber* and *A Brief Crack Of Light*. As musicians, it did us the world of good. I think, with this album, we were perhaps testing their patience a little bit. It's all right for me to talk about Albert Camus and Samuel Beckett, Charles Mingus and Ornette Coleman, or *Rosencrantz And Guildenstern Are Dead* and *Ecclesiastes*. But, you know, the average person on the street really couldn't give two fucks.

They want to know if the riff is catchy, and if they can sing the chorus.'

In March, the band were forced to postpone shows in Dublin and Cork until May; Neil had injured his hand, and a doctor advised the drummer to take two weeks of recovery time—no movement, lifting, or playing—to give himself the best chance of recovery.

A short run of shows in Germany, Slovakia, Holland, and Belgium followed almost two weeks to the day after that resounding crack. Then, on April 10, the band headed out on a five-date, five-quid-a-ticket Jägermeister-sponsored tour, as special guests to headliners Skindred. Black Spiders and The Defiled rounded out the four-band bill.

'We'd known Benji [Webbe, Skindred vocalist] since he was in Dubwar, and we all liked Skindred,' says Michael. 'That tour was a lot of fun. I didn't see much Jägermeister backstage, I have to say. Plenty of banners and promotional items, but not many bottles. It was probably for the best.'

On the afternoon of the first date of the tour—Leeds O2 Academy— the band made their way to Leeds General Infirmary to visit their friend Diamond Dave, who was recovering from a heart attack and a stroke.

'It was a bit difficult,' says Diamond, 'because I couldn't remember people's names, and I was a bit confused. We said our goodbyes, and then, about five minutes later, Andy came running back and said, "You're coming out tonight!" all breathless. So my missus, Cathy, and her friend Laura got me dressed and took me to the gig. Andy told the crowd that I was there and hadn't been well, and they gave me a massive cheer. It made me feel like a million dollars. That's the type of people they are. They're such decent people.'

The Brixton Academy show was the biggest date on the trek, and the trio quickly went about converting some of the uninitiated to their cause. 'Therapy? seem rejuvenated, slimmed down and full of energy as they bounce from the classic power of "Teethgrinder" and "Screamager", via an adorable take on "Half Way Up The Stairs" by Robin The Frog from *The Muppets*, and a heartfelt attack on the government ("fuck David

Cameron and fuck his government, fuck them all")', wrote *Classic Rock*'s Emma Johnston. 'It's seventeen years to the day since they first played the Academy, and time clearly hasn't dulled them in the slightest.'

For Andy, the following night at Bristol Academy was the highlight of the tour. 'Probably three-quarters of the crowd were there for Skindred,' he remembers. 'By the end of the show, people were going fucking nuts. When you've been doing this as long as we have, there's a satisfaction of playing to somebody else's crowd and winning them over. I like that challenge.

'The whole tour was fun,' he adds. 'There was none of that bullshit that comes with playing on a package tour, where everyone's bitching about each other. Everyone was just really chilled out.'

On June 10, the band played their first ever festival in Russia. The Maxidrom Festival was held over two days at the Tushino Air Field in Moscow, a sprawling site synonymous with Metallica's 1991 Monsters Of Rock performance, which featured heavy-handed military personnel doling out harsh punishment to its attendees.

'There was a heavy security presence,' says Michael, 'but it was a really well-organised festival. On tour, we sometimes organise football matches. You'll occasionally play the local crew, or the promotions company will put together a team. When we played at the Tushino Air Field, the promoter basically rounded up the Russian equivalent of the Red Arrows. So Therapy? and a couple members of Clawfinger had a vodka-fuelled kick-about in the mud.

'We crucified those guys,' he adds. 'We played it after the gig, which is crazy as well. They were obviously fine physical specimens, but Bård [Torstensen, Clawfinger guitarist] was a fantastic footballer, so we destroyed the locals. It was a very surreal end to a very surreal day.' ('Forget Bård, I scored a hat-trick,' adds Neil, clarifying his part in the band's victory in Russia. He didn't get to keep the ball as a souvenir, however.)

In July, LaFaro drummer Alan Lynn stood in for Neil, who was on paternity leave—yes, even a rock'n'roll entity such as Therapy? allows for such employee benefits—and played Austria's Castle Clam and Forest Glade festivals, Holland's Bokpop, and Glasgowbury in Northern Ireland.

'Alan—and Adam Sinclair, who played in August—really helped us out,' says Neil. 'We were all fans of LaFaro. I'd seen Alan play a few times, the first being in a coffee shop in Derby a year or so earlier. I hassled LaFaro as I wanted to put their records out on my label, Stressed Sumo, but they had arrangements elsewhere. I knew they'd both do a great job and add their own spin on things.' (Stressed Sumo's releases to date include You Slut!'s twisted instrumental albums *Critical Meat* and *Medium Bastard*, plus the compilation *Pledge: A Tribute To Kerbdog*, featuring the likes of Frank Turner, Jamie Lenman, and Northern Ireland trio Dutch Schultz.)

'My mind was on my son being born, so to be able to step away and leave Andy and Michael in capable hands was perfect for my head at that point,' Neil adds. 'I "drum-talked" them through the tunes and wished them luck.'

Glasgowbury took place on July 21 at Eagles Rock, just outside of Draperstown in Northern Ireland. 'It started out as small festival with a stage and a generator and it got a lot bigger over the years,' says Andy. 'It doesn't exist anymore, but it was one of the most anticipated events on the Irish rock calendar. They staggered the day so people could go to the main stage and the other stage and see all the bands. When we were about to go on the main stage, the field was quite empty. Then a few minutes before we started, all these people dressed in animal onesies started coming down the hill towards us. It was like something out of *Where The Wild Things Are*, seeing the silhouettes all of these animal ears. It was like a positive spin from that scene from Ingmar Bergman's film *The Seventh Seal*, where people are holding hands on top of the hill, dancing to their deaths. I saw zebras, giraffes, lions, and leopards.'

'Alan put in a double shift that day,' Michael remembers. 'He played with LaFaro and then had to run over to our stage. We always wanted to play Glasgowbury, and it was as much fun as we expected.'

After the summer run, the band spent most of the rest of the year on the road, culminating with a thirteen-date UK tour, with support from Hawk Eyes and LaFaro. 'You know when people don't like standing near the edge of a tall building, because they get a compulsion to jump?' Andy asks. 'It's the same for me when I'm watching a shit-hot band open for us, because I get the urge to run on stage and join in. That feeling sums up that tour. I had the same feeling when we toured with Clutch and The Jesus Lizard and Helmet. LaFaro are one of the best bands that Northern Ireland has ever produced. Just as they were getting amazing they decided to call it a day.'

'We're fans of both bands, and there was a lot of mutual respect on that tour,' adds Michael. 'Everyone had their own thing to take care of, but every single crew member, Hawk Eyes, and ourselves would watch LaFaro every single night; their chat between songs was full-on. It would get worse and worse as the tour went on—borderline inappropriate. Alan would count songs in to get Jonny [Black, frontman] and Herb [Magee, bass] to shut up. They turned alienating audiences then winning them over into an art form. Hilarious.'

The year 2012 was a successful one. Therapy? had expanded their sonic palette with *A Brief Crack Of Light*—a creative risk that was largely met with acclaim and was well-received by their fans. Even so, following their lengthy closing tour of the year, they knew that some changes were necessary if they were to survive as a touring band. After all, the cash cow of the 90s music industry had been left somewhat emaciated and begging for scraps.

'We all realised as a band that we were wasting too much money much on stuff we didn't really need,' says Andy. 'Up until now, we'd fallen into the habit of using tour buses. On paper, they're an expensive hotel on wheels, equipped with bunk beds, toilets, stereos, large screens, games consoles, and fridges. These are seen as the one-stop shop for a hard-working band on the road. The problem is, unless you're Metallica, the mobile dream palace is likely to be a piece of shit that stinks of fuel, is noisy, doesn't have fully-functioning tech, and a leaking toilet.

'You also have to hire a driver—sometimes two, if the schedule is hectic, so they can take turns driving,' he continues. 'You pay their wages, provide hotels on days off, flights, and a huge per diem—a daily allowance for breakfast, lunch, and dinner. Add to the wages of the working crew—a tour manager, two technicians, a merch seller—and your outgoings for the day are huge before you play a note. This is all fine when you're playing in countries where you are popular and make enough money to pay it all. The problems begin when, as a touring band like us, you venture out into the unknown, the less-chartered territory—the countries where they couldn't really give a fuck about how big you were in the 90s. That's when you lose a lot of money. We knew if we were to survive we would have to offload the trappings of a previous lifestyle and work within a method that would benefit the band, not bus companies.'

Henry Rollins's memoir, *Get In The Van*—an unflinching look at life on the road with uncompromising Californian punks Black Flag—would no longer be a luxury coffee-table book but something of a refresher course over the coming years.

YEAR 2013
TWENTY-FOUR/live without
a net

Following the completion of the band's 2012 touring schedule, a decision was made to put live engagements on the back burner to some extent, in order to allow Michael and Neil to spend more time with their young families.

'Normally, when we had time off, it was spent writing material for the next album,' says Andy. 'But Michael and Neil needed to be at home. I thought, *If I stay at home, I'm going to drive myself mad*, because I live out in the middle of nowhere. It's not very rock'n'roll, but it does my psyche the world of good. But I looked at this big yawning chasm of time off and asked our manager if there was something I could do, so I wouldn't drive my wife and son nuts. I thought about doing some acoustic shows, and I phoned both the boys to see if they would mind. They thought it was a good idea, so our agent booked a tour.'

In the spring, the band played just two shows, both of them in Greece: at Gagarin 205 in Athens on March 15, and Thessaloniki's Block 33 the following night. Then, on April 23, Andy headed north from his home in Cambridgeshire to record a solo album at Newcastle's Blast Studios. The one-day session would be later released as a souvenir CD.

'When the shows were booked, I wanted the tour to be as self-sufficient as possible,' he says. 'Our manager suggested some merchandise, but I didn't really feel right selling shirts with my face on. That's when I thought about making an album. They wouldn't be available commercially, or on iTunes or Spotify. You could only get them from the gigs.'

Titled *53 Minutes Under Byker*, the album was recorded in six hours and ten minutes with the assistance of engineer Mark Broughton. It features a mix of stripped-down Therapy? songs and songs written especially for the release: 'Lost In Care', 'Mean', 'Bedridden', 'Self Help Books', 'Bootstraps', 'Jesus Doesn't Live Here Anymore', and a cover of Love's 'Signed D.C.'

'Mark just put up a couple of mics in the room and I did it all live,' remembers Andy. 'The whole thing was a blur, because I drove up the night before, stayed in Gateshead, and didn't sleep very well. I got to the studio, recorded the album, thanked Mark, and drove back to Cambridge.

'It still blows my mind when I think back to bands in the 60s who would record entire albums after a gig,' he adds. 'They'd play somewhere in London, drive to a studio and record all night, then go to the next gig.'

The first leg of the tour was comprised of thirteen dates and began at Birmingham's Hare & Hounds on May 13. With the band's decision to cut back unnecessary touring expenses still in mind, Andy teamed up with guitar tech and touring guitarist Stevie Firth, and the pair drove themselves to each show with a couple of guitars and copies of *53 Minutes Under Byker* in the boot.

'I thought, *If I'm going to do this, I want to do it really old-school*,' remembers Andy. 'It was so good for me as a musician; I had to be creative, and I couldn't drink alcohol, because I was driving. I had to have my wits about me to make sure we got to the venue, checked in, set up my guitars, and make sure everything was working. It was a real hands-on experience, and it reminded me a lot of what it was like when the band first started.'

By the time Andy reached the Borderline, a now-closed basement club in Soho, he was on a roll. 'The acoustic treatment strips Therapy?'s songs of their noise and metal thunder, and focuses instead more on the menace, the mood, but also the sheer melodic punk-tastic sing-alongs that they've crafted over the years,' wrote Mark Williams for the *God Is In The TV* zine. 'The latter part of the set is, as Andy describes it, "a cavalcade of hit". It feels less like a Therapy? concert, and more like a fun evening at a mate's house. Both of you are old enough to know better, but when you've got tunes this good … well, you've just got to belt them out haven't you?'

The following show, which took place at the Haunt in Brighton on May 23, is etched into the frontman's mind, albeit for very different reasons. 'That show remains one of my nadirs,' he says. 'It's one of the few things in my musical career which I detest.'

Andy remembers learning that forty-eight tickets had been sold in advance for a venue that holds three hundred people, but it wasn't the number of tickets that was the problem. 'I wasn't going to pull a rock-star tantrum and refuse to play,' he says. 'It was OK. Some shows sold more on the door, and I was looking forward to playing. We were told that there was a club after the show, and we had to make sure we were off stage by half past ten. We played the show and finished at around ten, and people wanted an encore. I was talking to the audience, and one of the bouncers waved at me and reminded me about the curfew. During one of the final songs, the bouncers and bar staff started stacking chairs and dragging them across the room. This is in the middle of an acoustic song. You could have heard a pin drop. It was really rude and fucking horrendous.'

Spare a thought, then, for the fan who'd travelled from Norway. 'I met this guy after the gig and he was really depressed,' Andy remembers. 'He told me the bouncer said, "If I was you, I'd turn and go, because it's going to be shit tonight." A couple from Finland said he'd said exactly the same thing to them. I will never fucking set foot in that place again.'

Following a full-band show at Camden Rocks—a multi-venue, one-day festival set up by 3 Colours Red guitarist Chris McCormack—Andy's solo adventures continued into Belgium and Holland until the middle of June. 'A lot of the European shows were bigger than they were in the UK,' he remembers. 'They were proper seated theatres, and there were a lot of people who'd come along. It was fucking terrifying because I realised that, without the band, it was up to me to keep people compelled. I really enjoyed the challenge.'

Andy reconvened with Michael and Neil later that month for a series of European festival appearances and club shows, before the band ended their year's live activity in late October with a run of shows in Ireland. 'I'm really proud of Andy for doing those solo shows,' says Michael. 'I can't imagine it would have been an easy thing to do, to get up there and play a ninety-minute show with just a guitar and voice. I saw him play in Dublin, and what struck was how good the songs sounded, stripped down like that. And, coupled with some insightful and, in cases, hilarious between song stories, it was a brilliant show.'

'I felt it was a great move on Andy's part,' says Neil. 'Michael and I had family stuff going on, and it made total sense for Andy to stay busy, keep the name out there, and give fans something new to get their teeth into and enjoy. I went along to the Nottingham show, and he invited me up to join him and play "Nowhere" on snare and brushes. During the gig, I was in the audience, watching everyone respond to the stripped-down versions of the songs and his stories behind the songs. It was something really special.'

The following month saw the biggest release of Therapy?'s career so far—quite literally. *The Gemil Box* was released on November 18. 'Gemil'—the band's triangular mascot—had, until now, adorned various items of band merchandise dating back to the start of their career, not to mention the cover of *Crooked Timber*.

Andy recalls the moment his equilateral hero was conceived. 'In early 1990, myself and Fyfe were in a mutual friend's apartment near Queen's University in Belfast,' he explains. 'She was in Dublin and had given us the keys. I was up all night tripping and watching television, laughing my head off. We knew we had been thinking of designing some t-shirts for some time, so I drew the angry triangle guy on a piece of paper, and Fyfe liked it. We'd been watching a history of the World Cup, and it featured the famous goal scored by Archie Gemmill for Scotland against Holland in 1978. Both of us remembered the goal and were marvelling at the audacity of the fella. We decided we should name it Gemmill in tribute. I don't know how it came to be spelled *Gemil*.'

The black, twelve-inch, silver-embossed box set housed remastered CD versions of *Nurse*, *Troublegum*, *Infernal Love*, and *Semi-Detached*; two discs of unreleased material; a disc of demos and reworked songs; a DVD of the band's Sonisphere performance in 2010 (yes, that one), plus two video bootlegs; a twelve-inch titled *Listen You Fuckers*, featuring sixteen original demos; a cassette of a Dublin show recorded in 1990; and a twenty-four-page hardback book.

'We'd been working on that since 2009,' says Michael. 'It escalated from a few remastered CDs to this huge box set. There's always unused songs flying around, so we thought, if we were going to do it, we may as well do it right.'

Although the set offered a treasure trove of classic and unreleased material, the band's first two mini-albums, *Babyteeth* and *Pleasure Death*, were conspicuous by their absence. 'That's one of my only regrets,' admits Michael. 'They were meant to be part of the package. The relationship with Southern had always been a bit weird since we'd left. Harvey Birrell, who recorded *Pleasure Death* and *Nurse*, had done brilliant remastered versions, and it was all approved, in theory, at their end. Our manager asked the label for the paperwork and was told they hadn't looked at it yet. By this stage they'd had it for a good twelve months, so I have no idea why they decided to start messing about so late on. I was really excited about people hearing those, because those were the two albums that, sonically, needed a bit of a scrub up. Southern was a great label—they put out brilliant music, and gave us a great start—so that felt a bit petty and unnecessary, to be honest.'

Limited to one thousand copies, and with a reasonable £90 price tag, *The Gemil Box* was quickly snapped up by fans. Copies can now fetch over three times the original value. 'It was such a labour of love,' says Michael. 'I think most people got the intent behind it. In true Therapy? style, once we committed to it, it got to the point where it became ridiculous and we had to scale it down to make it manageable.'

As the band's archivist, Michael has over a thousand live tapes, as well as recordings of practically every rehearsal and demo. 'I think I was part of the reason there ended up being so much stuff,' he admits. 'It would have been easy just to farm it out to someone, but it certainly wouldn't have had the quality or depth of stuff to it. We could easily do a second box set with the amount of stuff we've unearthed since then.'

YEAR
TWENTY-FIVE/sweatin' to
the oldies

In mid-February, Andy performed three solo acoustic dates in Finland, before joining Michael and Neil at Newcastle's Blast Studios to begin pre-production of the band's fourteenth studio effort. This time, they had secured the services of Tom Dalgety, who had produced Royal Blood's debut album the previous year. Together, they spent two weeks honing pre-existing material—'Still Hurts', 'Tides', 'Idiot Cousin', 'Insecurity', 'Words Fail Me', and 'Deathstimate'—and working on a handful of embryonic ideas.

'We knew what kind of album we wanted to do,' says Andy. 'There was one song in particular that needed a lot of work. After Tom heard the original version of "Vulgar Display Of Powder", he thought it needed to be tougher. We did it in a slightly heavier tuning, and with a completely different arrangement.'

On March 31, Universal released a three-disc deluxe version of the 1994 album *Troublegum* and a two-disc edition of the 1995 follow-up, *Infernal Love*. 'As well as doing *The Gemil Box*, we were collecting bonus material for the reissues,' says Michael. 'I was involved with all the shenanigans going on there, approving B-sides *and* demos, and making sure there was no overlap between the box set. With the *Troublegum* anniversary shows coming up, it was perfect timing.'

The band marked the twentieth anniversary of *Troublegum* with eight UK shows in early April. Kicking off with a date at Bristol's Trinity Centre on April 2, the tour ended almost two weeks later at Southampton's Mo' Club. 'When you think back to when we started and what our ambitions were, it was crazy to think we'd be celebrating the release of an album two decades after it was released,' says Michael. 'I mean, fucking hell. Twenty years! When people tell us how they related to the album when it came out, it always blows my mind. I can remember when I first heard bands like Black Sabbath, AC/DC, and Motörhead, so it's always interesting to hear people tell similar stories about us, of all bands.'

Two weeks after the *Troublegum* and *Infernal Love* reissues were released, *Stories—The Singles Collection* emerged from the Universal Music Catalogue. Meanwhile, Therapy? headed back to Blast to resume work on their new album with Tom Dalgety on April 17. Tom's first taste of the band came when he purchased Ozzy Osbourne's 1996 single 'I Just Want You', which included Therapy?'s cover of 'Iron Man' as a bonus track. 'After hearing the "Iron Man" cover, my next step was borrowing *Nurse* on cassette from my local library,' he recalls. 'I have to confess I didn't get it straight away, so I went back the following week and switched it for *Troublegum*.'

At the studio, Tom presented the band with a photograph he had taken with the band after a show Terminal 396, a venue in Cardiff University's Student Union on December 12 1999. 'On that tour, Andy had been getting kids from the audience to come and play guitar on either "Screamager" or "Nowhere" with them,' he remembers. 'That night, I was the lucky one who got up and did "Screamager". Playing your favourite song with your favourite band aged fifteen is a pretty crazy feeling. I still have the plectrum somewhere.'

The band recorded the eleven-track *Disquiet* over fourteen days, the results fizzing with not only the energy but also the subject matter that informed *Troublegum*. 'Tom was just what we needed in the studio,' remembers Michael. 'He was really into it and was really positive. There weren't any mind games or an agenda. He just wanted the songs to sound really fucking good. We had maybe sixteen songs at the start of the year, and Tom picked the ones he felt he could do the most with.'

'I don't think there were any massive changes,' adds Tom. 'I just curated the content, really. Out of the songs they'd written, I picked the eleven darkest and moodiest ones. They were really receptive to any suggestions.

It was a really nice, open collaboration. We all have a lot in common when it comes to music and film, so we were often on the same page when it came to references. Michael and I also developed an unhealthy obsession with Malteaster chocolate bunnies.'

'Tom was really good at getting the best out of each of us when recording,' adds Neil. 'He'd always push the performance and remind me of fills or rhythms I'd played in rehearsals or live that worked better. The lads recorded their parts as a guide to a click track and left me and Tom to record the drums proper. He'd always make me laugh. I remember recording "Still Hurts", and it was one of those takes when you get to the end of the song and you know it's killer. I was thinking, *Awesome, that's the one*, but was met with silence. All deadpan, he said, "Nah, I'm not feeling it"! He did a such great job on that album.'

The band debuted the album's opening track, 'Still Hurts', at Cork's Cyprus Avenue on October 25 2013. The song quite literally picks up where *Troublegum* leaves off, beginning with the same crunching chord that concluded 'Brainsaw'. 'I was playing "Brainsaw" in my garage, and, as soon as it ended, I started improvising on the guitar,' says Andy. 'Within half an hour, I'd come up with "Still Hurts". The lyrics are a continuation of the person in *Troublegum* and how he feels twenty years later. The music's very *Troublegum*; it's got that stop-start thing and little bits of Big Black in there.'

'Tides' is a slice of melancholic, Hüsker Dü-esque pop, propelled by regret and chiming guitars, which Tom describes as 'Geordie Walker meets [post-punk guitarist] John McGeoch'. The lyrics were inspired by a quote from Samuel Beckett's one-act play *Krapp's Last Tape*: 'Spiritually a year of profound gloom and indulgence until that memorable night in March, at the end of the jetty, in the howling wind, never to be forgotten, when I suddenly saw the whole thing. The vision at last … the fire that set me alight.'

'Before I met my wife, I'd moved from Bray in County Wicklow to a place called Dún Laoghaire in 1995,' Andy explains. 'It's a rough-and-ready port town. When I lived in Dún Laoghaire, I felt like I was right in the middle of everything; our management and a lot of my friends were in Ireland. At this point I'd been using quite a lot of narcotics, so I'd be up to all hours. I smoked heavily and would often need to go and find some cigarettes at four in the morning. There was one shop that was open twenty-four hours. The only people who'd be out would be me out of my mind on coke, some drunks and prostitutes. When I couldn't sleep, I'd walk down to the pier and watch the sea. I took that low point in my life and how I managed to dig myself out as the basis for the song.'

'Good News Is No News' is a slow-burning song about the 'Eeyores' of the world—people who thrive on negativity and petty drama. 'I was trying to write a song that would be a bit like The Cars or something like that,' says Andy. 'I don't think it quite hit the nail on the head—it's one of my least favourite songs on the album.'

Like 'Tides', 'Fall Behind' is an autobiographical, pop-inflected song wrapped in bold, distorted riffs. 'If I'm not careful, I can get wrapped up in myself too much,' says Andy. 'I always felt this song was like a second cousin of something off *Semi-Detached*.'

'Idiot Cousin' recalls the band's early days in Northern Ireland and Andy's conversations with co-workers at his job at the Michelin factory. 'When we started, you had the sort-of chubby guy singing, a guy who looked about twelve on the bass, and a skinny, lanky guy on the drums that never spoke to anyone,' says Andy. 'We'd had a gig the night before, and there was this guy who was about sixty, who said, "You don't look like a boy who would sing." I think some people thought that if you were in a band, you had to look like David Bowie or Paul McCartney, not someone who looked like me. I should have been carrying the cases around. Actually, that reminds me of a time I went to see The Almighty while they were playing on MTV in the mid-90s. The band were at lunch, and Davina McCall saw me. She came over and asked me if I could move some amps so they'd be out of shot. She had me moving flight cases as well. About ten minutes later, she came over and apologised—she thought I was one of the crew. The band pissed themselves laughing.'

Whereas 'Still Hurts' picks up from where 'Brainsaw' left off, 'Helpless Still Lost' is a companion piece to 'Unbeliever'. 'Whenever I was writing lyrics, I'd think about what the protagonists of *Troublegum* were doing now,' explains Andy. 'This song is about the narrator of "Unbeliever": slightly older, slightly saggier, but still in the same position. I wrote the song after watching the [2013] Robert Redford film *All Is Lost*. He's at sea, and it's just him on his own. It sounds like a hard sell, but it's absolutely stunning.'

'Insecurity'—described by Andy as 'a real in-your-face thumper'—has an insistent riff that's reminiscent of Therapy?'s cover of Joy Division's 'Isolation'. 'That's about dealing with everyday problems, from the moment you open your eyes to the moment you go to sleep,' he adds. 'The song itself is pretty literal, just describing the litany of things that can go wrong, especially if you're hungover: "*I woke up screaming with the devil on my chest.*"'

The title 'Vulgar Display Of Powder' had been kicking around in Andy's notebook for a long time; here, it's paired with a blunt, Helmet-like riff buoyed by a chorus that wouldn't be out of place on a classic Ozzy Osbourne album. 'This song is about liggers, the kind of people who'd walk on broken glass to get backstage,' says Andy. 'There's a certain type of sick desperation. Even when we're playing smaller regional gigs, there are still people who see backstage as the Holy Grail, this mythical place of wonder. There's times when someone's told some story to security and we'll let them through and go, "Look, have a can of beer and make yourself a sandwich. No one's doing coke. Axl Rose isn't here, and Slash isn't pouring Jack Daniel's for everyone. There's a packet of cheese and some half-eaten chicken; this is life backstage."'

Samuel Beckett makes his presence felt on the flailing 'Words Fail Me', a song informed by open chords and a sense of mischief. 'Tom had a lot of input on this one,' says Andy. 'Originally, it was very *Bleach*-era Nirvana and had big, mucky power chords. He suggested I let the notes ring, like Geordie Walker from Killing Joke, so it would sound more like Therapy?.

'Sometimes I'll wake in the night and be upset about something someone said to me about ten years before,' he adds. 'It's more about the feeling than the actual words. What I've always really liked about Beckett is he wanted to get rid of language so he could get to the pure essence of being, and describe it in a scream, a sound, a movement or a gesture. Words can cause so much trouble. There's a line that goes, "*Cruelty comes so easy to some / On others it leaves a mark.*" Whether something said is intended to hurt or not, it can actually stay with you and deeply hurt for a long, long time.'

'Torment Sorrow Misery Strife' is a distant cousin of *Infernal Love*'s closing track, '30 Seconds', with Andy taking aim at the promises of a better life perpetuated by advertising billboards. The working title was 'I've Had 18 Straight Whiskies, I Think That's A Record', the last words uttered by the Welsh poet Dylan Thomas, who died in New York City, aged just thirty-nine, in 1953.

'I had Social Distortion in mind when I wrote "Torment Sorrow Misery Strife"; it was almost like something that would have been on their album *White Light, White Heat, White Trash*,' says Andy. 'I don't think Neil liked the middle tempo. It was too Americana and verging on Bruce Springsteen, maybe, so Tom made the call to make it really full-on, like something on Metallica's *Garage Days Revisited*.'

For the album's closing track, 'Deathstimate', Andy told the producer that he wanted it to sound like a Black Sabbath song as performed by Bristol trip-hop pioneers Portishead, unaware that their vocalist, Beth Gibbons, had recently recorded a cover of Sabbath's ominous title track with the UK metal band Gonga. 'I've got Fugazi's *Red Medicine* to thank for this song, because I started out trying to write a riff that wouldn't be out of place on that record,' he explains. 'I used to hate that album. When I first heard it, I was like, "Jangly guitars? Get to fuck! Who the fuck do they think they are?" But it's now my favourite. I absolutely love it.

'I was going to turn fifty the following year, and I was thinking a lot about that,' he adds. 'With lyrics like "*The road ahead looks shorter than the one behind*", it's quite a depressing song, but I think just the triumph of the riff kind of anchors it, so it's not completely wallowing in self pity. I think it's one of the best riffs we've ever written, and it's a joy to play it live, over and over.'

On June 20, the band made their debut appearance on the main stage at Hellfest, an annual open-air festival in Clisson, France. There, they shared a bill with headliners Iron Maiden, Rob Zombie, Queensrÿche, Sabaton, Satan, Crossfaith, and openers Nightmare. 'When we got the Hellfest slot, people were like, "How did you get on the main stage?"' says Andy. 'People forget that *Troublegum* sold over a million records, and it was massive in France. You don't sell hundreds of thousands of records in France without nobody knowing who the fuck you are.'

'I'd always looked at the Hellfest bills with much envy,' Michael adds. 'We had it in our head that we might not be heavy enough for some bizarre reason, but the show went really well.'

'Metal has really changed over the years,' Andy continues. 'Iron Maiden could play the same stage as Jawbox, but no one's going to bat an eyelid. We had a really good turn out and it was a fantastic day. We toured France the following year and got the biggest crowds we'd had in year, and I think a lot has to do with playing Hellfest.'

In July, the band returned to Sonisphere at Knebworth to play a special *Infernal Love* set, headlining the Bohemia Stage. It was a chance to lay some demons to rest, following the near disaster of their *Troublegum* set four years earlier. With no warm-up sets, *Infernal Love* was played in its entirety for the first time, including 'Bowels Of Love', which the band had omitted from their setlists following the release of the album in 1995.

'The tour following *Infernal Love* was brilliant, don't get me wrong, but the whole thing had been tainted by that never-ending feeling of pressure while we recorded that album,' says Michael. 'Everyone took the Sonisphere in the right spirit, and Andy even played keyboards of "Bowels Of Love". The set went brilliantly, and it never sounded this good when we toured it back in the day.

'What we've noticed is this groundswell of appreciation for the album over the years,' he adds. 'Some people said they hated it at the time and grew to love it. There was a real buzz when we played that day. They could have easily went, "Oh dear, not that pile of old goth bollocks." So that set was really validating. There was no hurry to rush out *Disquiet* at that stage, so we were sitting on a lot of good stuff. It was a good position to be in.'

With a number of solo acoustic shows booked for September, Andy returned to Newcastle's Blast Studios on August 19 to record his second solo album. With engineer Liam Gaughan at the desk, Andy performed eighteen songs in under six hours. Like *53 Minutes Under Byker*, this latest collection featured a mix of Therapy? favourites and a batch of new songs written especially for it: 'I Fucked Up', 'Armed With Anger', 'Demons! Demons!', and 'Meltdown Bound'. There are a number of ambient interludes threaded throughout, including a phone sample recorded on a beach in East Anglia and a snippet from *The House Is Black*, a short film by the Iranian director Forough Farrokhzad. The album itself was titled *"Fuck You Johnny Camo"*.

'I have to be careful how I put this, but we have a phrase in the band to describe a certain type of music fan,' says Andy. 'When you see them approaching, you know that the first thing they'll say is, "What the fuck was that dub mix all about?" or "When are you going to do another album like *Troublegum* again?" We'd nicknamed them Johnny Camo. It's not just in the UK, it's worldwide.'

A few days later, the band played two shows in Holland: at Poppodium Volt Sittard on August 22, and the Huntenpop Festival the following day.

Michael sat out those two shows as his wife was expecting their second child. A call was made to LaFaro bassist Herb Magee, whose second ever show as a fan was Therapy?'s gig at Belfast's Ulster Hall on December 30 1995 (his first was Def Leppard).

'I was watching Michael playing bass, thinking he was having the time of his life,' Herb told BBC Radio Ulster, in an interview about the formative influences that shaped his electronica project, Arvo Party. 'I wanted to do that. He's kind of the reason I wanted to be a bass player. When LaFaro ended, I was living in Bushmills with my parents, and I got a phone call from Michael [asking me to join the band temporarily]. It was incredible—like a weird dream.'

Following Andy's eleven-date trek around the UK in September—and an appearance at Holland's Breda Barst Festival—Therapy? reconvened for another *Troublegum* set at Belfast's Mandela Hall on November 15, as part of the Northern Ireland Music Prize 2014. The band were awarded the Oh Yeah Legend Award on the night, joining previous winners The Undertones, Stiff Little Fingers, and the late Gary Moore. 'Therapy? fully deserve a Legend Award,' remarked Stuart Bailie, journalist and then CEO of Oh Yeah Music Centre, in the run-up to the ceremony. 'They completely transformed our music scene in the 90s and are respected internationally. They continue to make great records, and it will be such a thrill to hear their *Troublegum* classic performed in its entirety.'

'That meant a lot to me, because the Oh Yeah centre is one of the symbols of the new Northern Irish music business,' says Andy. 'Because people forget just how bad it was when we started, and it wasn't really until after the Good Friday Agreement that all these little ships of hope popped up. There were always brilliant musicians and a brilliant music scene, but it wasn't until after that that people really took it by the horns: record labels, proper nightclubs, proper gigs. We didn't expect the award, which made it all the sweeter. We got a phone call out of the blue, and we were so made up.'

'When we started, we were very much outsiders, especially in Belfast,' adds Michael. 'The people that run Oh Yeah have a genuine passion for what they're doing. It was really nice to be recognised with that award.'

'I fully understand what Michael's saying about being outsiders,' adds Neil. 'That's a viewpoint we all share. I've always felt musically completely out of step with my hometown, and, for me, either with Therapy? or, years ago, when I was in The Beyond or Cable—it's a belligerent mindset you find yourself in. It's got to be one of the reasons why Michael, Andy, and myself see eye-to-eye on so many things.

'Stuart's so genuine and enthusiastic,' he adds. 'It was great hearing his speech. He knows his stuff and spoke about the band's whole career. He said some really nice things about me joining the band, which is always nice! The acknowledgement meant more to me than I expected, actually. I've always loved playing in Belfast and have always felt welcomed, but this was like an official acceptance in a weird way. Essentially, though, what I really enjoyed was watching Michael and Andy being recognised for what they've achieved over the years, and how they changed a musical landscape on their home turf. That was awesome.'

After receiving their award, the band played *Troublegum* in full before a packed crowd, including family, friends, and old faces from their early shows. Snow Patrol's Nathan Connolly joined the band for 'Die Laughing'.

'I remember lying down in the hotel afterwards,' says Andy, 'and I just felt grateful. To be honest, there'd been quite a lot of doubt since 2002. There were points when I thought, *Does anyone actually give a fuck any more?* I'd always want to be recognised—maybe by *Kerrang!* or something like that—and it never came. But to get the Oh Yeah award gave us a sense of vindication, and the realisation that what we've done hasn't been in vain.'

YEAR
TWENTY-SIX/there is a light at the end of the tunnel

The eleven-month gap between finishing *Disquiet* and its release was due to Blast Records' Eric and Ged Cook diverting their attention to their recording studios. In the interim, Eric took on an advisory role at Amazing Record Co, a new label founded by Gateshead-based Amazing Radio.

'Eric introduced us to the people behind that, and we told them what we wanted to achieve,' Andy explains. 'We were still working with Eric and recording at Blast, so it would be the same in all but name on the back of the record.'

'Still Hurts' was the first single to be released from the album, appearing on March 9 alongside two non-album songs, 'Demons! Demons!' and 'Armed With Anger', which had previously featured on Andy's *"Fuck You Johnny Camo"*. *Disquiet* was released two weeks later.

'[The album] shares certain lyrical themes with *Troublegum* and there are echoes of earlier tracks and even callbacks to certain riffs,' wrote J.R. Moores of *The Quietus*. 'Fortunately, the songs themselves are strong enough to be of great comfort to those who felt lost twenty years ago and found some degree of solace in *Troublegum*. And particularly by those of us who still feel lost today.'

Classic Rock's Paul Brannigan awarded the album four out of five, suggesting that the band sounded reinvigorated on the eleven-track effort. 'There's something perversely life-affirming about this salty bleakness, particularly when it's accompanied by some of the sharpest riffs Cairns has crafted in years,' he wrote. 'Yet amid all this doom, Therapy? sound reborn, utterly at ease with a sound they largely abandoned twenty years back. If this brilliant set propels them from the margins once more, that would surely be the greatest irony of all.'

Benjamin Bland echoed that sentiment in his review for *Drowned In*

Sound: 'If *Disquiet* proves anything, it's that Therapy? still have plenty of life in them. This shouldn't be seen as a concession to those that have been waiting for a more pop-inflected follow-up to their 1994 fan favourite [*Troublegum*], but instead as a bullish reminder that not only are Therapy? still here, but they still do what they do better than almost anyone who has attempted to copy them in the intervening two decades. When they do eventually depart—and I hope it is many years from now—it will be a sad, sad day for British rock music.'

The album earned four *K*s from *Kerrang!*, too—'weird, arty, heavy excellence, thy name is (still) Therapy?'—while *Record Collector* felt the album 'crackles with a credible contemporary energy and parades a succession of brutally accessible would-be hits courtesy of "Still Hurts", "Insecurity" and the soaring, Hüsker Dü-ish "Tides".'

For Andy, the positive press response and resultant placing in the UK album chart at no. 79—making *Disquiet* their most successful album since *Semi-Detached*—'kick-started the band's third act. Before that,' he admits, 'the shows were doing well, but in terms of sales, we were idling. I think, with *Disquiet*, there was a lot about that which reminded older fans what they'd fallen in love with: unusual riffs with hooky choruses, lyrics which were written like punch lines, and great artwork by Nigel Rolfe. We have a great hardcore fan base, but I think we reached a lot of people who maybe hadn't bought a Therapy? record since *Semi-Detached* or earlier.'

On March 31, the band kicked off a series of live dates, beginning with a show at Brighton's Concorde 2, ahead of one at London's Scala the following evening. Support came from Belgian trio Triggerfinger and Midlands punks Thirty Six Strategies, featuring bassist and punk historian Ian Glasper, whose band Decadence Within headlined Therapy?'s first ever show in 1989. 'I've kind of been in touch with Ian pretty much since 1989, which is nuts when I think about it,' says Michael. 'He's a lifer, and I've a lot of respect for him; he's really straight up and really knows his stuff. It was a real pleasure having them along on the tour.'

Buoyed by the reaction to *Disquiet*, the band's setlist leaned heavily on their new material, and they soon discovered it slotted neatly alongside established fan favourites. 'I bloody loved *A Brief Crack Of Light* and *Crooked Timber*,' says Neil. 'In hindsight, you get a clarity to what was going on at the time. We were making a point of doing what we really love, and we went unbelievably insular, but in a good way. They were really dark records. With *Disquiet*, the songs felt like there was a light at the end of the tunnel, and the crowd responded to that.'

'I definitely felt that, after we released *Disquiet*, there was a groundswell of people who'd not seen us for years,' adds Michael. 'Every night, people would tell us that they hadn't seen us since 1993 or 1994. As the tour went on, I'd hear it more and more.

'The reason for people returning to the band was, to paraphrase my good friend Elton John, a circle of life,' he adds. 'People maybe got into us when they were teenagers and then, twenty years down the line, their attentions turn to family, jobs, and stuff like that. It's understandable. But with the rise of social media and streaming, people can reconnect with the music they used to like. Doing the *Troublegum* and *Infernal Love* anniversary shows brought a lot of people back into the fold. We'd made a lot of good albums since, so there was a lot for people to get into.'

Following an appearance at Serbia's Gitarijada Festival on August 1, Michael and Neil worked on two new songs without Andy's knowledge. Enlisting the talents of the band's former merch seller 'Diamond' Dave, Tom Dalgety, Ash frontman Tim Wheeler, Black Star Riders' Ricky Warwick, Robyn G. Shiels, Stevie Firth, and The Black Halos' Rich Jones, they recorded a brand new song, 'Purveyor Of Quackery', and a cover of The Only Ones' 'Another Girl, Another Planet'. They pressed up ten seven-inch copies of the two songs, billed to The Gemils, with artwork parodying the Ramones' 1976 debut album. The single would be the second ever release on the band's own Multifuckingnational record label, originally set up to release their debut, *Meat Abstract*. One copy was set aside to present to Andy for his fiftieth birthday the following month, with the remainder going to those who'd taken part.

'Andy wanted to have a birthday party in London, with us, Michael's old band Evil Priest, and The Beyond on the bill,' explains Neil. 'That was poo-poo'd by management, because it would clash with London dates. And on a business level, I get that, but I was talking to Michael and thought we had to do something.'

'Andy's a big Ramones fan, and he loves The Only Ones, so we thought it would be fun to do a limited single made by his friends,' adds Michael. 'I had some riffs, Neil did the drums, and Tom played guitar and mixed it. Rich Jones—who's credited as Johnny Blunders on the record—did some lead guitar on it. I'd emailed him and he was on a train somewhere in Eastern Europe, but he turned it around in a few days. Tim and Ricky did a chanty thing, and it all came together.'

'I had the job of writing the lyrics about Andy,' adds Diamond, 'and I threw them together in my own inimitable way. It was a bit of daftness and a lovely thing to be a part of.'

On September 22, Andy was woken by his son, Jonah. First came a cup of green tea. Then a laptop. A video began to play, featuring some familiar faces. 'There was Frank Turner, James Dean Bradfield, Barney from Napalm Death, Tom Dalgety,' he begins. 'Michael had been collecting messages in the months leading up to my birthday, and covertly sent them to my wife, Kris. It was brilliant.'

Kris handed him an envelope. Andy, who regularly travels to Stamford Bridge to support his beloved Chelsea Football Club, was shocked to discover a letter from the club's then-manager, José Mourinho, wishing him a happy birthday.

Then came a gift-wrapped seven-inch single. 'I thought it might have been a rare single by a Belfast punk band I'd mentioned,' adds Andy. 'Then I looked closely at the artwork and saw it featured "Another Girl, Another Planet", which is one of my favourite songs of all time. It slowly dawned on me what this gift was. I was in tears that morning. It was such a fantastic way to start my fiftieth birthday, and I was so grateful. It blows my mind that everyone went to so much trouble.'

Therapy? spent much of November touring Europe—the Netherlands, Germany, Austria, and Belgium—before returning to Ireland for three *Infernal Love* anniversary shows. The Membranes—the legendary Blackpool post-punks led by one-time Therapy? producer John Robb— were in support. 'They'd just released *Dark Matter/Dark Energy*, which was such a stunning record,' says Andy. 'We all got on with John. He's good to be around; he's proactive and positive, which is infectious.'

Neil had previously worked with John, when he was a member of Cable. The Membranes frontman produced their 1996 album *Down-Lift The Up-Trodden* at Monnow Valley Studio in the appropriately named Welsh village of Rockfield.

'While we were on tour, we were laughing about the last time I'd had a night out with him,' Neil explains. 'To celebrate the end of the recording session, we went out for some drinks in town. On the way back, we'd ordered a mini-bus to pick us up, and the driver said he was picking up someone who was staying at Rockfield Studios, which wasn't far.' The passenger was Liam Gallagher; he recognised John and invited everyone back for a nightcap at the studio, where Oasis were working on their second album, *(What's The Story) Morning Glory?*.

'I started chatting to Noel Gallagher and [Oasis drummer] Alan White,' Neil continues, 'and we head down to the studio room for a look around and to have a bit of a play. While I was down there, Darius [Hinks, Cable guitarist] was drinking himself into a stupor. What I didn't realise was that, earlier, Liam had been playing their new album recordings, without Noel knowing. Darius said to Liam, "Why do you always have to rip off The Beatles?" which was the final straw. Liam replied, "I'm number one, me! I'm fucking number one! Who are you?" Darius replied, "No, you're not. Your brother's number one." That's when the punches started!'

'Darius was in no fit state to fight anyone at this stage, which made Liam's response even more comical,' he adds. 'The next day, we heard the band's session at Rockfield had been put on hold, and Cable were getting a bill for the damage to the property. It turns out that Noel flipped out when he heard Liam had been playing the rough mixes to everyone and ended up having a scrap with Liam on the grass, then drove home. Liam apparently smashed up the place, hence the bill.'

Let's go back to 2015. The band played two shows at Dublin's Button Factory on December 10 and 11, followed by a performance at Belfast's Limelight the following evening. For Andy, these special performances went some way to further bury the ghosts of the trying times at Real World studio two decades previously.

'The shows were great and helped me with coming to terms with that record,' he explains. '*Infernal Love* reminded me of having no sleep, loads of ecstasy and coke, feeling under pressure and feeling depressed. When I'd hear that wobble before it goes into "Epilepsy", I'd immediately want to turn it off and get out of the room. But I had to listen to the album, learn the keyboard part for "Bowels Of Love", and relearn the songs we rarely played. I'd judge the production or the songs. We rehearsed it for two days in John Henry's in London and made sure everything was just right.

'Everyone we met was so effusive about what that record meant to them and would show us their *Infernal Love* question-mark tattoos,' he adds. 'Those experiences rescued that record for me, but the most important thing was what it means to the people who keep this band alive and how they'd relate to it.'

The band's final show of the year took place on December 19 at the Electric Ballroom, a 1,500-capacity venue on Camden High Street in London. But earlier that day, Michael had other business to attend to. 'I went to see [the new *Star Wars* film] *The Force Awakens*, so I thought my day couldn't get any better from then on in, but it did,' he remembers. 'It was one of those shows were absolutely everything clicked.'

Or, as Andy told the crowd from the Electric Ballroom stage, 'I've enjoyed playing this far more than I did when it was fucking released. The demons are gone.'

The year's final run of shows further impressed upon Neil how important the *Infernal Love* shows had been for his bandmates. 'The lads were finding it quite therapeutic,' he says, 'and it put to bed a lot of baggage they were carrying from that time. I could see it each night. Watching your friends go through that is a good thing. I think those shows did the album justice.'

YEAR
TWENTY-SEVEN/strum kind
of monster

Following the *Infernal Love* tour, the band spent much of January touring Europe in support of *Disquiet*, playing shows in France, Austria, Hungary, Switzerland, and the Czech Republic. The next month, they spent a further three weeks touring the UK, playing their *Infernal Love +
More* set.

'I found it challenging to play that set after the *Disquiet* shows the previous month,' Michael admits. 'We had to get into a certain mindset to play the album still. I personally got a lot better at judging the mood and giving the songs like "Bowels Of Love" or "A Moment Of Clarity" the correct gravitas without dooming people out.

'It was a celebration of an album that people loved, but we didn't want to make it a harrowing trawl through the personal stuff me and Andy were going through at the time. I would have liked to do more shows like this in Europe, actually. It might be something to look at in the future.'

On April 15, the band released 'Tides', their final single from *Disquiet*.

It coincided with their debut appearance at the Whitby Goth Weekend, an alternative festival held on the North Yorkshire coast. The band headlined the first day of the weekend, on a bill featuring The Red Paintings, Lene Lovich, and Hands Off Gretel.

'A lot of our formative years were spent listening to Joy Division, Fields Of The Nephilim, The Mission, and The Sisters Of Mercy,' says Michael. 'Playing a goth festival was no more different than doing the Monsters Of Rock at Donington in 1994. We didn't know what to expect but just did our own thing.'

'What I liked most about that day was that the festival took over Whitby,' adds Andy. 'You'd go into a pub and hear bands like Siouxsie & The Banshees, Alien Sex Fiend, and The Birthday Party being played, and that was all good with me. We didn't change the set to play to a potentially partisan crowd, and while there might not have been people wearing loads of Therapy? merch or going mad down the front, I think they appreciated what we were trying to do. We were treated very well.'

On June 18, the band were invited to headline the Indigo stage at the Stone Free festival at the O2 Arena in London. On the main stage were the likes of Alice Cooper, The Darkness, Apocalyptica, and Blackberry Smoke. The Indigo stage featured former Hanoi Rocks vocalist Michael Monroe, The Virginmarys, Jackaman, and Jared James Nichols.

'It was quite surreal,' says Michael. 'I didn't realise it was in a shopping mall. It was a strange one for me—I flew in on the day, because London City airport was only a few miles away. We played around 4pm. I was back home a few hours later, and the phone kept pinging with videos from the lads, who were watching The Darkness and Alice Cooper. I was drinking tea on my sofa, which is proper rock'n'roll.'

On August 4, the band travelled to Wacken Open Air in Germany. Given the success of *Troublegum* in that country more than two decades previously, it was surprising that this was first time they performed at the metal festival.

'Michael knew it was going to be brilliant as soon as we got the offer to play,' says Andy. 'I thought we might have played to a half-empty tent, but it was rammed. It's such an iconic festival and has an influence on the rest of the rock calendar. The show was streamed, and "Screamager" featured on the Wacken souvenir album. It was great for us—the next time we went to Germany, the attendances were up.'

On September 5, the band performed at a party celebrating the thirtieth anniversary of the BBC's *Across The Line*, their set including a cover of Ash's 'Kung Fu'. The event, hosted by presenters Rigsy and Stuart Bailie, was broadcast live on BBC Radio Ulster and featured Soak, Villagers, The Divine Comedy's Neil Hannon, The 4 Of Us, Saint Sister, and R51.

'*Across The Line* was a flagship youth programme on BBC Radio Ulster which started a few years before Therapy? started,' Andy explains. 'Mike Edgar, who was the drummer with Cruella De Ville, was one of the presenters. Irish music was very much living in the post-U2 doldrums; a lot of the music was very windswept, with echoey, scratchy guitar, bombastic vocals and sentiments. Then bands like Therapy?, Pink Turds In Space, Pig Ignorance, Tension, and interesting pop and electronic came along. *Across The Line* became an Irish institution, and, from a regional point of view, it was very important as they played local bands' demos. It was a fantastic night.'

'*Across The Line* was on TV for a while, in a magazine format,' adds Michael. 'If you remember the "Nozin' Aroun'" segment on *The Young Ones*, it initially had that vibe to it. But they touched on a lot of things that affected young people in Northern Ireland, like drugs and homelessness, and social issues, as well as arts and cultures that were maybe a bit under the radar. We had a lot of support from them over the years. We did a session for them just before *Pleasure Death* came out. To go in and record a session was a bit of a coup for a band as noisy as us. They've been so good to us over the years, so that night was very important for us.'

On October 1, the band returned to Blast studios in Newcastle to record an acoustic album. Over the course of two days, the band recorded eleven songs with engineer Thom Lewis. The album *Wood & Wire* would be sold on tour. 'We rehearsed for a day, just sat in a triangle, and ran through the songs,' Andy explains. 'If they didn't work, we wouldn't spend time pursuing them.

'When I recorded *53 Minutes Under Byker* and *"Fuck You Johnny Camo"*, I had to approach songs like "Meat Abstract" and "Living In The Shadow Of The Terrible Thing" in a different manner,' he adds. 'There's a guitar player called John Fahey who plays this drone-y, fingerstyle guitar, and I looked up his tuning online. I was playing along with some of his records, and realised I could play songs like "Meat Abstract" in that tuning. If songs were more riff-heavy, I'd sing the vocal melody and play open chords and do it that way. There's no sustain, power chords, or walls of amplification to hide behind.'

Before the band headed into Europe for an acoustic tour in November, Andy played a one-off date at Cardiff's Brickworks on October 22. 'On the morning of the show, I phoned James Dean Bradfield to invite him along, then called him back later and asked if he wanted to play "Die Laughing" as well,' says Andy. 'There was sixty people in this tiny room. He was just standing with the punters and walked onto the stage. No one was expecting that.'

After recording the *Wood & Wire* set with a full kit, Neil wanted to try something different for their upcoming dates, so he called his old drum tutor for some advice. 'I stripped my kit down and visited Andy Boris, who gave me my first drumming lessons when I was eleven years old, to work on jazz stuff and brush work,' he explains. 'We listened to jazz albums and worked out what I wanted to do. He introduced me to the way jazz drummers play figure of eights and circles with the brushes on the snare drum. It's completely different to playing rock songs. I listened to people like Philly Joe Jones, and it really opened my mind up.

'Once we started playing the acoustic shows, our mindset was completely different to how we recorded *Wood & Wire*,' he continues. 'If you listen to the version of "Trigger Inside" on that recording, it's worlds apart from what we played on the tour afterwards.'

'Physically, it was an easy tour to do, but mentally, it was fucking hard,' adds Michael. 'If we need to change a song's key, I'll need half an hour to get my head around it. I can't really do it on the fly. There's nothing to hide behind. It's a very spartan show and you're just sat there and need to push some kind of energy out. It's hard. I think I was quite naive in thinking, *I can just sit on a nice stool, and we'll just play the songs a bit quieter*. But the shows got better and better, and I was pleasantly surprised they went as well as they did.'

By the time Therapy? arrived at London's Union Chapel, a working church and music venue on Islington's Upper Street, the band were a completely different beast; their career-spanning set also featured cellist Jenny Nendick on 'Gone' and 'Diane'.

'The first time I set foot in the Union Chapel was in 1997, when I went to see Sparklehorse with my wife,' explains Andy. 'I'd got the tickets quite late, so we were quite near the back. The show was really moving, and I remember thinking that I really wanted to play there one day. It was one of the few venues that I wished we could play but couldn't, whether it was because we couldn't fill it or they simply wouldn't let a band like us through the door!

'Our acoustic show was one of my favourite ever gigs,' he adds. 'It was completely sold out, and people left their seats to come and watch down the front. The feeling I had that night will never leave me.'

The success of the tour opened up another world of possibilities. 'I think that tour and that whole period, for me personally, gave the band a whole new lease of life,' says Neil. 'It's so easy to drift into a routine, where you do your thing and do it well. But this changed the way we approached ideas, and I think it set us up well for the next album.'

'To be able to do different things like this is important for a band like us,' adds Andy. 'We're reliant on touring to a certain extent, because we don't sell shitloads of records like we did in the 90s. If you've got the option of playing acoustic shows or "greatest hits" sets on top of a new album, it's a good reason to go on tour and celebrate playing these songs. If we went back to the same towns year after year, playing the same songs each time, it's no fun for anybody. I think our fans appreciate the acoustic shows; it's very intimate, and there's every chance you'll hear one of us fuck up. Depending on the mood of the show, we'll tell stories about the songs and give people an insight into the band. It's almost like playing in someone's front room.'

Two days after the Union Chapel date, the band released the remaining copies of *Wood & Wire* via their website. 'I think we should have recorded the acoustic album after the tour,' says Michael. 'Everything really gelled on that run. The songs sound great and it was a nice recording we did, but some of those studio versions are just the songs played without any distortion.'

Luckily for the band, Michael brought along his portable recording setup for the entire run of *Wood & Wire* shows, taping each night's performance.

'Sometimes you think you've played a good show and listen back to a board mix and go, *Ah, oh dear*,' Andy admits. 'When we all went back home, Michael listened back to the Union Chapel gig and called us to say said we should put it out. We got [live sound engineer] Richard [Baker] to make a couple of tweaks, and between the pair of them, they got it all sorted. We made plans to release the album ourselves the following year, on top of everything else we had planned to do.'

YEAR
TWENTY-EIGHT / 'well, it's one louder, isn't it?'

On April 11 2017, Eric Cook died from cancer.

Cook had begun his career managing Venom, before setting up Demolition Records and Blast Records with his brother Ged. Over the course of their eight-year relationship, Therapy? released *Crooked Timber*, *A Brief Crack Of Light*, and *Disquiet*, as well as their first live album, *We're Here To The End*. His loss was keenly felt throughout the north-east music scene, and by the bands who had benefited from his wealth of experience and unbridled enthusiasm for music.

'We were all shocked at the death of Eric,' says Andy. 'We found out about it the afternoon of a gig at Rotown in Rotterdam. Not only had he been the guy that had signed us to Demolition Records and given us studio time at Blast Studio, he was also a friend and supporter, and he would always have our back. He was always so full of energy, and his personality gave you hope and made you smile. He would never think anything was too big an ask, and he would try his best to make it so.'

'He'd apparently been ill for just a short time and hadn't told anyone, apart from his family,' adds Michael. 'Eric was such a brilliant guy, full of energy and humour. It was always a pleasure to spend time with him. Both he and his family welcomed Therapy? into the Blast family and made us all feel very comfortable during our time up in the north-east, and he also had the best stories about Venom—which, as a fan, I was always hassling him to tell me. On a professional level, he fought our corner hard, and his support and access to Blast studio meant that we were able to make the records the way we wanted. Even though he was the record-label boss, he never interfered in creative decisions and preferred to let us do our thing. That's rare.'

Later that month, the band played another brace of *Wood & Wire* shows in Ireland and Northern Ireland. Shortly after that, Andy, Michael, and Neil headed to Derby's Abbey Lane Studios—perhaps a distant relative of the facility made famous by The Beatles—to work on the follow-up to *Disquiet*. 'Those *Wood & Wire* shows really rejuvenated us, and I think that fed into the *Cleave* album,' says Neil. 'Changing the way we played and rearranging the songs made us approach things differently.'

'We wanted to get ahead of the game,' adds Michael. 'The weird thing was that everyone was going, "If you're doing these acoustic tours, is the new album going to be quiet and reflective?" It was the polar opposite—we couldn't wait to blast out some riffs in the practice room and let rip.

'There was no pressure,' he adds. 'We had quite a big pool of ideas which we worked on a various points in the year. One song that we'd record for *Cleave*, called "Save Me From The Ordinary", came from a soundcheck in Romania the previous year. I'd recorded it on my phone and saved it as "Romanian Shellac". My phone was full of ideas like that.'

Andy performed a solo acoustic show at London's Proud Galleries as part of the Camden Rocks festival on June 3. As part of his short set, he took the opportunity to play a new song called 'Crutch', featuring the lines, *'You once were the spark that gave me life / Now I wish that I'd just left you alone.'* 'I wrote this song at my kitchen table on my acoustic,' he explains. 'It's an autobiographical tale about the problems I've had with drinking. Alcohol has always been involved in any fuck-ups I've made.'

In July, Therapy?'s festival activity included appearances in Belgium, Russia, Holland, and Finland. On August 18, they played another acoustic set at The Levellers' Beautiful Days festival in Devon's Escot Park, which coincided with the self-release of *Communion: Live At The Union Chapel* four days later. The two-disc package would feature all twenty-four songs they'd performed on December 1 2016.

As free agents, the band discussed what to do regarding the release of their next album—their fifteenth—and made the decision to pool the money made from *Communion* and finance the new album themselves.

'The plan was to pay for everything ourselves, then shop it around,' Andy explains. 'Marshall were one the first labels to get in touch. One of the people there was a person called Steve Tannett, who was the guitar player for a band called Menace in 1977. They released some great singles, including "Screwed Up" and "GLC". He became friends with Miles Copeland and worked at IRS, and looked after The Alarm, Lords Of The New Church, early R.E.M.—stuff like that. Later, he worked at Ark 21, who released *Shameless*. He spoke to Gerry and mentioned that Marshall were setting up a record label, and because we liked Steve and got on with him, we were interested. It was a worldwide deal, which was important to us. We had a couple of meetings and one where Steve came to see the whole band.

'We could have split the money from the *Communion* sales and had a lovely Christmas, but we held onto it,' adds Michael. 'We wouldn't be beholden to anyone and if the Marshall deal fell through—we'd still own the album. Steve trusted us, and it was good to have him back on board; he really fought our corner with *Suicide Pact—You First* and *Shameless*.'

After deciding against making the album themselves, the band contacted Chris Sheldon and asked him to produce them for the first time since 1998's *Semi-Detached*. 'I was always keen to work with the band again, but they never asked!' he laughs. 'Actually, this was one of those cases when the stars aligned and it all came together. The band approached me to work with them, but I was already committed to another project. When I found out that they could put the start date back, I was in. I had been mainly concentrating on mixing, but it seemed like the right time [to return to producing]. I'd heard what they had been doing over the years and saw them adopting various styles of music, but this time around the songs they had been writing seemed like they would suit my style of production perfectly. It wasn't a tough decision.'

With a session booked at Blast Studios in January, the band forged ahead with writing new material and demoing songs in between their remaining live engagements. In September, they played four shows as special guests of The Sisters Of Mercy—two at London's Roundhouse and two at Ancienne Belgique in Brussels.

Much like the Union Chapel show the previous year, Andy relished the opportunity for Therapy? to perform at another iconic London venue for the first time. 'The year before, the Manic Street Preachers played three shows at the Roundhouse and asked me up on stage to play "You Love Us" with them one night,' says Andy. 'I really wanted us to play that venue, so when The Sisters Of Mercy asked us to support them, we said yes immediately.

'I can remember buying their records: "Body Electric", "Anaconda", "Alice", and *The Reptile House* EP at Caroline Music in Belfast,' he continues. 'After I had my initial flush with punk, I discovered Joy Division, The Birthday Party, Southern Death Cult, and The Sisters Of Mercy around the same time. I loved the guitar lines and the mystery. The drum machine—they called it Doktor Avalanche—made them sound quite unusual and dark, which suited me as a teenager.'

'We knew Chris Catalyst and Ben Christo, and had met Andrew Eldritch a few times, like on *Top Of The Pops*,' adds Michael. 'Those shows were great for us to do and I really appreciated the opportunity. It's always good to get in front of a new crowd. I didn't know whether we were going to be too abrasive or too lairy, or just not up peoples street. We had a different mindset, too, like backs to the wall. There's no point in suddenly deciding we need to play everything a certain way, or tweak the setlist to the bill. You just go out and do your thing. Belgium's a bit of a Therapy? stronghold, so we knew the shows in Brussels would be a lot of fun.'

On September 11, Therapy? headlined a Gig For Eric at the Cluny in Newcastle, in honour of the late Eric Cook. Support came from North Yorkshire quintet Avalanche Party and Wallsend NWOBHM five-piece Tysondog—two more acts that Eric had championed.

'The gig was, needless to say, an emotional one,' says Andy. 'His family were there with us to celebrate his life in a packed venue. It was a sensational Geordie send-off—there were as many smiles as tears. Eric, to us, was emblematic of the can-do attitude of the north-east of the country, and his part in bringing us up there to record is responsible for our love of the place to this day. Every time we play Newcastle-upon-Tyne, or any time I go to see Chelsea play at St James' Park, Eric is in my thoughts.'

In October, the trio embarked on a short run of *Wood & Wire* shows around the UK, which saw some bookings in more unorthodox surroundings. 'We'd played some unusual venues on the last acoustic tour,' explains Michael. 'We played a church in Rotterdam, and the Union Chapel, and we liked the atmosphere. We said to our agent, Paul, that we didn't want to play in the corner of a rock club, so we ended up playing in comedy venues like the Glee Club in Birmingham, the Komedia in Brighton, a cinema in Brynmawr, and Nell's Jazz & Blues club in London.

'Every night was really memorable, and there was always something going on—there'd be some wild card,' he adds. 'It definitely challenged us on a lot of levels, but it also really kept us on our toes and gave us a different kind of confidence.'

Neil reveals that the intimate venues and gentler amplification meant they could hear everything on the other side of the stage monitors— something that was best illustrated by their show at the Brudenell Social Club in Leeds on October 11. 'Just before the encore, Andy began to tell the heartbreaking story behind the song "Gone",' the drummer recalls. 'He hadn't mentioned the actual title at this point, but you could hear a pin drop. There were these two lads in battle vests, a bit smashed and completely into the show. Andy finished the story, saying, "This is 'Gone' …" and those two lads just went, "Oh, GET IN!" It was completely inappropriate, and we were trying so hard not to laugh at the situation.'

Next was a trip to Athens on November 24, where the band put in a double shift, playing an in-store at Syd Records and a full show at Gagarin 205 later that night, debuting a new song called 'Spat Out'. Two weeks later, they made an appearance at the Come As You Are festival in Eindhoven before heading home for the Christmas break.

'Looking back, it was a great mix of acoustic and electric shows,' says Michael. 'One highlight for me was the Rock For Specials gig in Belgium, which is an event dedicated to providing a festival experience for people with learning difficulties and their carers. The festival was extremely well organised, the atmosphere was amazing, and we had an absolute blast. I'll never forget that one.

'The new songs were sounding good,' he adds, 'and signing the new deal with Marshall was another step forward. It was really exciting knowing we had an album ready to record, Chris Sheldon was on board to produce it, and we also had a Stranglers support slot lined up for March.'

YEAR TWENTY-NINE/success?
success is survival

While Therapy? were setting up to record their new album at Blast Recording, something suddenly dawned on Michael. It was twenty-five years to the day since they began recording the *Shortsharpshock* EP with Chris Sheldon at Black Barn Studio in Surrey.

'It was so surreal when the penny dropped,' says the bassist. 'We were joking about the planets aligning. We were all raring to go because we'd done so much work beforehand. It was the first album in a long time where we actually did a production rehearsal, where you play the songs, in sequence, live in a room, with completed lyrics, solos, everything. Chris helped massively with arrangements and tempos—he really refined it without ironing out the energy.'

'Michael would send me rough demos of the songs they knocked together in a rehearsal room, and I worked on them in my studio,' Chris adds. 'I would look at the arrangements and try various edits and suggestions, then send them back to the lads to contemplate and try out. Most of my ideas seemed to gel with their sensibilities and worked out well. Consequently, by the time we hit the studio, we were already one step ahead of the game. Since Michael pointed out the date, it was fated that the album would go well.'

The trio's preparedness and long-standing relationship with the producer helped make light work of the task at hand. 'This was the first time I had recorded Neil, he says, 'but he's such a solid drummer and personality, the drums were seen off in pretty short order.' As on *Troublegum* twenty-five years earlier, Michael recorded his bass parts in a day and a half. They could even have been wrapped up a little earlier, had he not fallen in love with a Morley Tribute Cliff Burton Power Fuzz Wah Pedal, which he was sent to review for *Bass Player* magazine and eventually bought for himself. The pedal—which sounds exactly as described—is used to stunning effect during the beginning of 'Save Me From The Ordinary'.

'Michael's intro was a lot longer at the beginning,' Andy laughs, 'but Chris came in and said, "I know you like Cliff Burton, but this is ridiculous."'

'I admit I went *full Cliff* during that song,' says Michael. 'We spent about four hours getting that intro just right. In the end, Chris would do the pedal's rocking motion while I played. It's the sort of thing that, once you get into it, it becomes a whole house of cards and I kept fucking it up. The pedal sounds fantastic.'

With Neil and Michael's parts completed quickly, Andy had the luxury of spending two weeks on recording guitars and vocals.

'When I'm producing, I like to get singers in bands completing vocals as soon as possible, and not leave everything to the last minute,' Chris explains. 'Andy started laying down lead vocals as soon as we had enough musically for him to sing to. We experimented with a few different guitar parts and backing vocal ideas, which sometimes involved me plonking around on the piano to try a few ideas out then giving the rough germ of an idea to Andy. He would then modify and embellish the part until it resembled something that was actually usable!

'One of my greatest pleasures in life is working with Therapy? like this,' he adds. 'They are, as a band, completely open to ideas, however good or bad they turn out to be, which makes for a totally creative time in the studio. If I have an idea for a backing-vocal part, for instance, Andy is the first one to say, "Go and try it out."'

The opening track, 'Wreck It Like Beckett', was inspired by a thunderous riff that Michael had written and recorded at home and saved to his computer as 'She Watch Channel Zero'. 'Using the Public Enemy song as a reference point, Neil worked on his drum parts and I added some discordant noise rock to add a bit of grit at the start,' Andy explains. 'Samuel Beckett inspired the title, because every time he started writing, he would imagine pushing things off his desk so he had uncluttered space to begin writing.

'With *Cleave*, we wanted start afresh and not be held back or be distracted by anything,' he adds. 'The line "*Everyone's living all over each other / Everyone's living their life out loud*" is about tuning these frequencies out so you can only see the white page.'

The pace continues with 'Kakistocracy' (a term for governments run by unscrupulous politicians), a furious track highlighting the tensions created by the United Kingdom's recent EU referendum: '*Is this the end of empathy? / Turn away from the poor / Pulling up the drawbridge and bolting the door.*' 'Therapy? have tried to avoid writing overtly political songs,' says Andy. 'We try to do them with a bit of subterfuge, like "Potato Junkie" or "Church Of Noise". But with "Kakistocracy", that was probably the most obvious and blunt way of addressing the division between the haves and have-nots.'

'Callow' was inspired in part by a quote from Stephen Fry's autobiography, *Moab Is My Washpot* (1997), in which the actor and comedian writes, 'Heightened self-consciousness, apartness, an inability to join in, physical shame and self-loathing—they are not all bad. Those devils have been my angels. Without them I would never have disappeared into language, literature, the mind, laughter and all the mad intensities that made and unmade me.'

'I've never taken antidepressants,' says Andy. 'I've met a lot of people who've had them, and they've said they've taken the edge off their depression. I didn't think about it until I saw the Stephen Fry quote. I know they work for other people, but I like to deal with things myself. I like the rawness of lived experience. I like to feel it physically. It would strip a piece of reality away from me, and I don't want that. This is only from my personal experience, you must understand. I might be in a bad place for a while, and I might feel uncomfortable, but it's beneficial to me in the long run. I'm lucky to have my wife and son, Michael and Neil, and my friends to talk to. That helps me.'

The band had debuted 'Expelled' in Greece a couple of months before entering the studio. Back then, it was titled 'Spat Out'. 'The song is not a million miles away from something like "Nausea",' says Andy. 'It's written through a post-Brexit lens where people are getting left behind. When the Tory party is in power, they see things through Tory eyes: privately educated, well-off, nannies … they don't know what it's like to have to live the *I, Daniel Blake* experience,' he adds, referring to the harrowing Ken Loach film released in 2016. 'I don't know how they can empathise with a single mother who's trying to live on £40 a week.'

Propelled by a hypnotic, Killing Joke-esque riff written by Michael, 'Success? Success Is Survival' was sparked by a comment in the 1974 documentary *Leonard Cohen: Bird On A Wire*, after the singer is asked to describe what success meant to him.

'I thought that was gorgeous and wrote it down,' says Andy. 'The opening line, "*The cream of this country, rich and thick, will always rise to the top*", is paraphrased from something Samuel Beckett said about the

Irish establishment back in the day. Again, it's about the haves and have-nots. People go through an extraordinary amount of struggle to feed their families and keep a roof over their head. People can be two months' wages away from being homeless. I've heard how quickly things can spiral out of control.'

'Save Me From The Ordinary', which opens with Michael's fuzzed-up wah bass, was a phrase taken from one of Andy's notebooks. The lyrics came to him quickly, after he watched the Charlie Chaplin film *Modern Times*. 'In the film, Charlie Chaplin is working in a factory and literally becomes a cog in a machine,' he says. 'It's a classic scene, and there's a verse that goes, *"In modern times, a little man in the grip of change / Another cog in the wheel of the world."'*

Next come the grand pop sensibilities of 'Crutch', which was first recorded by Andy during a session for the Audio Production Workshop music gear YouTube channel in April the previous year, then debuted at Camden Rocks in the summer. The subsequent track, 'I Stand Alone', is the only one credited to all three members of the band. It takes its title and lyrical inspiration from Gaspar Noé's *Seul contre tous*, a French art film about a butcher who loses the plot. 'It's brilliant, but it's a tough watch,' says Andy. 'We thought about using the French title, but thought it would be pretentious unless I was singing in French!

'Michael sent through a drum machine idea, and it was like Young Gods or Ministry,' he adds. 'Neil said it reminded him of something from Metallica's album … *And Justice For All*. Like "Harvester Of Sorrow", I suppose. At home, I spent some time listening to the three bands and thinking of ways to make it sound more like Therapy?. I had some lyrics lying around, like *"I am only a cork floating on the ocean / But underneath everything has teeth,"* and I looked for ways to sing that over the riff. We had too many riffs and had to pare it back. The tension and the breakdowns work really well live.'

The music for 'Dumbdown' was composed by Neil. Despite the clatter of thunderous riffs, it was written in the peace and quiet of a library in Derby. 'Andy wanted Michael and me to come up with some tunes, so I went off and got some software and put some bits and pieces together,' the drummer explains. 'It got me into the mindset of writing riffs and adding my drums to them. I went with my laptop, mini-keyboard, and headphones, then recorded the drums and pieced it all together. I'm no Richard Clayderman—I was clonking away on the keyboard—but we managed to make a song out of it. I find it easier now to articulate any musical ideas. Andy gave me the push to do that.'

'Neil has a "guitar" setting on his keyboard,' adds Andy. 'It sounds like something from an arcade game—it's brilliant. He sent a riff, and I worked out how to play it on guitar. I tried a staccato riff over it, but it sounded too stilted, so Michael suggested I play big open chords, like "Potato Junkie".'

The lyrics were again written in the wake of the EU referendum result, following a polite dinner party that went awry. 'The divisions created by the Brexit referendum inspired a lot of the lyrics on *Cleave*,' he explains. 'My wife and I were at a dinner party in Cambridge, where we've lived for years. The referendum result had been announced, and I said I came from a country where division has ruined people's lives. A guy looked up and said, "Well, if you don't like it, you can always go home." It wasn't some numpty in an English Defence League shirt. It was a middle-class, educated man from Cambridge. I've been living in England since 2003 and had never been called a Paddy, and no one has ever said anything untoward about me being Irish. I love living here. As soon as Brexit happened, someone told me to go back to where I come from. That's where the lyric "*Some people like you hate people like me / I don't belong here*" comes from. A government should be there to advise, guide, and help, but with Brexit, they stood back and let people get what they wanted, even though it was bad for everyone.'

The album shifts gears with its closing song, 'No Sunshine', Andy's uplifting chorus punctuated by Michael's ominously slow verses. 'That was like a Béla Tarr movie—so bleak,' says Andy, referring to the director of *Sátántangó* (*Satan's Tango*) and *Kárhozat* (*Damnation*). 'Michael sent the opening bass line, and it was quite atmospheric. I'd written the lyrics out six months before, when I was really depressed. I was playing along with Michael's riff and came up with the chords. It was very cathartic and is one of my favourite songs on the record. The song is in a minor key, but it goes to a major, so there's a little bit of hope.'

Shortly after the album was completed, Neil re-joined his former band, The Beyond, for a reunion at the Venue in Derby on February 16. Frontman John Whitby had been appointed mayor of the city of Derby the previous year, and the one-off show was a fundraiser for the Derbyshire Children's Holiday Centre, Children First, Safe and Sound, the British Red Cross, and the Derby Museums Trust.

'It had been twenty-five years since we'd released our debut album, *Crawl*, and lots of people from the past showed up,' says Neil. 'I found it quite therapeutic to see them. As a nineteen-year-old, I was quite gobby, and I would often wonder if I'd said the right things to people, but everyone was very friendly. It was great playing the old songs, and we raised loads of money for the chosen charities.'

Following a warm-up show at the Crauford Arms in Milton Keynes on March 5 (where 'Callow' was debuted), the band headed out on a month-long tour of the UK as special guests of The Stranglers. 'When I played the bass, Joy Division's Peter Hook and The Stranglers' Jean-Jacques Burnel were two heroes of mine,' says Andy. 'One of my favourite albums of all time is [1978's] *Black And White*, and we'd recorded "Nice 'n' Sleazy" around the time of *Troublegum*. They've got a very partisan crowd: at the first gig, there was a guy who gave us the thumbs down sign and booed us throughout the set, but things like that make us play even harder.'

The band had a day off before their Newcastle date on March 28, so they spent the day at Blast, recording a cover of Venom's 'Possessed' (from the 1985 album of the same name) for an as-yet-unreleased tribute album. 'After Eric Cook passed away, his brother, Ged, hit upon the idea of doing an album with the aim of raising funds for Eric's widow and family,' Michael explains. 'I'm a huge Venom fan, and we'd actually met [drummer] Abaddon when he popped into the studio when we were recording *Disquiet*.

'"Possessed" was an easy choice to make as it was one of my favourite Venom songs, and to my knowledge no one had done a cover of it,' he continues. 'So many bands have done the classics like "Black Metal" or "Buried Alive" over the years—I felt it was important to look at something a bit more off-the-wall. I love the *Possessed* album, and I felt that the main mid-paced riff would sound good done *Therapy?-style*. It was also good fun going to town with the spooky intro noises and children's laughter, which was something we wouldn't normally get away with on a Therapy? album. There's also some nice noisy chords with drawn-out feedback in our version, which we thought was a nice nod to the end of "Warhead", another Venom favourite.'

While Andy and Michael stayed in the studio, getting the overdubs completed and prepping the final mix, Neil spent the rest of the day with The Stranglers and their crew. 'Normally, days off on tour are spent doing laundry and resting,' he says. 'We recorded the Venom cover, then their drummer, Jim Macaulay, who replaced Jet Black, asked if anyone wanted to play five-a-side and do some go-karting. As far as days off go, that was pretty special.'

By the time the band reached Manchester's O2 Academy on March 31, some of The Stranglers' fans had cottoned on to Andy's nightly announcement that it was Neil's birthday and that, as such, he was allowed to do a drum solo. 'They had a fan base which followed them around and we got to know their faces,' Neil explains. 'Once the tour got going, people realised that Andy was taking the piss. Someone collected all the birthday cards that were thrown on stage. There were loads in the dressing room.'

Remember The Stranglers fan who booed Therapy? on the opening night? He remained dedicated to his cause, and he kept it up throughout the tour. By the time they played in Manchester, though, he'd changed his tune. 'He'd brought a copy of *Troublegum* to get signed,' Andy laughs. 'We'd won him over, and that meant so much.'

Following the digital release of 'Callow' on May 25—accompanied by a zombie video directed by Sitcom Soldiers—the band toured the European festival circuit in the run up to the release of *Cleave* on September 21. In the weeks preceding the release, the press response was almost unanimous in its praise. *Kerrang!* gave the album a four-*K* review; *Planet Rock* went with four stars out of five. 'Informed by political and personal divisions, the spectre of Brexit and the evergreen appeal of downtuned, neck-bothering riffs, the impossible-to-pigeonhole Northern Irish icons' fifteenth opus is a rallying cry for this draconian age,' wrote *Metal Hammer*'s Edwin McFee, who also awarded the album four stars. 'Fans who enjoyed the feral, rampant riffola of 2004's *Never Apologise, Never Explain* will especially enjoy *Cleave*, and the likes of the bullish "Wreck It Like Beckett" and the combative "Dumbdown" already sound like pit anthems.'

'*Cleave* is reminiscent of their *Troublegum* era, taking cues from 90s contemporaries such as Helmet and featuring songs and lyrics that are as memorable as anything from their heyday,' wrote Eamon Sweeney of the *Irish Times*, in another four-out-of-five review. 'After all these years, Therapy? are a class act who won't go gently into the good night.'

Wayne Byrne of *Hot Press* dished out a nine-out-of-ten review and described *Cleave* as a 'collection of thrilling hard rock' that ranked among Therapy?'s greatest work. *Louder Than War*'s John Robb believed the album was the band's 'most definitive statement for years', adding that they 'still dare to bring the noise—that black T-shirt, high decibel noise to get lost in, they dare to riff and they dare to embrace the outer margins of post-punk, they also dare to infuse the noise with a remarkable sensitivity and a case of underrated lyrical smarts.'

The night before the band's first tour in support of *Cleave*, they were invited by *Kerrang!* to perform at Blondies, a small bar in Clapton, London, for a special show to be filmed before an audience of fifty ticket winners. 'We worked out this show was the smallest gig we'd ever played, even dating back to when we first started,' says Andy. 'We were among friends, and it was a great gig to do, but I don't think our crew would appreciate it if we did that every night. It was a bit of a squeeze. Things like that keep our interest piqued. We were still talking about that show a few weeks into our European tour.'

'The venue was tiny but the sound was actually OK,' adds Neil. 'I was set up facing the wall. If I'd set up normally, no one would be able to get in through the door. We only did five songs or something, but it was a great thing to do. Those quirky gigs are the best, because you don't know what's going to happen.'

The tour took the band through Belgium, the Netherlands, and Germany, then into the UK the following month. So far, so good. But no one could have predicted what would happen when the band played the Brudenell Social Club in Leeds on November 17.

'OK, this is a story in two parts,' says Neil. 'We played the Gorilla in Manchester the night before. My wife was going to come to that show, but she couldn't make it in the end. I was looking forward to a night out, so I went and got pissed up anyway. I was waiting to get a kebab and a fight broke out in the shop. There was blood everywhere, and some lads were trying to bite each other. Absolute carnage. I got my kebab and went back to the hotel.'

Oh, we see you're one step ahead of us. But, for the sake of clarity, we'll allow Neil to continue.

'In hindsight, the kebab was pretty rough,' he explains, 'and I shouldn't have had it. I was unbelievably ill the next morning, and, from about midday, I was sick ten minutes before every hour. You could set your watch by it. We did the soundcheck, and I worked out when we'd start the gig; I'd spew and evacuate myself, then go on stage. I had a bucket next to me, but the gig was going surprisingly OK.'

Halfway into the set, the band's sound engineer, Richard Baker, signalled for the band to stop during 'Screamager'; there was a crowd incident that couldn't be ignored. 'My wife and son came to that show, because my son was interested in going to Leeds University,' Andy explains. 'I saw my wife go towards what was happening, and I jumped off stage. Someone in the crowd appeared to be injured.'

An ambulance was called, and the band pulled the gig for safety reasons, promising the crowd they would return to make up for the shortened set. 'I went backstage and continued spewing, then headed back to the hotel,' Neil adds.

The tour ended on November 23 at Birmingham's Asylum. *Cleave* had struck a chord with the band's hardcore fan base, while the press' reaction to the release brought in new fans. 'It was a great year,' Andy reflects. 'We were playing new places, sold out gigs, and the response to the album was fantastic. We were in a really good place. After some years of uncertainty, everything seemed too good to be true.'

YEAR THIRTY/so much for the 30 year plan

'The last few years had seen a complete turnaround for the band,' says Andy. 'We had gone from no one giving us a break to having about twenty festivals booked that year.'

Much of 2019 was spent touring in support of *Cleave*. The band's festival run kicked off in earnest with two appearances at the Levellers-curated A Beautiful Day Out shows in Halifax on June 29 and Glasgow two days later. Next on the itinerary was a slot at 2000 Trees at Upcote Farm in Gloucestershire on July 13.

'It seemed to be mostly younger bands on the bill, so we weren't really sure how we'd go down,' says Michael. 'But the set was fantastic. We were there all day. You couldn't get into your dressing room until a certain time, so we checked out a load of bands: St. Pierre Snake Invasion, Milk Teeth, and Every Time I Die. There was a lot going on. Andy played an acoustic set in the woods, too.'

'Stevie joined me for that one, and I thought I'd do something a bit different,' explains Andy. 'I'd been listening to a lot of early R.E.M., and I did a cover of "(Don't Go Back To) Rockville", which is a brilliant song. I don't think one person knew what the song was. You can imagine a sad trombone sound—wah-wah–waaah—when we finished that song.'

Boomtown is a five-day annual bash held in the South Downs National Park near Winchester. The organisers claim that it's 'unlike any other festival', and this instalment, titled Chapter 11: A Radical City, featured over a thousand artists across thirty-eight stages. Therapy? played on August 9, just after Killing Joke.

'It was like if *Mad Max: Fury Road* had a festival,' laughs Michael. 'It looked suitably post-apocalyptic! They had these different zones that were like mini cities; old movie sets which had these facades and you'd drive through these muddy roads over an undulating landscape. A very different festival feel.'

'It had a great atmosphere,' adds Andy. 'It wasn't one of those festivals where middle-class caners in Puffa jackets spill out of the toilets.

'I was nervous about Killing Joke being on the bill,' he admits. 'Geordie [Walker] is one of my favourite guitar players of all time. His tech came over during their set and put his guitar on me and took a photo on my phone. I was like, *Oh my God, this guitar has made so many incredible riffs that I love.* I was too nervous to meet them, but they were amazing.'

On August 24, the trio returned to Belfast as special guests to Stiff Little Fingers, on a bill that also featured New Model Army and The Toy Dolls. Surprisingly, the last time they'd shared a bill with the headliners was the 1993 Féile festival in Semple Stadium, County Tipperary. 'We'd often bump into [SLF frontman] Jake Burns, and [bassist] Ali McMordie was Moby's tour manager, so we would run into him quite a lot in the 90s, during festivals,' explains Andy. 'They're bigger now than they were back in the day, and that's fantastic to see.'

That day, the band learned that their plans to record a special live set at Marshall's Milton Keynes studio later that year had been nixed, as the state-of-the-art facility would not be ready in time. 'This had been talked about for a long time,' explains Michael. 'We were originally going to record in the hall that Marshall were converting into a studio with pre-production and rehearsal facilities. You could easily do a gig in there. It would have been a different spin to recording another gig. We had two nights held, and would have it open during the day and play acoustic sets, do Q&As. It couldn't happen when we planned, and we had no gigs booked for the rest of the year.'

'There was talk of booking a small venue and doing it there,' says Andy. 'We didn't want to celebrate three decades with a hastily put-together small gig just to have something out. We had a meeting with the label and looked at doing a fan-club gig at a studio. We talked about what songs we'd have on there, and the elephant in the room was they wanted the most popular songs on a live album. Chris Sheldon got wind of this and suggested we do something at Abbey Road.'

On September 21, Therapy? began to wind up their touring activity for the year with an appearance at the resurrected Féile festival, also known as the Trip To Tipp. They had first played the festival in 1992, alongside Simply Red, Ned's Atomic Dustbin, and EMF. They were invited again the following year, playing on a bill featuring Iggy Pop, Stiff Little Fingers, Kerbdog, Rollins Band, and Manic Street Preachers. Three spots down the bill were Spiritualized, who they'd had a run-in with at Harlow's Square prior to the recording of *Pleasure Death*.

'Back in the day, every house near the Trip To Tipp had turned into an off license and sold cans from their gardens,' says Michael. 'It was good to revisit. It was pissing with rain, which was a concern, but the crowd really went for it.'

The band's final show of the year was a headline slot at the Indie Daze all-dayer at London's Kentish Town Forum on October 5. Joining them on the bill were Kingmaker, Back To The Planet, Utah Saints, Carter The Unstoppable Sex Machine's Jim Bob, Pop Will Eat Itself, and Swervedriver. 'That show was good to do, and it felt like an end-of-year party for us,' says Michael. 'We had an eighty-minute set, and, because we'd played lots of festivals, everyone was dialled in. It was good to reconnect with people who hadn't perhaps seen us for twenty years. It was a no-pressure gig, and it was fun to do. The band and crew ended up drinking cocktails in a converted public toilet after the pubs closed.'

On November 8, the band and Chris Sheldon convened at Abbey Road Studios in St John's Wood, London. There, they'd spend the day recording their twelve biggest-selling singles for a 'greatest hits' collection. As they arrived, they each noticed the early morning rush-hour traffic was held up by Beatles fans walking over the iconic pedestrian crossing. (Exactly three months earlier, the area had been packed as fans lined the streets to mark the fiftieth anniversary of Iain Macmillan's iconic photo session.) 'There must have been forty tourists getting that photo, even at eight in the morning,' says Andy. 'The person in reception said it happens twenty-four hours a day.'

The band set up in Studio 3, where The Beatles made most of *Revolver*, Pink Floyd recorded *The Dark Side Of The Moon*, Lady Gaga tracked part of *Born This Way*, and Amy Winehouse recorded the song 'Body And Soul' with Tony Bennett, just a few months before her death.

'It was a big ask for the band and me to be able to do [the album in a day] and keep the quality-control up, but I think we did pretty well,' says Chris. 'There was zero prep done before we met up at Abbey Road, apart from a couple of phone calls between Andy and me, and getting the tempos right for the clicks between Neil and me. I also discussed with the guys the idea of doing a band version of "Diane". That was pretty much it! I had to re-familiarise myself with some of the songs, particularly the ones I hadn't had anything to do with, like "Stories" and "Loose". Neil and I discussed using or not using a click track, but we decided to go ahead with using one for expediency's sake.'

This would be the first time Neil performed these twelve songs in a recording studio, having joined the band some four years after the release of their 1998 single 'Lonely, Cryin', Only'. 'I had to approach the Abbey Road versions with a certain amount of respect,' he says. 'We'd played most of the songs so many times live, but you've got to respect the fact that the original versions mean a lot, to a lot of people, so you can't fuck with them too much. But, equally, it was about us capturing the essence of how the three of us play them live now.'

To ensure the whole album would be done in time, both band and producer came to an agreement whereby they would record three takes of each song. '*Troublegum* was painstakingly put together over a few weeks, with multiple takes on each instrument and vocals to get the exact version we wanted,' Chris continues. 'This was done literally live in the studio—warts and all—then mixed quickly at my studio the day after. What it shows is the songs in their rawest state, as you'd hear them in a live setting, but with the benefit of studio quality.'

'We'd spent twenty-eight years doing the pre-production, so we really couldn't fuck up,' Michael laughs. 'I'd sent Chris the song samples ahead of the recording, and we were ready. The only stress we had was the time we had to do it.'

The album is saturated sense of urgency and confidence, and perhaps, gives some of their earlier recordings a renewed vigour. 'We could have gone into Abbey Road for a few days, but Chris said correctly that our focus levels would drop,' says Andy. 'He called it right—there's a focus and energy that remained intact. I actually prefer the new versions of "Stories" and "Lonely, Cryin', Only" to the originals. He'd also brought in the Vox AC30 amp that I'd used on *Troublegum* and slaved it with my amp.'

'When he started playing "Turn" through it, I got goosebumps—it was THE sound,' adds Michael. 'I was really pleased with my bass sound—my parts on "Teethgrinder" sound like the way they should, for example—and Neil just nailed it.'

The album was completed in about eleven hours. 'By the end of it, we were completely fried,' says Neil. 'Various people would drift in and out of the studio to see how we were doing. Luckily, Gerry was there to make sure we could get on with getting everything done.'

The only song on the record with any additional embellishments is 'Die Laughing', which features a guest appearance by Manic Street Preachers frontman James Dean Bradfield. 'He was going to come to London,' says Michael, 'but with the nature of the session, he would have been under pressure to perform in a very narrow window. So he recorded it at the Manics' studio in Wales. The joys of technology.'

'We'd discussed with James what we wanted him to do and he wanted to play the whole song,' adds Andy. 'He's always said that "Die Laughing" was his favourite song, and it was fantastic to have him on this recording.'

The band packed away their equipment and left the studio, pausing to watch tourists recreate the *Abbey Road* photo in the early hours of the morning. Their *Greatest Hits* set was done and dusted, leaving Chris to mix the twelve tracks for the release in the spring. With their schedule completed for the year, the band looked ahead to the following twelve months, during which they planned to mark their thirtieth-anniversary with a number of headline shows and festival appearances.

EPILOGUE/the world is fucked

Greatest Hits (The Abbey Road Sessions)—now retitled *Greatest Hits (2020 Versions)*—was scheduled for release on March 6 2020. It was later pushed back a week, less than a fortnight before the UK was effectively shut down to tackle the coronavirus pandemic, leading to the postponement of the band's spring and summer shows in the UK and Europe. It would debut at no. 40 on the UK's Official Albums chart, while the vinyl edition went in at no. 4 in the Official Vinyl Albums chart.

With the album release looming, Michael put the finishing touches to a special bonus disc that would be included with initial quantities of the CD format. With the thirty-six-track *We're Here To The End* live album from 2010 covering the bulk of the band's career, the bassist set himself the task of creating an official bootleg featuring deep cuts from their thirty-year tenure.

'I'd made a rule where it would be one song from each album that hadn't had a commercial single release or on a live album,' says Michael. 'So we had songs like "Body Bag Girl" from *Shameless*, and "Big Cave In" from *Suicide Pact*—that way, there'd be stuff for the die-hard completists, and stuff for people who maybe saw us for the first time at Boomtown. I was quite invested in the idea.

'I tried to think songs I couldn't really remember playing live, then look through the archives to see if there was a recording of it,' he adds. '"Jude The Obscene" would be taken from a tour in 2015 where we played *Infernal Love* in full. I didn't want to use gigs that had been widely bootlegged, either, so it was a process of elimination. I didn't want anyone thinking it was just one show, so we wrote sleeve notes to add some context to each song. The thing is, we had the cover art and all the sleeve notes written before we went to Abbey Road.'

EPILOGUE

And there you have it. Therapy? were a band whose ambition was to make a single and have it racked at Caroline Music in Belfast. Three decades on, they have fifteen studio albums to their name—including the million-selling *Troublegum*—and remain one of rock's most fearless acts, and show no signs of slowing down. So what's the secret of their longevity?

'Other than me?' jokes Gerry. 'They're three incredibly hard-working, very intelligent lads. They know what they want to do and achieve, and, to be honest, they work their balls off. Nothing is a problem, really. They're also the nicest people you can meet, and people respond to that. They also have incredibly loyal fans; in return, they wouldn't do anything that could be perceived as taking advantage of their fans. We also have an incredibly loyal agent, in Paul Bolton, who's been with us through thick and thin and has never wavered in his support. Paul and I work closely as a team, and, in twenty-eight years or so, we have never had an argument.'

'This is going to sound corny, but the obvious highlights could the summer of 1994, or how the band have managed to turn their career around in the last few years,' says Paul. 'But, in reality, the highlight is that after nearly thirty years of working together, we still haven't had a major argument, and I hope I can call the band and management friends, not clients.'

'We've joked about the ten, the twenty, the thirty-year plan, but there was no master plan,' says Michael. 'We made decisions along the way because they felt right, and we learned from them all. Life has ups and downs, and doing this book, and looking back at all the things that have happened in a logical manner, has given me a massive amount of closure on a lot of things. It's given me snapshots of where the band were, mentally and musically. On a wider scale, we get to do what we love, and we're surrounded by people we love. As far as life goals and "mission statements" go, it's been massively successful from my point of view. If it all fell to pieces tomorrow, I'd have no regrets. I'm so hugely proud of what the band has done.'

'The only thing I've ever regretted was not taking time off before we made *Infernal Love*,' adds Andy. 'But when we did those tours in recent years and saw what that album means to people, it changed my feelings about it. But from forming the band with Fyfe, to playing with Martin and Graham, to this line-up—which I love—it's been brilliant.'

'I often wonder, what would I have been doing now, had I not been at that Rival Schools gig in 2002?' laughs Neil. 'The last eighteen years have flown by. It would be easy for us to drift into doing something that would just pay the bills, but it's important for us to sleep at night with a clear conscience, musically. I'm lucky to have met two people who have the same mindset; the three of us are focussed and aim for the same things.'

'I say this on stage most nights, but if it wasn't for the fans, we'd be nothing; they've kept us alive for thirty years,' says Andy. 'It's been a strange, crooked, anomalous trip,' he adds, 'but if you know the kind of people we are, and the type of music we make, then you'll know that we wouldn't have been any other way.'

AUTHOR'S
NOTE/acknowledgements

Firstly, this book would not have been possible without the love and unwavering patience of my darling wife, Cassie, and our wonderful daughter, Rita. Thank you for everything.

Thank you to Andy Cairns, Michael McKeegan, and Neil Cooper for entrusting me with your story. Your time, patience, and assistance in writing this book has been invaluable. Unless otherwise noted, all quotations are from interviews I conducted with them between October 2019 and April 2020.

Thanks go to following for their participation, help and encouragement: Gerry Harford, Paul Bolton, Chris Sheldon, 'Diamond' Dave Thompson, Graham Hopkins, Herb Magee, Stevie Firth, George Smyth, Simon Glacken, Nick Holmes, Darren Edwards, Tom Dalgety, Peter Spiby, Hugh Kelly, Scott McCloud, Rich Jones, Andy Prevezer, Phil Alexander, Sam Coare, David McLaughlin, Luke Morton, Nick Ruskell and all at Kerrang!, Clare Dowse, Fraser Lewry, Kiran Acharya, Steven Campbell, Jon Raine, Caroline Fish, Paul Harries, James Hickie, George Garner, Jason Arnopp, Nick Sayers, Graham Whitmore, James Sherry, Mike Rampton, Ingrid Pryer, Emma Johnston, Ed Kirby and all at Beano, Steve Clarke, Ben Myers, Stevie Chick, and Jens-Peter Jensen.

Thank you to Nigel Osborne and Tom Seabrook at Jawbone Press for affording me the opportunity to write my first book. Special thanks must go to Tom for his patience, diligence, and thoughtful editing.

Thank you to my mother Margaret and stepfather Bill—who both now know more about Therapy? than they ever dared imagine—for their love, kindness, generosity, and support.

Thank you to Pam Young, Edna Nichol, Mary and Gerry Cahill, and my extended family, for their love and kindness.

Thank you to Paul Brannigan for his advice, encouragement, and inspiration.

Thank you to Helen Armfield, Siân Cahill, and Max Geddes for assisting me with the Herculean task of transcribing hours of interviews.

Thank you to my much-missed friend, Ashley Maile.

This book is dedicated to memory of my late father, Peter, whose unconditional love, gentle guidance, and record collection have shaped me into the person I am today.

And finally, thank *you* for reading this book.

INDEX

THERAPY?

INDEX

THERAPY?

INDEX